Over, Under or Through

By
Chris Robinson

Chris Robinson – Over, Under or Through

Over, Under or Through

Introduction: Land of Hope and Dreams

1. The Ghost of Tom Joad
2. Hungry Heart
3. Dancing in the Dark
4. Downbound Train
5. Roulette
6. Wrecking Ball
7. Brothers Under The Bridge
8. It's Hard To Be A Saint In The City
9. Living Proof
10. One minute You're There..
11. Chasing Wild Horses
12. Long Walk Home

Acknowledgements: Human Touch

Introduction: Land of Hope and Dreams

It is time to set it down now before I forget too much.

I have heard this story before, as well, of course, as having lived it. I have gone over it daily, rehashed it and rehearsed it all the way along, minute by minute, reflecting, remembering and reshaping, no doubt. I think I have always expected some day to actually write it out. What has held me back has mainly been the terrifying thought that no-one else could possibly be interested and I would just be embarrassing myself in my vanity if I thought otherwise.

It's not that I think it has been an uneventful ride. Four marriages, seven kids, various lives and careers, politics, bankruptcy, professional football management, running charities, travelling the world and then there is the Buddha in there, too, alongside Sir Bobby Charlton, Boris Johnson, Jose Mourinho, the Countess of Wessex and a cast of drunks, sisters of mercy of varying types, priests, professional and unprofessional footballers, assorted children and a lot of poor people. I have had some great jobs, been unemployed, been rich, been poor, lost a child, found love. No, I guess that's eventful enough for most. It's just that I have doubted I have ever quite finished anything, and I felt that was somehow required first. Then I wanted also to keep some things hidden but mostly, thanks to a leading newspaper, a lot of that is out in the open now anyway so I have lost that excuse.

So, why do it now? It just feels like time. Nothing more complicated than that. I have other stories I want to write but I need to get this true one out of the way first. Also, now, I probably worry less about what other people may think of me or of being embarrassed by my succession of mistakes than at any time in my life to date.

I wish I could bring you the music, too, that has been there as a soundtrack. You would get a lot of Springsteen, a lot of Otis Redding and delta blues, a lot of Chuck Berry, Paul Weller and Leonard

Cohen, and more recently some John Smith. But the technology is beyond me for now, so you'll have to add that soundtrack yourself. Or wait for the film?

Also, from time to time I have gone back to re-visit places and look at them as they are now. All of this is about how I now today see the past. It is not the past it is just my looking back at it. The past does not exist. There is only now. So, it is in this now that I stand and wonder at this life and what happened to my hopes and dreams. Most of all I wonder how I could have got it so wrong, so often, and still come out with a wonderful life – particularly these last two years when I have found the love of my life.

I have changed just one or two names to protect people who have not volunteered for this where possible. Many others have not volunteered their names either, but it would be pointless trying to conceal their names, for various reasons, so they are in. I am sorry if anyone is upset by what I write here. I can only say in my defence that I am trying to tell the truth as it appears to me now and I mean no harm. Reading that back it sounds a bit lame so let me try another tack: this is my truth, if you don't like it then you can write yours.

So much has changed. Not just where I lived but who I lived with. Most of all, I have changed. Perhaps more than most.

We carry the past with us all the time, or are reaching for it, if it is not already to hand. We remember or create our memories to order. We do it to validate our choices, to explain our present lives. We give our ghosts – those that we all carry with us – as our references for this new job of living this day now. Ghosts of family, lovers dead and gone into the past because even if they are still alive, those that are still living are somewhere else and are different people now, gone, removed, the ghosts of our dreams and ambitions, of our failures and embarrassments. These ghosts hover round us, every day, our constant companions, speaking to us as we speak to them, continuously.

Or is it just me?

"Worth the telling only if I dig deep into everything", so old Uncle Jack Kerouac tells me. Jack, the soulful scriptwriter of my youth. If Van Morrison's 'Astral Weeks' was the soundtrack of those teenage days, sitting there in the red lamplight in my little room in the council house in Essex, then Jack was the scriptwriter who gave me the plotlines I acted out, living it as I could, hearing him explain my life to me. So now, of an age he never reached, I sit in this lovely house and make a start with his mantra on my mind, one of his books again on the table behind me.

I have travelled so far, often alone, trailing wives and children, friends, careers, houses, pets, books, blues, footballs, guitars and lives behind me, in my often, disastrous wake. I must have learned something along the way, even if only how to come to terms with my ghosts, to be able to name them and nod at them in passing, like bikers flashing in opposite directions, sharing a brief connection.

I have stood on stages, on walls at factory gates, crying my songs of freedom as I understood them then. I have laid in a hospital bed, exhausted. I have held my new born children, saved a man's life, broken some hearts, stood at the back at my son's funeral and taken my blows in return. I have stood on a touchline hearing thousands of fans chant my name and also received death threats in the mail and on the phone. I have spent most of my life looking for a woman I did not think I would find, only to do so when I had almost given up looking, at this crazily late stage.

I have made so many mistakes. My only saving grace has been the ability to laugh at myself. I mean, you cannot take all this too seriously, can you? I feel like I have redefined the term 'fool' every five years. When I look back, I am stunned by my consistent lack of awareness of what was going on around me. I missed so much, its only now that the ghosts tell me what really happened or at least hint at it.

Some years ago, I stood in a suite at the top of the London Hilton on Park Lane, looking out the night-time full-length window back along the park, with the headlights flashing and red brake lights glaring, back towards Marble Arch where I had been homeless as a kid. I thought with a sense of puzzlement of distances travelled but then was distracted by the crying of the woman in the suite behind me and turned away from the black London night.

And then people ask me to explain this life to them, to share my calm, to give any clue of a sliver of an answer, to spill some 'wisdom', whatever that is. Or I see my children stumbling towards the cliffs, and I want to call out. On the radio, my mate Tommy Boyd called me the 'Radio Guru' and says 'you're good at this'. I feel a fraud.

Because all I can do is tell you about the ghosts. That's all, just the ghosts.

Ah, but what ghosts.....

In there, inevitably, there are the ghosts of Chris Robinson at four years old in London streets after the war, at seventeen at a party falling too deeply in love so that he never quite gets out, at thirty-something killing himself with two marriages gone at forty-two as a professional football manager frowning on the touchline as the TV cameras whirl, and many more. Many times, it seems, I was a man with a plan. I had something going on, I had some scheme, some driving aim. It also seems that for a lot of those times, there was a girl or woman next to me, and I was turning on the charm, getting them to buy the dream and throw in their lot with me.

And now, I am mostly writing this because having finally, ridiculously, found the love of my life, she keeps telling me to write this story. For my children if not for me.

Somehow, I kept going through it all. I kept picking myself up and rolling on, chasing those hopes and dreams. Alone, together, healthy, ill, rich, poor, happy, sad. Get back up and go again. I have said to my kids that it is the Robinson family motto –

Over, under or through.

1. The Ghost of Tom Joad

I hope I don't die too soon. I hope I can make a difference somewhere along this line. The ghosts plead with me for some repayment, for something approaching delivery.

I've always had this sort of chip on my shoulder. I am trying to work out why and how it relates to how I grew up so I can tell that story and introduce you to those ghosts with some sensible context.

To show you what I mean, let me take you back to a walk I took a while ago when I still had Diego the Dog to look after.

The leaves were nearly all off the trees, lying underfoot on the soaked ground as we suffered yet more rain. We trudged through the woods. Well, I trudged. Diego is not keen on the rain at all, but it was quite mild that morning, so he was quite cheery and bright-eyed as we had our long morning walk.

Unlike me, as I was up till gone midnight the night before, finally getting to bed about 1.00am this morning which seemed so bloody recent right then as I staggered on. What was I doing till the early hours, I hear you ask?

Was I carousing in a noisy back street bar as Northern Soul blared out from a sound system? Was I licking whipped cream off the honey-coloured body of a Cuban dancer?

No, I was sitting up waiting for the Christmas delivery slots on Tesco to open up at 00.01hrs. I tell you what, rock and roll? It was life in the fast lane at Bramble Cottage, I tell you.

So, I was a little less than bright-eyed. I can't do late nights any more.

One thing about the woods in winter is that you can see a lot further as the trees and bushes thin out. I know that might sound obvious, but such changes are very noticeable to me still and remain strangely surprising to a city boy like me. This means you can see people coming from a lot further away in winter.

There he was, walking up the path through the woods down by the corn field. Hooray Henry, as I inevitably called him. I often see him and his two dogs. One is a very keen springer spaniel, extremely well trained, obviously a gun dog, and the other is a scruffy bored little terrier of some sort.

The first time I met him out walking was last summer. I immediately noticed the cream cotton Oxford shirt with a broad check, the green gilet, the dogs' leads casually looped around his shoulders as if to broadcast the fact that his dogs were so well trained that of course he didn't need to have them actually on a lead. He wore salmon pink trousers.
Obviously, I took an instant dislike to him.

He was about forty, a cheery ruddy faced guy and, as certainly forecast by my sharp 'Toff Radar' when he spoke it was in a plummy matey voice, reeking of school dorms, old boy networks and casual racism.
"Morning! What a handsome dog" he said, referring to Diego, straining on the lead to get closer to his two, "what sort is he?"
"He's a Bloody Nuisance," I said.

Now I am very aware of my inverse snobbery and my almost unforgiveable jumping to a conclusion here. I have to work very hard to overcome my inbuilt class dislike of anyone with that public school accent, that almost physical sense of privilege, and salmon pink trousers. If I were a betting man, which I am not, I would bet Diego's pocket money that Hooray Henry has another similar pair in yellow at home. Possibly several.

I should have learned years ago how misguided I could be when I started a management training course fresh out of university. One of the other guys registering on the first day was a slim, athletic looking chap with fair hair, wearing a yellow cravat. Yes, even then it was old fashioned to an extreme. A cravat! When he gave his name – suitably double barrelled of course – I had to physically fight to restrain my sneer. But as the months went by it turned out this fellow was a real good lad. Yes, he was posh, but he was a bloody good cricketer, and good company to boot. However, I struggle to take on board some lessons and have done so throughout my life. In fact, I think I am getting worse. Maybe it was just the recent General Election that had sharpened the working-class axe which I grind and polished the veritable potato on my shoulder.

I should know better than judging on first impressions, filtered by my class consciousness. I am sure Hooray Henry could be a very nice man, kind to his children, attentive to his wife, working in a caring profession. He could be. I will probably never know. (I bet he's not, though.)

We do judge so easily. Everyone we meet can either instantly be a friend, an enemy or a stranger. Instantly categorised, without even consciously thinking about it. It may be hard-wired in, a primordial awareness of possible lurking dangers, I don't know. But we judge, we discriminate, we construct. All the time.
It is not helpful.
Just for the rest of today, just check yourself when you meet people, or pass people are you categorising them like that? Friend, enemy or stranger? Attraction, aversion or indifference.

Knowing that we do this, we expect other people do too – and are usually right, of course. So, we can be very aware of what we think others think of us, painfully so. I heard the wonderful late Leonard Cohen in a radio interview explain that as far as women were concerned men went through five stages of life.

At first, we are cute, we are little babies and cute. Then for some years we become invisible to the female population, annoying little boys not worth attention. Then briefly we are interesting.

For some of us that third stage of being interesting may be for a while, for others it can be a brief moment in the sun of female attention. I think mine was an afternoon in Accrington about thirty-five years ago.

However, we then become invisible again, for a long time. No more the lingering look from a passing lovely. Finally, at the end, we become cute again. A cute old man, harmless but possibly cute, also possibly toothless.

I think I am somewhere between the fourth stage of invisible and the final cute.

But, if our images of ourselves are illusions – I've said before I still think I am thirty-five until a mirror surprises me – and I've also said how we take mental snapshots or misleading impressions of virtually everyone else we meet and they can be way off the mark, filtered and adjusted by our prejudices, then what we think others think of us is really an illusion of an illusion, isn't it? Why do we worry so?

The antidote is an open mind, and a letting go of our own ego, and a taking of life and the people in it as they come and go. The path to peace.

Meanwhile, while I work on that, my class prejudice gets in the way. I don't suppose Hooray Henry worries about what I think of him, he probably doesn't know or care.

I know I should rise above it, too.

But salmon pink trousers. For fuck's sake.

I was born in 1954 when families were looking forward to a new life, something new and positive, in those London Street days. Going with my dad to the tiny old newsagents shop on City Road by the Central Street junction of my childhood, by the alley where I later made fearful appointments for fights that usually never happened and walked home with girls not knowing why. I was engrossed in my comics back then that we picked up as Dad bought his cigarettes, but the old newsagent couple called the Rodgems were talking to him about life. They had gnarled, lined faces which I remember as if they were now standing before me. They were both wiry, small people.

"You just want a better life for the kiddies than we had," I heard Dad say and I looked up from the 'Victor' or the 'Tiger', from Roy Race or 'Alf Tupper – the tough of the track'. I can remember it so clear, my Mum and Dad's intention and purpose and the accepted common striving for the working-class families after the war. Back when the gaps of broken buildings were still called 'bomb sites' and probably actually were. When all the men I knew had fought in the war in some way, and everyone had stories, some they told, some they did not, maybe some they made up. Heroes for their children, perhaps. I don't think that applied to my Dad who got in the tail-end of the war, in the Navy.

"What was the worst thing about the war?" I asked my Dad, my childhood adventure yearnings for more navy tales.
"Seeing your mates die when you could do nothing to help," he said and turned away.

Well, they achieved their purpose, that generation. They worked and worked, shifts and long hours, bringing us fridges and cars, holiday camp holidays and days out, all they never had and presumed we would need.

"Bloody hell", said my Grandad, Henry Charles March, Harry March from Somers Town, as I prepared to go skiing with my secondary school at twelve years old to Austria. "A day out for us as kids was Theydon Bois."

Footballs, cricket bats, toy soldiers for my endless make-believe football games on the thin carpet, as I wrote the programmes and match reports of games that only existed in my head and on that carpet with marbles and little figures. To make it real I had to write it down. It's been that way ever since.

Toys from Gamage's in Holborn, but more often Dawson Brothers, the department store down near Old Street. Nothing like the profusion, the obscene flood of things raining down on our kids now these days of course but it's all coal gas and violets, all relative. From wartime and ration books to some shiny choice, in weeks, that was a heady mix to deal with, a mighty brew, a future shock right there. I was taught the value of things, and the difference between right and wrong. May I do the same for my kids.

Old Street? When I was a kid, you couldn't give away a house on Hoxton Square, now there's artists there and seven figure estate agents' commissions. Ah, what the hell, it's better now, of course it is. It's just changed, the ghosts have moved on. Maybe.

But along the way, securing us all this, making these material advances, our parents created a generation of suddenly half-educated kids who thought the world owed them a living. Don't get me wrong, I have no complaints, I take responsibility for my own life. That has been one of the clearest lessons.

My earliest memory, though, is of being in the homeless hostel near Marble Arch with my Mum and sister. My Dad was coming to visit. In those days, husband and wife could not stay together in the hostels. I don't know where my Dad stayed. My Mum was ill, I remember, so I was cuddled up in bed with her, and maybe my sister, too. The staff were making the bed with us in it, telling us how my Dad was coming to visit and then he was there. I was about two, maybe three years old. We had nowhere to live. We'd stayed with my Dad's parents, in Northview Road, Hornsey, backing onto the Alexandra Park racecourse where later as a teenager I would blissfully play cricket, but that had not worked out. My Dad's sister stole my Mum's clothing, so the story goes. I don't know. My Dad's family was from Carlton near Nottingham, dirt poor. He would say later he had no time for any of them, they would only come to see him when they wanted something, usually money because by then he was working regular and doing well. But back then he was a lorry driver, telling me and my sister tales of his time on the road, driving down snow-covered roads in the black night.

Some years ago I had to go to Hornsey for a cricket match where I was presenting one of the trophies. Keir, my number five son, then aged eleven, came with me on a sunny late summer bank holiday afternoon. We drove round the area where I was born. The nursing home in Alexandra Park Road is gone now, replaced by a block of flats. We drove down Northview Road and parked up. It's not a bad area at all now. We looked up at the house where I first lived, it's a narrow terraced first floor maisonette, as I recalled. We walked through a pathway to the back, looking up at Alexandra Park. The horse racing track is long gone but there's a good open common space there. We walked over to the cricket ground I loved to play on later in my teenaged life. The fine old wooden pavilion is gone and there's an ugly modern changing room block there but at least the grounds were in good use with a football tournament taking place. We walked back to the car and drove around the corner to the Nightingale pub, now closed up.

It was all so long ago, fifty-plus years and I had not been back since. At the edges of my memory some things tugged or registered but it was another world, another time.

We tried living with my Mum's lovely parents, Harry and Lydia March, but their two-bedroomed council house in Courtman Road, Tottenham was just not big enough for this growing family. So, we were homeless. The plan was that we would get allocated a council house, but it never came, not for many years.

My Dad's employers came up with an offer of a three-bedroomed flat in Islington, one of two high above a rat-infested old transport depot on Macclesfield Road, facing onto City Road. 258a City Road, on the canal bridge, halfway between the Angel, Islington and Old Street. Old school London. Through an anonymous green double door in the blank wall of the depot frontage on the bridge you went up a gloomy grey concrete stairway, echoing footsteps, always cold and forbidding and dark with feeble bare light bulbs high above. At the top, to the right was our big heavy dark wooden door that showed us into the long corridor off which went the living room with small kitchen, then the lounge that we called 'the best room', then the three bedrooms and the bathroom and toilet. It was bleak, no garden just the roof of the transport depot with the heavy industrial glass skylights, one of which would later leave with a scar on my forehead I can find to this day. This roof, our garden, became football pitch, tennis court, cricket square (although the long passageway in the flat was favourite for that), western prairie, war ground and anything else my frantic imagination could come up with. At night, lying in my little strange shaped bedroom all angles, with the iron steps and walkway outside leading round to the huge drop of the fire escape stairway down to the depot below, the clanking green iron, I could hear all the scabby mongrel guard-dogs that used to go out on the parcel delivery vans barking below because the kennels were there. I could hear the night trunk lorries throbbing below as they drove out late at night and the returning lorries in the early hours. I don't know what my Mum made of it. Maybe it was just somewhere, our place, our home, anywhere will do. We moved there when I was four and lived there until I was 15 when the council house finally came up, out on the Belhus estate in South Ockendon, Essex, in the no-mans land of eastward sprawl.

Meanwhile, I spent the years there that meant this part of London would be where I forever after said I was from. Dad working as a lorry driver for BRS then a foreman and finally in a suit for a while managing some transport outfit or other, then back in the Docks on the Isle of Dogs where I eventually worked with him. Mum always worked, part-time at first then full-time, down in the City, office work, typing or whatever. Really, though, her full-time job was me and my sister, Pauline, eighteen months older than me. She ran our lives, she lived for us and vice-versa. She was everything. Our disciplinarian, our ever-warm comfort, our lives.

So, what day did you say? Will we ever know. Pick a day, pick a time, take me back to that security, that promise, with all my life before me, everything can be done. This is what she told me, the gift she gave me.
'You can do anything you want to do in this life.'
That is what she said, over and over. Until I believed it.
Such a gift, such a gift.
Oh, that I should be able to give my kids that same gift. May I try every day.

It must have been hard for her. One night me and my sister were tripping to bed along that long passageway in the flat towards our bedrooms, maybe having watched 'Rawhide' or some such. I was ahead, my sister following on. I guess we were headed to clean our teeth and our Mum would then come to 'tuck us in' because she always did. As she kissed me goodnight I would hold on to her hand. 'Can't you leave your hand with me?' I would ask and she would laugh at me.
Oh, Mum, can't you leave your hand with me now?
Anyway, this night my sister calls out and there in the passageway – I must have passed it by, blissfully unaware even then, probably still in my head shooting it out with Gil Favour and Rowdy Yates – was a big rat huddled against the wall of the passage. We headed back to the Best Room which presumably meant me hurdling the grey rat

17

on the way. Back in there, panicking and shouting, Dad was despatched to deal with it. Mum barricaded the door and held on to me and my sister. There was much banging and cursing. Eventually Dad gives the all-clear.
"It must have been someone's guinea pig that escaped." That was the story. No mention ever of a rat. It never occurred to me to question why then my Dad had hammered seven shades out of someone's pet guinea pig with our big broom. Even then, I was sailing through life ever looking up, ever dreaming.

"How much do you love me?" my Mum would ask when she tucked me in at night.
"All the money in the world…and tuppence." I would say. Same question and answer every night. Neither of us grew tired of it. I would answer the same now, given the chance.

My Mum, Phyllis Marie March, had been a singer and dancer in her teens, and met my Dad, Bernard Alfred Robinson, at a Dance at Hornsey Town Hall. She gave up the dancing and created a family instead. She was bright enough to pass the 11-plus, but her parents could not afford to send her to Grammar School as one of her elder brothers, Denis, was already there. She was a bright, determined, opinionated, warm-hearted striking brunette, probably the strongest-minded person I have ever met.

Years later, I am in Zambia and going through my wallet for some reason. I show an old photo of my Mum I have found there to a friend. A photo of my Mum as a teenager, I would guess, maybe twenty years old at most.
"But…. she's beautiful," my friend says.
"Yes," I say, taking the photo back, looking at it anew, "I suppose she was."

Sunday mornings, my Dad would take me and my sister out. I would love to think it was to give my Mum some time to herself but looking back I know now it was to give her a better chance to clean the home with us all out of it and to cook the Sunday dinner. I feel the ghosts telling me that. Dad would take us maybe to Club Row market to see the puppies and kittens there, then we would walk through to Petticoat Lane amidst the noise and colour of the mixed market there in the dirty, crowded streets. There would be chancers noisily selling dinner plates, cups and saucers off the back of a truck, or doing 'chase the lady' card tricks with one eye out for the police on street corners, men Dad called 'spivs'. Sights and sounds, music blaring from one of these new transistor radios, deep fried apple fritters covered with a shaking of sugar if we were in Chapel Street market along past DiMarco's Ice Cream parlour, if I could brave walking past the black wriggling horror of the fresh eel stall outside the pie and mash shop, blood on the chopping board, knives in the air. The apple fritters were worth it, though.

I can remember sitting with my Mum watching 'The Grapes of Wrath' film on TV. It's a great 1940 black and white film by John Ford with Henry Fonda in the lead role as Tom Joad. The film is based of course on the incredible book by John Steinbeck – my favourite novel. The screenplay was written by Nunnally Johnson and has some great lines in it. Tom Joad tells his Mum just as he goes on the run that wherever she comes across someone in need, someone poor, someone downtrodden, then he will be there.

'Look in their eyes, Ma, you'll see me.'

I absorbed it all in.

Listen, I tell you London was wide open then in the late fifties and early sixties. Everything was going to happen, it was all possible, there was a brave new world order on the way. That was the feeling. Some Tory bastard was saying 'You've never had it so good' and he was probably right for the only time in his old school tie, officer class, cut glass, shitblown life.

Sunday summer mornings in the city, the wide Islington streets behind the Angel there, away from the 'Blue Kettle' where there was a murder one time, Sunday summer mornings and radios blaring while someone washes their rare shiny car in the street outside their home. Wide open streets, sunshine, music from the radio blaring cheerful and loud. Breakfast inside, eggs and bacon, Sunday roast to come, couple of pints down the pub maybe amidst the smoke and laughter, crowding the serious old gimmers playing crib, Sunday papers flashing, 'Sunday People' and the 'News of the World', beer, cigarettes and roast to come, I tell you. Bright clear sunshine, city streets, Sunday morning optimism. Kids on old bikes, cheerful old lady with those shopping bags on wheels there used to be, still wearing a mac even in July. Passing the time of day, people that you know.
"Getting away this year, Bert?"
"Thought we might take the kids down to Clacton."
"Lovely. See you down the Arms later?"
"Yeah, might nip in for one."
"Righto, see you, mate."

My grandad Harry March signed up for World War One by lying about his age, only to come face-to-face with his older brother in the trenches. His brother grassed him up and Harry got sent back home to wait till he was of age. Never spoke to his brother again for the rest of their lives. Over the top eleven times in three years. Years later showing me the round bruise-like wound on his foot where he'd got shot way back in the 'first war'. Harry March, trade union man, council worker, laying down the paving stones through Stoke Newington park, near where his council depot was, where he used to take me to have my hair cut. Grandad, sitting with me outside the old Cambridge pub in Tottenham, on the roundabout, telling me stories. Teaching me to play cards and chess, endless patience as he sat in his chair in the little house in Courtman Road in Tottenham that was my second home. Whenever there was mention of the Royal family on TV or radio he would mutter and swear, "bloody royals, bloody spongers". A strange mix of patriotism and republicanism, the ghosts tell me now, a working man in his prime. A big bluff dark haired man who liked a drink and supported Spurs.

Take me back. Take me back to my lovely Nan making me my favourite rice puddings in the little kitchen, me and my sister fighting till my Nan was reduced to tears then me getting sent upstairs though it was my sister who within ten minutes would come up and play with me up there anyway. Grandad called Nan 'Squibbs' because that was her maiden name, Lydia Squibbs from Hitchin, a lovely, kind, quiet, patient woman.

Take me back..

My Grandad who, in later life, would have both legs amputated one after the other as his circulation got worse and worse. A big man reduced. My Nan dying of cancer, and I could not understand how she was suddenly gone.

Oh, but take me back, to me and Grandad bringing a Mackeson home from the pub for Nan, and she would pour me and my sister a shot glass each.

"When do you go to the big girls school?" he would ask me, and I would laugh.

He would ask me about my football.

"We won 5-0 and I scored three," I said.

"Who were you playing? The Blind School?"

When I look back on my long eventful life one of its features is that I have moved around a lot. I worked out recently that I have lived in twenty-five houses or flats. I take full responsibility for all that has happened in my life – good and bad. Regrets, therefore, rightly, are usually more focused on what I didn't do rather than what I did. Moving round, usually following work of one sort or another has, like a lot of things in life, brought rewards and also incurred costs.

One of the biggest costs is that I have not been local, nearby, available for most of my children – and now all of my grandchildren. Is that the sort of parent or grandparent I want to be?

It inevitably makes me think of my own Nan and Grandad and the relationship I had with them. This is my Mum's Mum and Dad – funnily enough we had relatively little contact with my Dad's parents – that's a whole other story. But my Nan and Grandad on my Mum's side were very important players in my early life.

So, Grandad. Harry March. He was from Somers Town, just north of Euston train station in London. It's now a very trendy area of course but was a rough old place back then around the turn of the 20th century.

He was a tall well-built fella with a great sense of humour. He was a bit of a mix because on the one hand he volunteered and joined up early for the First World War. He "wanted the adventure" he told me later. He signed up with his mates for the Middlesex Regiment of the old King's Rifles, an infantry regiment. Off he went to war.

In time he was back after being sent home for being under age and went over the top eleven times in three years. He told me stories of the trenches, mostly about the horses and the songs, kindly missing out the horrors, I am sure. Eventually he got shot through the foot.
"Did it hurt, Grandad?" I asked as he showed me the mark still on his foot, a small bruise on the side of his foot with a corresponding mark on the other side. The bullet went straight through.
"Funnily enough," he said, "not at the time. But it bloody well did when my mate was giving me a piggy-back to the field hospital!"

He was soon back in action and ended up a Sergeant and lived, of course, happily for all of us, to tell the tales. He was a crack rifle shot and won medals at Bisley after the war when he was in the Territorials and then was an air raid warden in the Second World War.

Harry came back home, worked as a labourer for the local council at Stoke Newington, laying paving slabs and met Lydia Squibbs, a couple of years older than him, when she was out walking in a park with a friend on a Sunday afternoon and there they were. Nan and Grandad.

They lived in Courtman Road in Tottenham, first at number 19 then at number 20. Council houses. They had two sons – Denis and Arthur – and three daughters – Vera, my Mum Phyllis, and the youngest Doris.

Grandad was a Tottenham fan (other than that he was a real good guy!). When Tottenham played Leicester City in the 1961 Cup Final Grandad and me had a sixpenny bet. Tottenham won and I had to pay up. Our sixpences were on the mantel piece above the fire. My Dad told me I had to hand mine over as I'd lost the bet, having backed Leicester. I was in tears and grabbed the silver sixpenny piece and threw it at my Grandad, much to his amusement.

I had turned seven years old the day before.

I've never been a good loser.

On the other hand, Grandad was a trade union man and had little time for the Royal Family or the other 'knobs' as he called them. He said something to me once that I thought was original to him, but it turned out later it was quite a widespread saying amongst the proper people of the time. Someone mentioned that word 'scroungers' again.

Grandad said, "If you took all the scroungers in this country and threw 'em in a big old pond, there would be more top hats than flat caps float to the surface!"

He taught me endless card games and to play chess too. We would play cribbage or rummy or whist for the buttons my Nan kept in a round biscuit tin. And he would tell me stories.

He and I would walk down the Great North Road in Tottenham to the Cambridge pub, and we would sit outside on a bench. Me with my orange juice and him with a pint. And more stories.

He had trouble over many years with circulation in his legs. He eventually had to have his foot amputated. Then his leg up to the knee. Then finally up to his thigh. When the other foot started troubling him and the Doctors said that would have to come off, he said "Bugger it! Take the whole bloody thing off, I don't want to go through all that again."

So, this tall, broad-shouldered man spent his later years in a wheelchair. When he had had just one leg, he had worn an artificial one, but he didn't bother when he had no legs left. He just had a blanket on his lap in the wheelchair.

He had a good sense of humour, always teasing. One day my Uncle took him, in his wheelchair with the blanket on his lap and no legs, to a department store. A young shop assistant held the door open so Uncle could wheel Grandad in.
"What department would you like, sir?" asked the shop assistant.
"Shoe department, "said Grandad, deadpan.

In these later years he was living with my Uncle Denis and Aunt Margaret in Knebworth, Hertfordshire, funnily enough not far from where my Nan was from originally. Funny how life can take you in circles. My lovely, gentle Nan died of cancer. Grandad lived on a while. He liked to go down the village pub now and then. When we were visiting and down that pub he introduced us to one of his drinking pals – the local undertaker.
"Now listen," he said to me as we stood with these guys," when I die don't let this grabbing bugger sell you a full-sized coffin – I only need a little one!"

I remember his funeral and remember noting it was actually a full-sized coffin, for a full-sized man.

So, as you can see, he was big influence on me. I could tell you many more stories. I think he was a formative positive influence in many ways too. He was a good hard-working man of his time and generation.

I wonder what stories, if any, my grandchildren will tell of me, their Grandad, who they see just a couple of times a year? Is this part of the inevitable change in modern life with our more mobile families? Maybe. Nan and Grandad lived about twenty minutes from us most of my childhood. We visited as family pretty much every week. My sister and I went and stayed there most school holidays as my Mum and Dad both worked full time. I spent a lot of time playing football in the street at Courtman Road.

So, what am I going to do about it?

I have my work down here with the long hours and major commitment. Football is a wonderful world to work in but unforgiving and not family-friendly at all. I work six days a week, eleven months of the year and the phone never stays quiet for long. I have two of my five sons down here. Julie has her family down here, too, and her lovely, lively grandson and granddaughter, who she looks after a few days a week, sharing those special times that can never be replaced or paid back.

Back in the day, as a kid, walking down by the Thames, with Dad and Pauline, me chattering away, along the embankment, autumn wind blowing clouds across the washed-out sky, leaves from the trees blustering past us. In St James Park walking round the pond where the ice was forming in winter, where I would walk in later life, as a teenager, hopelessly drowning in love so fierce and cold I could not bear it. In spring, on Tower Hill, watching the escapologist in his chains and bag, rattling and thrashing on the cobbles before his miraculous emergence, the stately Tower behind, beefeaters and crows, fewer tourists then. The smell of Billingsgate fish market, where later in another lifetime, I would make a speech before two thousand drunken city traders as the girls in bikinis wove through the tables selling raffle tickets in the spotlights. And the river flowing on behind, browns and greys, mudflats at low tide, living history.

Smithfield's, Billingsgate, Covent Garden, Spitalfields. All gone now. All gone to shit and Gap. Though that's gone now too, funnily enough. All gone. Everything changes, all the time.

The winter of 1963, I think it was, the snow so deep. We got to Turnpike Lane and then had to walk from there through to Courtman Road, such snow, you don't see that any more in London. All gone. All fucking gone to shit, all globally warmed to hell, all gone. And that ain't coming back.

Down on the docks where me and Dad used to work, the awful Isle of Dogs with scruffy pubs, rat-infested wharves and dockside, poor people, I mean poor people, working hard for fuck all, all their lives, Freddie Rock telling me "the office people get a turkey at Christmas, you know? I think we might get a fucking seagull if we're lucky!"
Hard work and trouble, getting drunk most every night. "Had a great night last night" says young Lenny, "six pints and a fight then I puked up." I watch my Dad throw him over the wharf wall into the Thames on the first day I went to work, wondering what I had let myself in for, who was this hardworking, swearing man I thought was my kind old buffy Dad. This was the working life, and all bets are off.
As we drove there for my first day's work, me at seventeen, Dad says:
"They're a rough lot. You'll have to stand your ground." That was it. Thanks, Dad.

I would read Kerouac, pulling a battered paperback from my jeans back pocket and the guys would rib me "for always having your nose in a book". But I learned the ways and just like my Dad said, I learned to stand my ground.
Freddie Rock on a forklift, me on a trailer and I drop something.
"Bloody hell, you're alright with a book but fucking hopeless else," he would shout.
"Fuck off and come back when you can count me 'O' levels," I would shout back and he would wheel away on the forklift, chortling aloud with his raucous laughter.
The Kingsbridge pub there on the island – well, shit, it could just as well have been the Nightingale back in Northview Road, Hornsey, before I was born where my Dad and his brother used to drink, my Uncle who was a real losing boozer who kept his Nottingham accent unlike my Dad. Uncle Harry who once said to me, "Now your Dad, he were a boozer before he met your Mum, he really were." On the island, when we worked together, my Dad would go in the Kingsbridge every lunchtime, two or three pints, then every night, I mean, every night would call in another pub, the Anchor, I think it was called on the way home, another two or three pints. He would not go out again, mind, but every working day I am telling you he had six or seven or eight pints and I knew none of this till we worked together. So what was he like before when he was a boozer?

And, you know, my Dad was a quiet man till he had a drink and then he talked some crap, hell, yes, he did. I have always been aware of that and wary of it in myself. One of these reasons I stop drinking from time to time, just got to choke off that bullshit line spinning. That slippery boozer slope is always there close at hand to me. And I know a drinker don't tell no truth, don't look after anyone, does nothing worthwhile and real and I have feared for my life to go that way because, I tell you, I could smell how close it was now and then, breathing old beer fumes behind me.

How did I grow up to love the Blues? My choice in music and football. I don't know on either count. No idea.

Growing up I learnt Mum liked Frankie Vaughan, Joseph Locke and, later, Elvis and Dad liked truly, deeply awful music by Mantovani or the Frank Chacksfield Singers or some shit, oh, Jeez, that Sunday night radio programme, 'Sing Something Simple' how I hated that with a passion! That dead Sunday afternoon, early evening time and this wretched sickly music. To be fair, Dad did like a bit of Nat King Cole and Ray Charles so there was some hope.

I remember being at the Arsenal one time and in the crowd, me going off for a wee then going back, searching for my Dad, and then seeing his face as he watched the game, standing there in the crowd and I can remember thinking, ain't that funny, all these faces here, thousands and thousands here and that's the face I look for and then feel safe? Oh, life is strange, there is no doubt. He was a good man, a hardworking man. When I spoke at his funeral, not so long ago, I said that I knew he would not want me to get too serious.
"Tell 'em a story, boy," he would say. So I did. I told them a story about my silly, lovely old Dad. Some years ago, I had a canal boat of sorts and needed it taken down from Lancashire where I was living to the Midlands because I was moving down there. Dad, the old salt, the old sailor from the war, said he was up for the job. He gets two mates together and they set off from Chorley although the two mates soon abandon ship – it was a crappy old boat.
Next I hear, Dad is down in Cheshire somewhere and phones up.
"Going alright, boy, just got a bit of a problem. Got this tunnel coming up and I've worked out the boat is about four inches too tall. Anyway, not to worry, I've worked it out, I'm going to saw the top off the cabin, that'll drop it down a few inches, see, and I'll get through, then I'll nail it back on when I get out the other side."
I'm sort of stunned in silence, then he's saying:
"Well, gotta go, boy, speak to you later." He hangs up.

I turn away from the phone and must have looked a sight. My eldest son, Pat, then about fourteen, asks me what's up and I tell him the tale.

"Why doesn't he just get a big rock or something, or a couple of people, on the boat, that will lower it down a bit and he won't need to saw the roof off?" says Pat. Good point.

I wished I had thought of that when the old man was on the line. Frantic phone calls, British Waterways and all sorts, trying to catch the saw-happy old fella before he does the damage. As it turns out, the boat breaks down before the tunnel is reached.

That was my Dad.

I told this story at his funeral about ten years ago and his old drinking mates laughed, though some of the more polite neighbours – this was long after Mum had died and Dad was living in the same village as my sister down in Somerset and had for some years – looked like they wondered what the hell was going on. But my Dad would have laughed, he liked me telling the story, it was true, and he would enjoy the telling. I knew he would not have wanted any sentimental stuff. One of his mates came up to me after the service and shook my hand and said how much he liked the story.

"That was your Dad, that was."

See you on the far post, Dad.

I have a lifetime of these phrases in my head, this music in my veins, this pain speaking to me across continents and time. These ghosts.

On the dusty London boyhood streets, in the markets, the smelly alleys, the bombsites and school playgrounds, I would occasionally see a big shiny Rolls Royce gliding by. Maybe up the West End – the 'Other End', as my Mum called it – waiting outside a fancy shop or sailing along the Mall. There was something about this that stuck with me, something I just could not figure.

"Dad, why have some people got Rolls Royces and us lot got nothing?"

Chris Robinson – Over, Under or Through

It was not envy, let me tell you, it was puzzlement, and a sense of unfairness. There was them and us then. Then?

Out in the docks, on the road where my Dad was, or working for the council, mending streets like my Grandad, it seemed there was only the Unions on our side, in our corner. I learnt these lessons well.

In my primary school – Moreland Street Primary School – just off City Road, just around the corner from our flat, along by the Gordon's Gin Distillery – there were concrete playgrounds around the big old Victorian school building, and dank gloomy playing areas underneath the school, too. I would run to school early to get time to play football and stay after school to play in those spaces under the building. I had my first fight there, I guess, but I don't remember, though I do remember losing a fight to a mate of mine, Costakis Makrakis, under there. More kids from that school went to prison than went to University, I can tell you that.

When I was first there, the cock of the walk was a kid called 'Dixie' Deans. I think he'd just left the primary school and I'd just gone up to the Junior school making him about eleven and me about eight, I guess. He was a tough kid. He breezed into our after-school game one night with a few mates down in the cellars beneath the school where we played out of the rain. Someone grabbed our ball and he had us marching up and down like soldiers.

"Attention! Stand at ease!"

We went along with it. There was not much else we could do and besides it was almost fun.

He comes and stands in front of me where I am standing to attention.

"You like all this, don't you?" he was almost surprised.

"Yeah," I said, "but I'd rather play football." For a minute his eyes glared, and I wondered if I had gone too far but then he just laughed and turned away, calling out to his mates, slinging our ball back and they left us to our game.

Me and my big mouth didn't always work out so well.

Years later I read how another classmate of mine from those days was sent down for life on a murder rap. Also I recall the elder brother of a girlfriend of mine getting ten years for robbery.

But this is no hard luck story, not at all. My Mum taught me to read before I even went to school. She marched me down the local library at St John's and she told the librarian I wanted a library ticket for the children's library.
"How old is he?" asked the woman librarian, glasses on a chain around her neck, frizzled hair in a bun, cut glass accent. Islington always had a posher end, even then.
"Four."
"So he's not at school yet?"
"No."
"Well, I'm sorry but we only give cards to children that can read."
"He can read," said Mum.
"But you said he doesn't go to school yet, he's only four?"
"That's right, I taught him."
Bloody librarian did not believe Mum, clearly. Mum takes a book off the desk and gives it to me.
"Read it," she says with a smile.
I read it out loud. I get my library card. You did not mess with my Mum.

That's stayed with me. Everywhere I go, my first step is to join the local library. I read two maybe three books a week. I am sat here in my little office at home, books round the walls, a pile of library books waiting for me to take them back later today. Nowadays I buy books as well as borrow them, of course, in this Home Counties comfortable life. In airports, foreign cities, the big bookshops of the West End. Amazon makes it too easy, my only temptation these sorted days, perhaps. Another one for Mum, then.

Moreland Street School. My wonderful teacher, Miss White, grumpy old Mr Hodgkinson, the frightening, blustery teacher who took the football and set me on the way, who had a soft spot for my sister so took it easy on me, Mr Hunter the Head Teacher, Arsenal fan but otherwise all right. The feedback from the teachers was always the same, - bright lad but talks too much. About right. I loved it all, bring on that learning. Miss White used to get me to come out front of the class and tell them stories that I made up as I went along about this explorer and a witchdoctor called 'Gluepot'. Christ knows where I got all that from. I had no nerves and a lot to say. 'More rabbit than Sainsbury's' as the saying went back then. ('Rabbit and pork' – talk.)

Some of the kids struggled for shoes so we were not the worst off by any means. Mum and Dad were both working hard, making their way for us, for me and my sister, building that life.
We had school medical inspections.
I remember standing in the Head Teacher's little office as this Doctor examines me. There's him and a nurse and Mr Hunter, all stood there staring at my scrawny legs. I wonder what's so interesting. I look down, usual scabby knees, bruises from endless football.
"I think there's a touch of rickets there," says the Doctor, pointing at my bandy shins.
"Surely not", says Mr Hunter, "he comes from a very good family." They all nod and murmur. "He's maybe curved his legs round a football too much! He's forever kicking a ball", Mr Hunter is cheery, defensive.
They all relax and laugh.
"What's rickets, Mum?" I say when I get home.
Here we go.

We would go to Holiday Camps. My Mum would get me up on stage in the talent contests, singing old ballads like 'Slow Boat to China' and 'Lucky Lips'. I would never be keen, feigning stomach ache until the rehearsal but once I got the mike I was away, couldn't wait for the show and the audience. One time at the rehearsal the pianist

didn't know anything I knew. My Mum suggested song after song. No luck. So my Mum says to him "What do you know then?".
"How about 'Who's Sorry Now?'" he says, small tubby fella, brylcreemed hair, elastic bands holding the sleeves of his grubby white shirt back off his wrists.
"Okay," says Mum.
"But Mum," I'm mortified, whispering, "I don't know that."
"Don't worry," she says to me. "You play it", she tells the pianist, and turns back to me "and I'll tell you the words, you'll follow the tune, it's easy, you'll pick it up." She sang the first line to me. So off we go, he plays, she whispers each line in advance to me, and as she predicted, I just picked up the melody as we went, she had me so well trained, though I did not know the song at all. I mean, how can you not become confident with that?
Up on stages, laughing holiday crowds, family entertainment, pick up band behind me, I was seven or eight years old, maybe younger at first.

You sling these ingredients into a pot and it ain't no surprise what comes out. I've been a socialist all my life and see no reason to change now. I started going to the Labour Party's 'Young Socialist' group – mainly for the discos at first, to tell the truth, in the old Red Lion at the Angel where Lenin used to attend meetings (a while before me – steady, Tiger!) – when I was about sixteen, I think. I studied my history books and tried to make sense of them and also what I saw around me, searching for the underlying patterns. Nothing explained it really till I read me some Marx and the world suddenly fell into place.
My friends were all Labour supporters though we cursed the leadership. I knew then I was on the edge of the Party, that my views were not the mainstream but more than that I was totally convinced that they should be and believed that they could become the mainstream. At sixteen, seventeen and on, I was so sure. I knew the answer just like I knew the answers in class. It was all black and white. You were with us or against us. I had such certainty. Such clarity.

When I was about thirteen or fourteen, a teacher at my secondary school – Dame Alice Owen's School for Boys, at the Angel, down the road – says "you need to start thinking about your course options if you want to go to University."
Me? University? This is the first time this has ever been mentioned. No-one in my family has been to university, kids like me didn't go to university, no-one from my Primary School; had gone to University before. But, of course, in fact, we were beginning to do just that as the system began to open up a bit, and the working class broke out of their hovels, even if in a strictly supervised and limited way.

Geez, Owens School, though, where to begin? Originally a Brewers school, set up in 1613, a grammar school then run by the state, vestiges of old faux public school in the Rowing Club, the house system, the school song and traditions. Dusty dark old classrooms, a dusty 0.22 shooting range in the gloomy basement, across the playground there's the newer girls' school, full of distant promise. And hidden heartache, (but that's all down the road, hidden round the bend, those ghosts are sleeping for now, sshhh, stay quiet). Teachers in robes, tall corridors with clanking grey radiators, honour boards with the names of past cricket captains and football captains and Head Boys, little me looking up in my new school uniform, black blazer, red and black tie. They still had this ceremony where some old guy from the Brewers – Charringtons I think it was – comes along and we all lined up in silence – and he gives us 'beer money' – it used to be beer even further back – I remember getting a 'Churchill Crown'. Crazy mix of history and street kids, middle class kids from all over North London, plus ragamuffins like me, chancers and Jewish kids and some black kids, tradition and energy suddenly meeting head on in sixties London when the world was exploding, and we were there. Exams, lessons, detentions, Latin lessons which deteriorated to where the teacher, Mr Reeves, who we called 'Enus' for some reason, would leave me alone to read my 'Melody Maker' if I would not cause trouble. Slung out of Physics at thirteen, no sciences for me, give me that History and English, let me argue, let me play football, cricket, hockey and anything else I could have a go at. I was just a little kid, bright brown eyes and dark hair, all chat and energy, just one of many.

Kids had nicknames, teachers too. Because I was dark I was called 'Bubble' – from 'Bubble and Squeak' – Greek. I looked Greek, hence 'Bubble'. My best mate was big Gordon 'Griz' Phillips, called that cause he was big and black like a Grizzly Bear, I guess, even the teachers called him that. The teachers – 'Fanny' Cast (no idea why), 'Gym' Chant (the PE teacher), 'Rocket' Stephenson.

Once it had laughter, once it had dreams. Now, it's all gone, they closed the school because they were going to build a flyover at the Angel, which never came. All gone. Knocked down.

I was back there recently at the Angel, eating a lunch in the old Angel Inn café we used to frequent as teenagers, and walking round to the site of our school. The girls' school building is still there, part of a sixth form college now and where our playground was is a small park. I sat there on a bench. I could see the old wall that marked out the side of the playground where every day I would throw myself into football or cricket games at any opportunity, arriving back in class after break, sweating buckets, breathless and mark time till I could get out again and kick that fucking ball. Sitting there again, I just felt a sense of loss.

There were school bands, kids will make music given the chance, I watched them in awe at the school shows when I was younger, was up there on stage playing the drums and singing myself when I was older. In bands called 'Manhood's Home' and 'Willie The Pimp', playing with good musicians like Anton Pyzakowski, Bob Cranham, Frank Bortoli, Danny Newman and Bill Benfield, all way better than me, (probably the worst drummer in rock music history). Me, Danny and Bill played at a pub in Upper Street one time doing an acoustic thing with them on guitars, me on bongos and Danny and me

singing. We couldn't think of a name so Danny says to the guy, 'Can we just call ourselves 'Three Friends?'
"You can call yourselves 'Three Cunts' for all I care," he says.
He was keen on us once we played though because the other two lads were good.

'Willie The Pimp' played the White Lion Theatre back of the Angel, me on the drums, whacking out a crude rhythm to Frank Zappa and Who songs, where I heard my ex-girlfriend, Linda Murphy, was crying over me in the girl's toilets. My mate Dave Sutherland says, "I wish I had girls in the toilets crying over me," but I just felt confused, not at all sure what to make of it all. Why would she cry over me? Little me from nowhere, as Bruce says.

There were plays and shows where I was Stage Manager, making sets, running backstage, organising my mates, skiving lessons with permission now!

There was another kid called Robinson in my year, Geoff, a mate of mine, a big lad, good keeper. One day I'm in the playground playing football, what a surprise, and I see my Mum and Dad walking in to the school. They spot me and come over.
"What are you doing here?" I asked amazed. They never missed work.
Turns out Geoff is bunking off and the school office called the wrong Robinson family out. So, my Mum gets my Dad out of work, and they come straight up, no messing. They were more relieved it wasn't me than angry at the school. One thing, though, if you were their kid, you could never get the impression they didn't care, could you?

There were older boys who were the heroes when I was first there – John Sullivan, Tony Martin – top footballers and cricketers, the kids we looked up to. Did I become one of them later? Maybe, I can't tell. I never noticed, as usual, if I did.

Julian Berger, one of the editors of the infamous schoolkids issue of 'Oz' the underground paper and he was in the year below me. I remember reading 'International Times' or 'IT' as it was called, printed in different directions across the page, tightly packed print, photos or designs underneath, I tell you, we ain't seen nothing like this before. All the rules were being broken all the arguments were there to be torn down. What are you protesting about? What have you got? Indeed.

Of course, there was the boredom, the grind, the growing up, the pains and mistakes, I am not glossing over them, no rose-tinted glasses here. But there was escaping round the corner to the 'Angel Inn' for a bacon sandwich and a cup of tea with my mates, school trips, and football, football, football, cricket, too. Most of the kids were Arsenal or Spurs fans but there were a few other Chelsea fans like me and some West Ham, too, and the banter was fierce.

In a class examination now aged about thirteen, I guess. I finished my exam and there was still some time to go. I just get my library book out my brown leather satchel, I was reading the cricketer Godfrey Evans' autobiography at the time and start reading, the form teacher, little Mr Williams, military moustache, sprightly, kindly manner, comes round, hissing:
"Put that book away, you can't read in an exam!"
I put the book away, bemused, it never occurred to me to cheat, I had just finished so I got my book out. I guess he knew that, too, because he took it no further. I sat there thinking about other people's standards, trying to work it all out. I still am, I guess.

Rocking and rolling down the corridors, always something going on, forgotten my homework, thinking about that next football game, talking nine to the dozen, Leonard Cohen, Rolling Stones, Chelsea beating Leeds in the 1970 FA Cup Final replay, John Snow bowling from the Nursery End, bloody lucky Arsenal, what's in your sandwiches today? This book I'm reading, he had a right go, best guitarist in the world, I hate fucking Latin, what a laugh, old Morecambe and Wise gag, wasn't it, have you got a school atlas, I've lost mine again, did you see?

I wrote out a whole play about kids playing football, longhand, in green ink on some sort of ledger paper Mum had brought home from work, I was twelve, I sent it to the BBC, they sent a nice encouraging letter back, ever onwards, rolling, hurtling home, speeding towards the light, always wanting to be sixteen, that was the chosen age.

Then it was past me in a flash. And I never saw it go.

Just a kid, one of the throngs, black-blazered, grey trousers, sweating faces, ties askew, white or grey nylon shirts, going through shoes because of incessant playground football with tennis balls, just one of the boys. An Owens boy.

On the demonstrations, against the Vietnam War, marching and shouting, all together. Learning the cause. Goodbye, old London.

Then it was Political Theory at Sheffield University, working for the Party, learning the game, slogging the streets, canvassing on doorsteps, going to the endless meetings, do your time, learn the language. I took to Yorkshire like a mucky duck. Living out in digs at Jordanthorpe with a landlady who had a crazy daughter who one day threw something at my mate, Dave, who shared the digs with me, apparently because he was always having a go at me (I hadn't noticed, I think it was just our direct London humour). Anyway, whatever she threw, a plate I think, missed Dave and hit me! We left those digs as soon as we could.

We made friends at University easily. Contrary to my fears about pink gins and class divisions, we found kids just like us, working class kids with a half-decent education, football nutters, music fans, all out on the pull. They happened to be from Durham or

Birmingham or Manchester. Once we fathomed out the accents, the one thing that divided us, we were left with all the similarities.

I studied the cause in the library stacks and on the sloping streets of terraced houses. Knocking door to door, long dark hair now and a London accent. I argued in the seminars and in the student union debates. Thatcher's side kick Keith Joseph came to deliver a careful, intelligent lecture about society and the Tory way forward, packed lecture hall with the tidy hair cut Tories out in force, and a few denim boys like me, hovering, simmering with the inarticulate rage of class hate. Question time was polite, too, till I let rip into him saying how the society he was describing – that a few years later Thatcher would bring to fruition, of course – had nothing for my old man back working on the docks and how this was simple class politics and we can play that game, too, and then hell broke loose and it's all up in the air and he was hurried away. Love it.

Now, I have to fess up here in advance and say I have a bit of a downer on alcohol generally and I have alluded to some of that background. The whys and wherefores are a bit tortuous so I won't bore you with all the background just now but suffice to say I have seen the damage the stuff can do and am not keen.

I have never met anyone who is a nicer person for having had a drink.

I have met people who are louder, more expressive, more talkative, more aggressive, more flirtatious even – but never anyone who was nicer. Now you may not value being nice but for me it is probably the most underrated of human attributes. I am a big fan of 'nice', as it happens. If I were to have a gravestone (extremely unlikely) when I die (extremely likely) and someone put on it 'Here lies Chris Robinson, a nice man' then I would rest in peace.

I had noticed with myself that, like many others, when I had a drink I tended to get louder. I reflected on this and decided I was probably loud enough anyway when sober and have more or less stopped drinking alcohol for some years since. I may still have the very occasional glass of Sancerre or an ice cold extra dry champagne but that's about it. I think I do that just to remind myself that I can if I want to.

I come from a long line of boozers, however. My Dad was a case in point, as explained. It was only really once I started working with my Dad on the docks when I was about seventeen that I really got to know him. He was generally a really nice, good-hearted, hardworking silly man who I loved dearly. However when he had had a drink he was different. He spoke gibberish fluently.

I learnt, from my Uncle, as I have said, that Dad had been a real boozer and brawler in his younger days when they were growing up in Nottingham and later in Hornsey in London. Mum sorted him out, I guess, to a large extent.

Now I don't want you to get the idea that I am pure as the driven whatsit here. What, you didn't have that idea anyway? Thanks.

Anyway, I have had my drinking days and nights, and lost weekends. When I went up to Sheffield at eighteen to go to University and play football I walked into a familiar drinking culture. It was the times, it was being eighteen in the early seventies, it was a working-class group of lads in a fine working-class city.

The first away trip I went on introduced me to the pattern of football then. We were away at Newcastle, my first visit to yet another fine working-class city that I would visit many times, usually for football purposes, over the following years. Anyway, at the time, to give you an idea, on away trips we had what was called a 'puke draw' and this Newcastle trip was my first experience of it. We all put a pound in the kitty and names were drawn from a hat. You got a 'puke partner'. If your nominated puke partner was the first to throw up then you won the kitty – a sizeable sum in those days. So you tried to get your partner drunk double quick, buying as many drinks as he would take. Now, of course your name had been picked out by someone else so they were trying to get you drunk as quick as they could as well. The purpose of all this is hardly disguised, is it?

Back in those days, back at home in London, I drank 'brown and bitter' – a half pint of draught bitter with a bottle of brown ale mixed in, making a pint. It was quite a common southern drink at the time. I don't think you can even buy brown ale now? Anyway, my name had been picked out by a lad called Geoff Magowan, a scouser, and very good midfield player as it happens. He asked what I was drinking, and I said:
"Brown and bitter, please, Geoff."
Now the closest they could get to it up in Newcastle that eventful first night was a half of 'Federation Best Bitter' (which you could run your car on) and a bottle of the infamous 'Newcastle Brown Ale'. Suffice to say that I was later told there was a ward in Newcastle General Hospital dedicated solely to drinkers of Newcastle Brown Ale.

I took a sip of the combined pint and lost the power of speech.

I don't remember anything else from the evening though I do remember at one much later stage looking up from the gutter wherein I was laying and thinking to myself;
"That's our coach parked just over there. I can see it, but I have no chance of getting to it."

So you get the idea. Our social lives revolved around the Broomhill Tavern at Crookes just up from the University and the training ground where we trained twice a week and in the area where most of us lived in squalid bedsits and unspeakable flats. The 'Tav' was a really good typical Yorkshire pub. I could go in there at just about any time of day and find someone I knew. We went there after

41

every training session and game and all the big weekly nights out would start with someone saying, "I'll meet you in the Tav then."

One such set piece was the annual 'Pyjama Jump'. This was held at the end of each Freshers Week in September. It was held at the huge Top Rank dance hall in town, a massive place holding two thousand frenzied dancers. The hook was everyone had to wear night wear. Pyjamas, nightdresses – you can imagine. Anyway we of course had to do it differently so tended, as I recall, to wear girls' nightdresses borrowed off girlfriends or female classmates. I don't know why. This particular year I have in mind I was in fact wearing pyjama trousers but with some sort of Disney princess top. No doubt a fine sight.

The festivities at the Top Rank went on till 2.30am or thereabouts. We met at the Tav at 5.30pm. When we rolled out of the Tav at about 9.30pm I felt I'd had a really good night and was absolutely bladdered and we hadn't even got into town yet let alone to the Top Rank. A noisy walk down into town, stopping at a pub or two en-route, we were very partial to the Drifters 'Saturday Night at the Movies' for some reason and would sing it at any opportunity en masse. I think a stop into one of the local chippies – 'chips and curry sauce' perhaps? – on the way would have helped settle the eight or nine pints of lager.

I have always blamed those many pints in the Tav, followed by more on the way down, and even the chips and curry sauce, let alone the more lager at the Top Rank or the Searchers playing live and certainly my mate Stevie Johnson from Manchester who was supposed to be looking after me, for the fact that the girl I met that night I ended up marrying. Far too young.

Oh, people, you see I have drunk my fill and paid the price. I am not preaching from any raised high holy pulpit here but more from the dirty gutter, the stale taste of last night's beer on my breath. Been there, done that, brought the t-shirt, threw up, drank again.

Chris Robinson – Over, Under or Through

A few years ago I was back in Sheffield on business, still a fine city. I went up to Crookes and the Broomhill Tavern is still there, of course. The small cosy little rooms have all been converted into one big room, as is the modern way, and the décor has changed but it was still the Tav. I was about to step inside when I looked into the window. I saw this young kid in his late teens, with long dark hair, with a strong cockney accent sat inside, drinking lager, surrounded by a mass of other working-class lads from all round the country, all with scruffy jeans and t-shirts, all shouting and laughing as he told some silly story, random football kit bags strewn at their feet as they roared and sang.

I turned round and walked away.

I left University with a decent 2:1 degree in 1975, was getting married, was offered Ph D courses at two Universities – Sheffield and Bristol – but thought I should get a proper job and got a place on a Management Training course run by the National Freight Corporation. Mistakes all round there then. Transport management, my Dad's familiar world of lorries, transport yards, docks and drivers. What was I thinking of? I was soon bored rigid and applying for master's courses. I ended up at the LSE, a hectic one-year M.Sc.(Econ.) in British Politics, mainly by a thesis ('Syndicalism and the London Dock Strike of 1911'). Living in a flat in Walthamstow, working a full-time shift on the Docks with my Dad, coaching and captaining the University football team, learning I had made an even bigger mistake in getting married so young.

I became a full time Trade Union officer at 23 years of age for NALGO, working in the Health Service in Lancashire in 1977. Soon I was chairing the Trade Union Committee representing 26,000 health workers in Lancashire and negotiating on their behalf. What did I know? No-one told me I shouldn't be doing this. No-one challenged me, asking what did I know? I talked myself into these jobs, got up on the platforms and the meeting rooms and sang, picking up the melody as I went along, just like Mum had taught me.

Everything was for the cause. I got promoted to Manchester in the Union as a District Officer, decent money and a good car. I wanted to be General Secretary. I was living in Bacup in East Lancashire by then, from 1978 and the poor souls of that old mill town at the end of the Rossendale valley must have wondered what hit them.

I took the decrepit local Labour Party by storm, me and a group of young locals, powered up in reaction to Thatcher's May 1979 victory. We could see the writing on the wall. We produced newsletters, distributed them ourselves, out on the streets, waging campaigns to save the local swimming baths when the ruling Tory council gave us a gift by saying they were going to close it, bombarding the local paper. A year later I am in cheering crowds at the public hall above those baths in Bacup, having defeated the previously impregnable Tory leader of the local council in the Rossendale Council elections. Our people are going nuts, young guns, energy, drive, cheering and shouting, arms in the air, stunned Tories, I'm up on the stage giving it large in my acceptance speech and a mate of mine can only get just in the door at the back, the press of people is such. He hears the old police Sergeant at the back turn to his colleague and say "someone ought to shut that red bastard up." That red bastard was me. And still is. I'm just quieter now.

They really thought I'd been flown in from Moscow. (I mean, apart from anything else, even a Soviet leader would have been hard put to pick Bacup out on the map as a likely place to send a revolutionary). Of course, I played up to it, what did I care? I sprayed a hammer and sickle on my big sliding patio door in the bungalow on the hill overlooking the town. When the Tory opposite alerted the newspapers, and the News of the World turned up, I got wind of it and by the time the journo arrives it's changed to a 'Solidarity' graphic and 'Happy Xmas to all our readers'.

One night, around midnight, all the family in bed, the phone goes. I get up, bleary and tired, still half asleep.
A woman's voice.
"My husband's got a shotgun and he's coming to kill you."
I was wide awake now.
'I'm sorry," I said, "you'll have to narrow it down a bit."

She had a scottish accent and was slightly slurring her words, so I suspected a drink or two had been taken. She said they lived up on Fairview – the main council estate ion my ward which I could see across the hill from the lounge I stood in with the phone. They had problems with their windows or something and I had not done anything to help and her husband who had been drinking in a late-night bar behind Stacksteads had come back for his shotgun and was on his way to kill me. I could not get any more sense or info from her; she wouldn't tell me her name or address. I hung up.
I was scared. The threat seemed bizarre but in the dead of night, at that moment, who knew?
I phoned the police. The local station (the one used for the external shots in 'Juliet Bravo', a TV series of the time, as it happens) was at the bottom of the lane where I lived, down in Bacup.
I stood by the big plate window and waited.
Then I saw a car slowly driving up the hill, the headlights slowly heralding the approach up round the bend. My heart was in my mouth. Was this him?
I went outside. I don't know why really. I just instinctively felt if there was to be a confrontation it would be better outside, away from my sleeping family. In my pyjamas and slippers with a sweatshirt on, I crept down the outside stairs to the road.
It was the police.
One officer walked along the road, coming up the hill, with a torch searching into the shadows of the houses and the police car slowly followed him. The police officers said they would have a good look

round and would come back and check regularly but there was not much more they could do. I said I would call in to the station the next day.

It was an uneasy night for me.

The next day a few Labour Party friends gathered, and we went over what information we had. I had checked my notes and there were no outstanding complaints that fitted the bill. I had checked with the Housing Manager too. We were all mystified.

"Bloody Fairview!" I ranted. "After all I've done for people there! Someone up there threatens to kill me!"

O ye of little faith….

"Hang on," said Paddy Niven, a great character, fellow labour councillor, ex-Tory funnily enough, who knew everyone in Bacup. In a council meeting Paddy once raised a complaint about a council house in Bacup.

"I'm not saying it's damp but one of the kids went down t'cellar and got bit by a dolphin!"

Anyway, Paddy had a glimmer of an idea…

"You say she had Scottish accent?" he asked.

"Yes."

"OK…well, I've a bit of an idea. Let me go and see someone."

He went off. Later that day he came back. He mentioned the Tory County Councillor we had deposed from his seat a few months before.

"Well, you know his wife?"

"Yes," I said, "vaguely. I've met her at the count I think."

"Right, well, she used to live in Scotland and that got me thinking. She has..how shall I say it? A bit of a drink problem - and I know she's taken her husband's fall from office right hard. So I went and saw him. I asked if it might be her and he went pale as a ghost. 'It could be" he said. Anyways, he said he will sort it."

"So it was her?"

Paddy nodded. "Definitely. I don't think husband knew anything about it. I'm sure he didn't. He were mortified."

I was stunned – who knew someone's loss of social status from being a councillor would affect someone so much – and relieved, of course.
"Are you going to tell Police?" asked Paddy. I thought about it.
"Nah, " I said at length, "she clearly has her problems. Let him deal it."
"Aye," said Paddy. "Sounds right."

Meanwhile, for the union or the Party – it was all the same gig for me – I was being stood up on walls to make a speech outside a striking factory gate, ripping it up at the Labour Conference calling for a republican Ireland, getting elected Secretary of the Lancashire Association of Trades Councils, more platforms, more smoky back rooms in pubs, and with panache and passion, I give them more socialism than they were comfortable with. I get Dennis Skinner to come and share a platform with me in Bacup, I drive to Derbyshire to pick him up, I listen, and I learn. At the Labour conferences I follow Tony Benn from meeting to meeting, following his developing arguments.

When the steel strike is on, I am running support in Lancashire. When the Miners are in the final struggle, our final hoorah, I am running the local Strike Coordinating Committee. I am told the police are tapping my phone. I get another death threat late one cold night. There are not enough hours in the day or night. I am constantly working, everything for the cause, while my class is locked in deadly battle and losing and only some of us see it happening.

I bring agit-prop theatre groups to Bacup like the Red Ladder group, the 7:84 people, the New York Labor Theatre (who the council ban at first, to our glee, and the Americans all get t-shirts that we make saying 'Banned in Bacup'), hire a hall for local punk bands to play a gig when the Council will not support them. I walk out into the night in the ward I live in where I am Councillor, walking up to the teenagers herding round the bus shelter on Fairview Road – a road the Daily Mail calls, with some exaggeration, 'the worst road in Britain.' I ask them what they want, they say somewhere to just sit and hang out with their mates, out the rain. I organise it, battling the police, the council, any fucker that gets in my way. Travellers come and park out on the rough common ground in the shadow of the huge Ross Mill, now derelict along by Stubbylee Park. The phone starts buzzing, the local Tory supporters see this as a chance to embarrass me, the defender of the travellers. I go down there which is just what they do not do, of course. Fronting up again. I walk over, talk to the families there, they tell me they are just passing through, on their way to a family funeral further north. I talk a while then go home and phone the complainers. "They'll be gone tomorrow," I say, and of course they are. They whisper about me even more, my apparent power of influence confusing them. I put the phone down and laugh.

Bacup, decaying mill town at the rough end of valley going nowhere. The land that time forgot. You drive along that valley road and the years slipped away like it was a time warp. In the Joiners Arms, you saw fashions you thought died out years ago.

But not so long ago, nearly thirty years later, I read of a gang of youths who kicked to death a 'Goth' girl called Sophie Lancaster and battered her boyfriend just because they looked different. In Bacup. In Stubbylee Park. I talked that night to my son, Nye, brought up in Bacup. We work out I played football years ago with two brothers who were from the family of one of the convicted murderers and how Micky, another of my sons, had a mate from that family.
"It's poverty," says Nye, "poverty locked in with class 'A' drugs. It's a bad combination, we know that." We agree it's not about Bacup as such, it could be anywhere.

"The sad thing is," says Nye, "it's not really surprising. It's awful, it's shit, but it's not surprising."

As a councillor, I went round knocking on doors.
"Is there an election coming up?" they asked mystified.
"No," I say, "'ve just come round to see if there is anything you want me to do."
It blows their minds, but did it do any good?

It's not just me, of course. There are others working hard, too – Rae Connell, Barry Castell, David Edmondson, David Easton, James Hennighan, Lyn Cook. I guess I'm the face of it, though, there, at that time, in that little place, for a while. I get nominated as the Parliamentary Candidate for the constituency, mowing the other candidates down. The pace ratchets up a notch. I'm then Deputy Leader of the Council Labour Group. When I get elected the local radio asks if this is a left-wing takeover of the Labour Group.
"I don't know," I replied, "I'm the only left winger in the group so I doubt it."

When my friend, Barry Castell, a fellow Bacup councillor, dies suddenly of a heart attack in his forties, his widow, Maggie asked me to speak at his funeral. The Tories said later I sang the 'Red Flag'. I would have done if Maggie asked me to but as it happened I just quoted from it, "we'll keep the red flag flying here". They lied anyway, though.

It had to end. The General Election came in June 1983, and I was standing in my home constituency of Rossendale and Darwen. I was in the midst of an affair and my marriage was falling apart though maybe only I knew it at that point. I was already heading off down a losing path. I battled through the election, but the times were against me and like everywhere else Labour suffered in Rossendale. I wonder what difference it might have made to my life if the times had been different, and I had got elected. Who's to say? On Election Night, I made a fighting losing speech, but the moment was gone. In my heart I knew I had blagged it all, I knew my politics were a long way beyond what my colleagues in the Party thought or wished for.

I did not believe in parliamentary democracy, as such, not in the way they did. I just felt that getting a socialist committed Labour Party elected was a necessary precursor to the Tories and the Establishment showing their teeth and casting aside their façade of respectable belief in such elected institutions and then the real revolution could begin. I was ready for it.

In fact, the bastards did not have to wait for that process, Thatcher got elected and the electorate got presumably what they wanted, the destruction of the organised working class. And my political career, such as it was, died away, too, with the movement I loved.

Kinnock came along, and I could see Blair and all that bollocks down the line, though I did not know who it would be. I could see the form if not the face. I could see they would sell their souls – or no, not their souls, which were never on the line – but my soul or anything else in order to get elected. Power at any price. No guiding principles. And I wanted no further part in that.

I walked away from the Union when it became clear my politics would prevent me from getting any further and I tried to focus on my increasingly chaotic personal life. I walked away from the Union and the Party with no regrets, no bad feelings. I knew the score all the way through. Nothing lasts forever. I was always out on a limb, and it got chopped off. All that changed. I didn't win but I never doubted I was right.

But now, talking with Nye, reading about that murder and that lost life, those stunted kids who did the thing, whose families apparently laughed when the police were charging them, so they papers say, I just don't know.
"Did I do any fucking good at all?" I ask Nye. But I can't take all that on myself, of course, because that would be a final massive vanity.
"You and a lot of others thought you could make a difference, you said' we can do this', you had a go. It's not your fault it never worked out that way, you did have a go," says Nye. I did, I guess, I

don't know. There are just some new ghosts to add to the queue now.

But my feelings, my beliefs, my passionate connection with the politics of my class, as I understood it, did not change. For the next six years though I wasted my career in dead ends and impossible positions, trying to make some money, getting more and more unhappy, and finally more and more ill as everything imploded. My Lost Years. I lost my way and my purpose. I'll tell you about them later.

I ended up in the Lake District, with a second mistaken marriage collapsing under me, businesses in ruins, debts drowning me through little fault of my own as a business partner ripped me and the bank off, in 1990.

Football rescued me, and a good woman or two, but more of all that later. For now, I smile at those ghosts from those days of politics and passion. Those lovely red ghosts, trailing history, Tom Mann, James Connolly, Dennis Skinner, Tony Benn, Rosa Luxemburg, Antonio Gramsci, Arthur Scargill and Regis Debray. They were all there with me then. I felt I was marching along with them, the bands playing, our banners flying, our red flags fluttering in the breeze. I could hear the singing, I could feel the arms linked in mine, smell the cordite in the air. Was I wrong?

In the midst of the Miners' Strike I put on a benefit gig in a working men's club in Stacksteads, near Bacup. I persuaded the best local musician, a great Irish singer and guitar and banjo player called Donal Maguire to play for free. The hall was packed, he was a hell of singer but rarely played locally. Just before he went on I asked him if he would sing a favourite old Irish song of mine called 'The Red-Haired Man's Wife'.
"Jesus," he said, "that's an old one."

He played a great set. At the end he said he'd play a song someone had asked him to do called 'The Red-Haired Man's Wife', but he could not promise to remember it all.
Some years later I heard a tape that someone had recorded of that night, that great gig. Donal sang that song unaccompanied in absolute silence – which takes some doing in a working man's club in Stacksteads. As he finishes, you can hear him say:
"Ah, Chris, that's all I can remember..." and the crowd explode into cheering and applause.
I know what you mean, Donal. We sing as much as we can remember, as well as we can, then. We don't not sing, do we?

For some reason, I remember standing in a booth in a deserted record shop in St Peter Port in Guernsey when I was on my last holiday with my parents. I was sixteen. I stood there, it was summer night-time, listening to Leonard Cohen.

Can I really hope to do that? I ask you ghosts now. Did I let some people down? Certainly. Did I inspire some? I hope so.

A couple of years ago I went to Rio. I was on a trip to Brazil, part of a team designing an international sport programme related to London 2012.

We'd been to the country in the north east, inland from Recife. A small town called Quebrangulo, I recall. Poor people but a warm welcome. Walking round the town with the major, a good guy, it seemed, trying to get something going. Just about everyone in the town either came out to say hello or put on their party act for us. Strange local traditional dances based apparently around when the local women, slaves, would be asked to go up to the big houses to serve at big dinners and events and how they often got molested. So the local guys dressed up as women and took their place. Now this local dance commemorates all that, (and they call British panto strange?).

My photos record saddled horses in dusty streets, resting under the shade of a tree. Children in costumes. Some old guys trying to keep a traditional form of music and dance together, roping in their grand-daughters and nieces. A gorgeous blonde girl of about 15, with honey skin, and flashing blue eyes in captured in digital memory for ever, smiling at the camera. Or was she smiling at me?

In Rio, I stayed in a hotel down at Copacabana beach. Each morning I would go out and run from one end to the other and back. As I recall it's 4 kilometres each way. Golden, golden sand, with football pitches and volleyball nets as far as the eye can see, recalling for me the old Hackney Marshes childhood heaven of everlasting football pitches, though a different climate and time.

Outside of Rio we visit a sports complex now being put to good community use. I meet a guy called Andrezinho there, an ex-footballer. He and I gravitate to each other, even with no common language other than football. He gets his scrapbook and shows me his history, a good player clearly, ex-pro, now late thirties, playing for a good vet's team. He and his son aged about ten show me round. The language thing is not an issue at all.

When it's time to go, I give him my prize 'Right to Play' cap. He is overcome. He dashes off then returns with a shirt, his shirt from the vet's team with his name on it, for me. We hug but then I have to go. We met for about fifteen minutes, yet the football gave us enough common ground to be friends.

I grew up hard but loved and given confidence. In these later years, I have had the chance to travel round the world and I see my people wherever I go. I got the chance to go to the poorest countries, to the poorest parts of the poorest countries, and meet great people there. I saw the poor, the refugees, the city slum kids, the hungry.

They have it worse than I did. But I feel this connection, singing through the years. Some are cheating, some are stealing, robbing, killing, just like always. I have no illusions left. There is no dignity in poverty. I have been poor twice in my life and I did not like it. But for all that, these are my people, for good or bad.

Now I spend my working life trying to make a difference to these kids, in my small way, back home in London, following the bouncing ball. But to me it's the same old cause. Different names and languages, different climates and smells. But the same kids, the same people. The same old song, just a different singer?

When I went to these slums, these favellas, these barrios, these ghettos, I didn't feel any different from those growing up days, or those days on platforms, in my boxer's stance, side on, giving it plenty, or in the meeting rooms arguing my corner, standing my ground. No, to me, I'm just playing out my part in the same old game. Maybe in a different position, playing in a different way, but it's the same game, and the same player.

I guess it has been a process of me finding the tools to enable me to deal with life, to enable me to press on when the going gets tough.

Years later I would hear a Buddhist story of two monks, one old and one young, making a long journey across difficult terrain, barefoot and tired. They crested a hill and in front of them as far as they could see there was a huge vista of a field of sharp stones.
"Oh no," the young monk sank to the ground, head in hands, "all those stones, we will never get across, it's not fair."
The old monk sat down beside him and smiled:
"You have two choices in life now. You can wish that the world was covered in leather. Or you can put some shoes on."

It took me many years to find a pair of shoes that fit.

2. Hungry Heart

Oh, it's easy now, sitting here, knowing a beautiful woman is here in this house which is our home. It's easy having now finally found the answer when I had almost forgotten what the question was.

Of course, it's a bit of a bugger that it has taken me so long to find who I was looking for. And along the way, love has been a losing game for me more often than not.

However, we all like a happy ending, don't we?

I stood on the platform at Paddington station, sheltering from the rain, not heeding the storm I was living in. I had been waiting something like four hours because the train from Wales seemed to be going somewhere else, anywhere but here where I was, much like her, I guess. I had waited and waited. Santana's 'Samba Pa Ti' echoing in my head, over and again, mournful, slow and pure, as it was the last song I had listened to before I left my mate Griz's flat in Swiss Cottage to come here. That long April Sunday afternoon and early evening. I wandered around and around the dusty old station until even the scrawny pigeons became fed up with me. It was 1972, I had not yet hit eighteen, but everything was already coming off the rails.

Long time gone, years passing it felt like, my hair turning grey inside my head and the train finally came in. I walked down the station against the tide of people finally reaching their delayed destination, searching for her.

When I finally saw her amongst the flow of people carrying cases, my heart leapt. She looked up at the same time and she saw me through the crowd and the look on her face told me everything, everything that I did not want to know. Suddenly it was all too clear to me though, of course, while my young, battered heart then would not accept it out loud, deep inside I somehow knew. It was over and gone. I could tell by the dead look in her eyes when she saw me. Whatever it had been, that teenage romance, it was over and gone, and my life would strangely be forever marked by it all, and I would search for whatever it had been, or I thought it was going to be, from then on. It had been there, and then was gone. Like life itself, of course, but I did not know that yet so that lesson, like many others, was lost on me.

Oh, our little saga, our teenage vignette, had not played out completely, of course, no, not at that stage, we were only half way through, I guess, but the die was cast, the song was sung, the ghosts were beginning to swirl and take terrible shape.

Everybody knows. Age old stories yet not when you are living them. You are inventing them anew, of course, surely? Each time, each new heart, each silent telephone, each empty street corner.

It had started down in Sussex, ironically, we were both seventeen, a week away with the school, late autumn, a geography field trip. Suddenly noticing her, it seemed. Not a classic beauty, surely I would have seen her before if that had been the case? There was something in the air, though, something waking me up all of a sudden and there she was. I struggled to get next to her as we walked across the Sussex Downs. That night we all trooped out the mile to the local pub. I must have made my pitch, but I cannot remember now, probably thankfully. Walking back, the beginning of the civil war, armies engaged. By the big tree halfway back, early December night still soft and warm enough to stroll slow, a kiss. I quote her Leonard Cohen as we walk which she misunderstands, or says so later when even then, later that night, she was looking away, somewhere else.
Our steps will always rhyme, I said, but I guess they never really did. Or maybe they did but just for such a little while.

The song begins, then.

Back at school it must have been me that suggested we meet straight after school and go round together to the favoured hang-out, the Angel Inn café. Then later I walked her to Upper Street for her bus up Holloway Road. It must have been me because that is the sort of thing I would do. It was also probably me that said let's meet at lunchtime and go for a walk and we walked to the nearby square and sat on the bench by the church. It was no doubt me that phoned first in the evening when I got home. All those things, yes, it must have been me, I must be the guilty one, the needy one. I did not know why, but now ignorance is no defence. All those things and then I locked us into a pattern that drove her crazy. I was frightened to miss one chance to see her, I held her too close. I was too desperate from the start. I had no idea what this thing was, but I knew I could not let it go. I was so sure. So, it had to be every night from school, every lunchtime, every time, every moment.

"You can never get enough, can you?", she said to me once, as we lay on the rug in her front room.

Stumbling on the heart of Saturday night.

At first, though, it was sweet as light. God bless your crooked little heart. At Danny Newman's party at his house in Barking, just before Christmas 1971, not long after we had met, we sat together, by a sofa, lost in each other all evening as the party went on around us. Just talking, talking. I looked deep into her champagne eyes and dove right in. We had eyes and time only for each other. What could ever go wrong, her in her black midi dress, long and stylish, she was slim and curvy. This was before she had her hair cut, her black hair still long just past her shoulders, free flowing and mine. What did she see in me? I never dared stop to ask or wonder, I was in free-fall.

Her name was Sharon Garnon. I'll change some other names on the way but not this one. Sharon Garnon. Except it wasn't, as I later found out.

There were rare nights when she would phone me, or when I phoned her, and she was right and just by the tone of her voice I knew it was sweet time.
'Hello,' she would say, soft and honey-like in love. It drove me cross-eyed. Otherwise, her tone was neutral or harassed with her complicated family pressures and times.

Walking on Hampstead Heath on a Sunday in spring 1972 - after all walking was cheap and I had little money. Walking, hand in hand laughing, joking, me entertaining, suddenly wrapping her close, kissing her soft red lips, crazy with it all. It started to rain; we sheltered a while but got wet. Back at her house, in her grandmother's kitchen, she says "give me your jumper" so I just take it off, not thinking twice, so unselfconscious it must have been painful. I sat there in the kitchen, in just my jeans. She says she'll wash it and get it back to me. She finds one of her brother's sweaters for me after a while, she's in no hurry, we smile at each other. On the Monday at school, she returns my neat-ironed now clean jumper to me. Somehow it all takes my breath away.

When you get something, you then have to hold on to it.

I'm gonna love you till the wheels come off, as Tom said. Oh, yeah. But not yet.

There was a party above a pub off Seven Sisters Road, someone's birthday, I recall. All the gang was there. I went to Sharon's grandmother's house where she lived, in Alexandra Road, off Holloway Road to pick her up. We walked through the back streets to the party pub, and she walked close to me. This would be February 1972.

In the party there was seventies music loud. The Sweet and Johnny Nash, some Alice Cooper, some Temptations, some early Rod Stewart who'd lived with his parents nearby in Archway. Disco lights and cheap beer. A mate called Chris Burt from the year below me in school had a girlfriend we all called Angela Orgasm, I don't remember her real name. She could dance. Late in the evening and Angela Orgasm is up on one of the tables, giving it large to the rocking beat. You'd think most guys would be happy with that, but it just embarrassed Chris.
"Bloody hell," he says to me, ruefully, nodding towards Angela gyrating her hips in her hot pants, "look at her." And no doubt we all did.
My friends there, Griz, my soulmate and blood brother, tall, gangly, black in his early Afro phase.
But it was about me and Sharon at that stage, for me, nothing else. We were together, a couple, connected and it felt so good.
She loved to dance as the girls do.

Some girls flash cold eyes despite the hot messages their bodies send.
But this girl just broke my heart in two.

Lying at home, writing to her, listening to Don McLean singing 'Vincent', I tried to understand. An awful syrupy song but I can still barely stand to listen to it. She was complicated and I never really knew before that people could be. My first, but sadly not my last, complicated woman. She was changeable, sometimes warm as summer, melting me with those champagne eyes. Other times cold and distant. Like the turning of a switch. A switch I could not locate. I did not understand. How could I?

Her parents had a hotel at Finsbury Park called the 'Penrhyn Hotel', I think. I never went inside. She worked there most weekends. There was some big complication about her family that she would allude to now and then, get dragged down by on occasion. She lived with her grandparents. They were all fiercely Welsh from a town called Llandyssul, a place I learned to first pronounce, then spell and finally hate. Sharon had been born there but had no Welsh accent yet spoke lovingly of the Carmarthen hills and fields. She told me of her great friend there, Diane, who was a few years older than her and married. I was a city boy, what did fields and lanes mean to me? Fields were Hackney Marshes, the only lane I could think of was Petticoat Lane.

One day, on the top deck of a 104 bus, going along Upper Street, she told me what this big family secret was. Her parents were not married. Her father's name was Jones and she said when she went back to Wales that was what people called her, Sharon Jones, not Sharon Garnon. Her brother, Ian, who I had met, he was about twenty, I would guess, was not actually her brother but her uncle. Her mother's brother. The school knew as did her best friend, Ann Adams, but no-one else. I can remember wondering silently what the fuss was all about. OK, her parents were not married. It was not as commonplace in the seventies as now but even so it was not earth shattering. I made sympathetic noises but could not understand why this fact seemed in some way to be at the heart of her difficult family life and the effect it had on her. All sorts of identity stuff, who she was if she had two names, one at school and one back in Wales, I guess. Her father and his connection to her. All that stuff. I was just left dealing with the changing moods, the untouchable depths, the reserve, the secrecy, the split personality and the hidden feelings.

I was just a poor boy, football and cricket crazy, a sports nut, avid reader of Kerouac and Hemingway, listening to Van Morrison, James Taylor, the Stones and Leonard Cohen, quoter of poetry and song lyrics, occasional singer and bad drummer, big brown eyes, straggly dark hair, scuffling along, plenty of chat, ready to rage against the capitalist machine, but still starry-eyed, friend to all. I was way out of my depth.

Many, many years later, way after it had all gone, I was in Finsbury Park and walked past the hotel. I could not bring myself to go in for some reason. I went to a pub down the road a little and had a drink and sat there nursing the pint of lager, and I was still trying to work it all out, maybe twenty years later.

And still, every lunchtime, back then in school, I would wait for her, standing on the steps of our school main entrance, looking across the grey playground to the girls school, waiting for that first glimpse of her coming out. Waiting to go to our bench in Middleton Square, in the park by the church, where I would hold her hand, and we would talk about our lives. The same after school, waiting to go to the Angel Inn where the gang would be. Sharon and me, drinking coffee, smoking Embassy Gold cigarettes, playing hangman on the cigarette packets, spelling out our questions. We used the game to communicate.
"When will we make love?" I spelt out.
"God Only Knows" she replied, as I worked it out, letter by letter, another of our signature tunes, of course.
And then I remember her putting down a phrase which I gradually spelt out but did not understand. She would not explain it to me, of course, either.
"Love The One You're With," it said.

One day at school, a half-term end day, we'd been in the Angel Inn with the gang, this was early days when her eyes still flashed and sparkled at me, and she held me tight. We were walking back past the front of the school; I was trying to tell her something, but she was teasing me.
"You're not helping me, are you?" I said, smiling, mock desperation.
"You're making this difficult."
"Making what difficult?"
"Making it difficult to say I love you."
There it was.
"I love you, too", she said, so all was settled. I kissed her yet again.

I didn't know what it was. How could I? I had no idea. The word came easily really. It was in every song we listened to, just about. Bandied about. Then it became a constant in every conversation we had. Strange thing, though, as it turned out, I was telling the absolute truth. If I had known what it would mean I would have run from her then, jumped a 43 bus down to Moorgate and run to Fenchurch Street and got on a train to my family home and never came back…..or would I? Or could I?

I can't make you love me, if you don't, I should have said, though I would not hear that song for many years yet. But she had said she did, so I believed her. I believed that because she said the same words as me, she must mean the same as me, feel the same as me.

Fool.

Somehow the rest of my life was churning by, too. It was 'A' level year, I was playing football and then cricket for the school. Hockey, too, where I played in goal and I can remember we played the girls team once and Sharon, a good player, was competitive and strong. My mate Pete Morbin played for the school cricket team that I captained and sometimes his girlfriend, Alexis, whose parents owned a greengrocer on Seven Sisters Road, and Sharon, would come out to the school playing fields at Totteridge and meet me and Pete after a cricket match. Later on summer evenings me and Pete would play Sharon and Alexis at tennis back at school. I was playing music in the band, badly banging the drums, maybe singing with Danny and Bill in the acoustic band on the side. All that was happening, I was applying for Universities and living life. But none of it registered. I only say it happened now because I know it must have. I only had eyes for Sharon.

I didn't have much money, working shifts at weekends when I could in a petrol station in Upminster for 'The Guv'nor' Len Groves. But many Saturday nights across those vivid years I would stay up in London at my mate, Griz's council flat, Burnham Tower, off

Adelaide Road in Swiss Cottage, one of those soaring towers looking over the city. Griz's Mum, Trudi, would often go out on a Saturday night visiting a friend in Belsize Park, having cooked us great Austrian strudels, and Griz would be maybe out with the lads or his girlfriend, leaving the flat to me and Sharon. Or I'd be walking back late from Sharon's from Holloway Road along to Camden and up past the Roundhouse along Adelaide Road.

Late Saturday nights, walking home on my own, North London nights, that soft spring, then balmy summer, jeans and a Wrangler denim jacket, walking back from my girlfriends, seventeen years old, ain't that right? Taxi cabs and the odd late red bus passing by, the sound of my steps echoing in the backstreets, early hours, maybe still feeling the buzz from the alcohol, still tasting Sharon on my lips. Just walking back, oh feeling every nerve in my body tingling, thinking about my girl, maybe tired, sometimes drunk, always in teenage high focus, such certainties and royal emotions raging inside me.

We walked through St James' Park one spring Sunday, the flowers blooming red and purple in the neat beds, grass so green, around the lake, watching the little kids feeding the ducks. Us holding hands, talking trash, made me feel that Park was just ours to have and hold, there just for us.

No, no, the pain had not come yet, we're still back in the few weeks when it was all so damn right, tidal wave time, Tsunami of love.

One night, soft velvet light, we walked from Griz's flat just across to Primrose Hill. In the park, the lamp posts along the path strung out like fairy lights in the dark, pools of yellow light on this spring night. There was a bench at the top then and we sat there, looking down over London, the Zoo and Regents Park beneath us, the lights of the city stretching behind, St Paul's lit in the distance. Soft night, we sat together, I had my arm round her, she was sat real close, head on my shoulder, her dark hair beneath my chin. She turned her face up to me and I kissed her lips.

Just hold that moment. Just freeze it there. Because that was all the magic wound up in one second. And it would not come again for her and me.

I have learned that the big mistake we make is wanting desperately for something not to change. We grasp that person just as they are right then, that smile just then, that taste of their lips, the person we are then and they are then and we yearn for it to be held. We act as if it not only can be but actually is going to stay the same, hell, even should stay the same. Then when she changes or we change or the moment changes, we feel cheated. We build our lives on those shifting moving sands and wonder why we fall. We grasp and want to hold. But there is nothing to hold onto, the river runs, the image changes, it's all smoke and mirrors. Everything changes. All the time. Especially us, whoever we are, because we kid ourselves there is some real finite presence here, too, in the mirror or in our heads. Yet we, like all these ghosts, are not real, not a given, not something with any permanence at all, just collections of memories, prejudices, imagination clustered around a changing, failing body. Yet more smoke and mirrors.

Everything changes, all the time. If we don't take that truth into our lives we will suffer. We don't and so we do. I didn't and therefore I did. I am not sure I have ever really learned that lesson, even yet. My life story would suggest not.

Who do you love?
Do you love me?
Tell me.
Reassure me that this has not changed.
Was it good for you?

I have been back to Primrose Hill a few times since all those years ago. I have walked along from the Zoo like Sharon and I sometimes did when we could not afford to go in, watching the wolves watching us from the outside, hearing the animal calls. Recalling my 'Perfect Day' back before Lou even sang about it. I have walked on up to Primrose Hill, seen those curving paths around the shoulder of the hill still there with their black painted lampposts and wondered whether if it was night-time would the pools of yellow light look the same? At the top they have some sort of panoramic guide to the city beneath you now but there is still a bench or two more or less on the top. I have sat there, having maybe escaped briefly from my working life, stealing a minute or two to revisit my past. I have sat there, with the years stretching back just like the city stretches before me, right back to me and Sharon Garnon sitting there. What is the power that has pulled me back there, not sure what I was looking for but maybe it was my past I half hoped to find, knowing it was impossible?

Further on up the road, I found it was all an illusion.

Was it there still when I went back? Did I find something of the past other than the view? No, of course not, but by then really, I knew I carried it all with me actually. I brought it along. The place just sharpened the focus, brought my attention to bear. These ghosts are always with me, sometimes they shine brighter, some places make them vivid to me, but they are there, waiting, always, whispering, singing old songs in my ear.

It had to end. I would not ever have accepted that back then, but it was so.

The end of the Easter term, 1972. Last day of term. The school had run out of sports awards and colours to give me, so they had discovered this 'special colours' one from somewhere, not given out for years, and presented me with the badge for my blazer at the last assembly. A woven circle with the school emblem in the middle, if I had got it sown onto my school blazer, I would have had a different school badge from everyone else in the school which would have been a bit weird. But I didn't, of course. The school day finished at midday. We ended up back at Sharon's house. Inevitably, I gave the 'special colours' to her. I wonder what happened to them.

We were sat in the lounge, old high-backed armchair and sofa, dark wooden sideboard, maybe drinking coffee.

"What would you say if I said we should finish?" she suddenly asked. I gasped a little for breath, stunned, seeing in her face she was serious. The world tilted. Everything began to slip away.
"Are you saying that?" I finally managed to say. (When I told Griz about all this later, he nodded and said, "good answer".)
"I don't know," she said, and looked away.
There was a clock ticking somewhere.

She would tell me later, when the unravelling got to be really messy, that she should have gone through with it then, that day, March 10th, 1972, but when she saw the pain in my eyes, she could not do it, could not see it through.

For me, I would never feel so old again. The realities, the unfairness, the unremitting suchness of life finally hit me all at once. At seventeen.

I went out of the room and sat a while on the stairs in the gloomy hallway. I was just reeling from the shock, barely able to think at all. I was aware that she came to the doorway of the lounge after a while, leaning against the doorframe, head down, in the shadows, the light from the lounge windows behind her. She'd had her lovely long hair cut, that very day, as I recall, into the fashionable layered cut which I never liked. Maybe my memory fails me, it was maybe not that actual day, but around that time. In time for her forthcoming trip back to Wales at Easter, it later occurred to me, for sure. Whatever, I have always associated her long free hair style

with the brief sweet time and the layered, centre parting cut with all that went progressively bad from then on. Silly, of course, but there it is. It reminds me of a great Billy Bragg song about teenage romance where he says:
"And then she cut her hair and I stopped loving her."
Well, I wish it had been that way for me, but it was not. Maybe it was the other way round. She cut her hair and maybe stopped loving me then. If she ever did.

"I'm going for a walk," I mumbled and went out. I walked round the block a bit, trying to clear my head, trying to make some sense of it. She'd said – many times (even if not as often as I would have liked) – that she loved me so how could she be finishing with me? A simple conundrum, repeated on every street, on every town probably every week, but new to me then. I could not work it out and I was used to being able to work most things out.

I went back after a while, knocked on the door and she let me in. She put her arms round me and we made up of sorts but the die was cast. There would be other times she would say again she loved me. Other times when I would hear that softness in her voice when I phoned her. But that day was the watershed. For the first time, even I could not pretend there was nothing wrong. Into my little teenage heaven had come a shadow that would never quite go away and indeed would become bigger and darker in fits and starts until it eventually shut out all the light.

I think we had two weeks off for Easter. Sharon was going back to Llandyssul for the first week, staying at her friend Diane's. A whole week. I was distraught, particularly in the circumstances. Time went on so slowly, she occasionally phoned, I wrote every day I think, she maybe once wrote back. She told me that Diane's brother was in a country band, and she'd gone with him to Swansea one day to pick up a new amp or something. I'm thinking: yes, yes, so what, when are you coming back?

Sunday is slowly limping round. I am working at the petrol station and my workmate there is used to me counting the days off.

"I can't wait till she gets back," I said.

"Yeah," he said, looking at me, thoughtfully, "sometimes a big reunion doesn't work out."

Hell, what does he know? Looking back, how come he could see things I couldn't?

Sunday, she's due to be driving back with her grandparents. Around five she phones.

"Guess where I am?" she says.

"I dunno, Bristol?" I figure she's en route by now, surely.

"No, I'm still here in Llandyssul. I'm staying another week. Diane's asked me to."

What? I go crazy.

Later that night I write her a letter, pouring my heart out in desperation. She writes back later that week saying I should never write anything like that to her ever again, she's fed up and confused, she says, every day she hears 'I Love You' and she is just too pressurised. What is she talking about? I haven't seen her for ten days, I've written a few times, we've spoken a couple of times on the phone (when she calls me, as I don't know Diane's number) so how is she hearing 'I love you' every day? I don't understand. She must be really confused. In a letter she tells me she and Diane went to see the brother's band playing a holiday camp at Newtown and she and Diane were dragged up onto the stage to do ' the splosh'. How embarrassing, she says. Never mind all that, when is she coming home? The next Sunday, by train. I work out the times.

I cannot see the writing on the wall.

I can't eat, I can't think about anything else. My Mum is going nuts. The Saturday night before Sharon is due back my Mum asks if I am going to meet her – I presume the events have been quite clear to Mum although I don't recall telling her what was happening. I say I am. Mum says:

"I like Sharon, but all this is making me hate her. You are so unhappy. Don't go and meet her."
I say again that I am going to meet her. Nothing Mum says can dissuade me.

So, that Sunday finally comes round and there I am waiting at Paddington, Santana in my head, waiting and waiting. And I see her disappointed face.

We stumbled on. I get ten out of ten for persistence if nothing else. It gets so she must be dreading coming out of her school at lunch time and evening as I always waiting there.
"Me and my shadow", she says in one of the nicer times. We fall into being sarky and cutting in public and in private, I don't know, sometimes good, mostly bad and always me falling apart.

The wife of one of our teachers, called Geoff Clarke, knows us both quite well, at a school event, me and Sharon sparking off each other.
"Why can't you two just be nice to each other?" she asks, as Sharon glares at me.
"Oh no," I say, "that would never do. We might get to like it, eh, Sharon?" She looks away.

One minute it's fine, next it's all off again. It must drive Griz round the bend the number of times I come into the Angel Inn and slump beside him, moaning, "it's all over."

My birthday is in May, hers in June. On my birthday she buys me a pewter tankard. She has it engraved but she won't tell me what. 'It's five words' is all she says.
When the birthday arrives, the tankard says, 'Happy 18th Birthday from Sharon'. I am devastated. Nevertheless, I keep the tankard for over twenty years till finally it disappears or one woman or another throws it away.

For her birthday, I bust my bank to buy her a beautiful little gold cross with 'Love Chris' engraved across the arms. I can never decide after if it was a good wish or a desperate instruction. I also buy her the hit of the day – 'Without You' by Nilsson. Shmaltzy stuff, I know. "I can't live if living is without you."
To this day, I can hardly bear to listen to that record either, of course.

In the midst of all this, 'A' levels are looming. In the better times, Sharon and I had decided she would go to Lanchester Poly – her choice – in Coventry and I would go to Sheffield University, not too far away. I can remember us telling a friend of hers that when the friend asked what we would be doing after school. In the better times this clearly was a relationship that we both thought was going on beyond school into the future, we even talked about kids, she wanted a boy called Jamie, for example. So she said. Or so I believed. I cannot know, of course, or now be sure. In the bad times, though, I would walk away from her not knowing if she would ever be speaking to me again let alone whether we were still going out together. There were more bad times than good.

As I come out of the showers after cricket. Geoff Clarke asks me how me and Sharon are getting on. "Great," I say, "we're getting engaged."
"Really? Congratulations."
"Yeah, either that or splitting up."
He laughs. I'm glad I can help other people see the funny side. It escapes me.

School staggers to an end, the summer limps on, there's the confusion and hiatus of waiting for exam results and your future to start. Sharon are I are drifting further apart, she paddling away and leaving me drowning, I think. She tells me we are finished. Again.

On the phone one summer day. Me at home in South Ockendon on my own.

"I've got something to tell you," she says. "I'm going out with someone else. Someone you know."
"Hang on," I said. I put the phone down and walk to the toilet down the hall and throw up. I walk back and pick the phone up again.

It's my best mate, Griz. Now I really am fucked up.

He tells me she was at the Old Boys disco and some other guy we know was trying to chat her up so, like, what could he do? She says we had finished after all so she can go out with someone if she wants. Yeah, but why my best friend?

I am way out at sea now. I know Griz is going out with some other girl, too, so I say he has to tell Sharon he's also seeing someone else. He doesn't want to; I threaten him that I will. As it turns out, I can't bring myself to, but the damage is done. He has to tell her and she and him are really pissed off at me now. How does that work out?

I end up losing the girl and the best mate, for a long time anyway.

I am way out in unchartered seas no, adrift, alone. I am working in a rough pub called the 'King's Head' in Romford. An awful place but it has music every night and is packed with young people, many of whom I get to know. There are drugs everywhere. I get handed tabs with the money people pay over the bar. I am a good looking, long haired tortured sad poet and the girls in their short skirts and hot pants are lining up. I barely notice.
I work the lunchtime shifts and am on again in the evening. I scull around Romford for the couple of hours in between. I sit in the hot library writing letters to Sharon, some of which I send, none of which she replies to. She is back in Wales over summer.

I hit the drink at the Kings Head, the music loud, the crowd three deep all along the bar waiting to be served.
"Chrissy! Here, mate!"

Five hours a night. Driving on.
Heavy times.

The last time I saw Sharon Garnon was in September 1972. I was waiting for University to start and to go up to Sheffield. She was back from Wales, going out with Griz. He had her 'S' ring on his finger that I used to wear. There was another club night at the Old Boys. I went with the guys. Dance floor stares.

Eventually she walks outside with me. We walk down the field by the Old Boys club in the dark late summer gloom. There's some wooden bench there. Dark night, the music from the club in the distance, the black space of the playing field in front of us.

"What do you want?" she says to me.
"I want you; you know that."
"Like this?" She grabs me and kisses me passionately, but she is playing a part, pretending. I pull away.
"No, I want you to mean it."
She shakes her head.
"Oh, I'm fed up with fighting all this," she says. "Do you want me? Then take me now. You can have me now. Right now."
I look up at the night sky, tears in my eyes.
"No, I want you forever, not just now."
I walk away.

I am beginning to understand it is ending. A while before, some weeks before, back before school broke up. I had sat with her in our churchyard at a last lunchtime and asked her to marry me. We had finished by then.
"Why do you ask me now?" she says in despair.
"Because I wanted to have asked you," I said.

There were maybe a couple of letters from her later down the line. I wrote to her still when I was off in Sheffield at University. We lost touch. I would hear word of her on one or two occasions from friends. She was a buyer for Marks & Spencer. She had an operation for an ovarian cyst. Obscure fragments. She maybe got married.

Some years later when me and Griz were sharing a flat with our respective girlfriends, wife in my case, actually, Griz says:
"I got this weird phone call. It was this geezer saying he was Sharon's husband."
"Sharon?"
"Yeah, your Sharon. Well, he says she was a bit depressed, and he was trying to get in touch with some of her old school friends to link them up with her again and did I know of any of their numbers."
"So what did you say?"
He shrugged and looked over across the room towards my wife. He looked back.
"I told him I didn't know any," he said.
I nodded.

It sounds ridiculous to say but it took me years to work out that she had a boyfriend in Wales all that time – Diane's brother presumably. All the clues were there but she never told me outright. Maybe she was sparing my feelings. Maybe I just did not want to face it. Either way, I blocked it out.
Maybe it was that boyfriend she married. In a way I hope it was.

Sitting here at my desk. John Lee Hooker on the headphones. Forty-plus years down the line.

It was a good three years before I woke up one day and realised that the previous day I had not thought of Sharon at any time in the whole day, for the first time ever.
I still dream about her from time to time. Vivid dreams when she is as real as ever to me. All these years down the line. I could still tell you her phone number back then – 01 272 5938.

A couple of years ago I walked down her old street, Alexandra Road off Holloway Road as I was nearby for a meeting. What I think was her grandparents' house has been knocked down now to make space for a small park. Everything changes.

Would I like to meet her again? No, definitely not. I remember her so well but it's when she was seventeen, and I was, too. When her hair was long and dark (and mine was, too!), walking beside me up Camden Passage at the Angel, laughing together, on our way to the Camden Head. Too many years ago. We are not those people anymore.

I have sought that fierce overwhelming feeling of total love every day though. And it has hurt me. And it has taken me a long time to find it, and even better it.

Ok, so let's fast forward over all sorts of drama and angst, marriages, lost years and family, that I will cover later, and find me much nearer home now. Ironically back in Sussex though. Something like fifty years later. Is that right? I add the figures up again. Yes, it is. Fifty years down the line.

When I was away on my own in Tenerife in January 2020 I thought seriously about my future. Having been single then for eight months or so I realised that I was finally quite happy on my own, and that I could make this state work. I enjoy the independence and the ease of it. However, I also realised that if I was really given a choice, if life now will actually give me another choice, I would choose to find someone special to share my life with. Knowing myself quite well though I do also realise this would be a real longshot because I want an impossible mix. It really would need to be someone special – or else I'd rather not bother. And where am I going to meet this probably mythical special person?

I work in a male-dominated environment – I do meet quite a few women, but they are invariably the mothers of our young players or triallists and I kind of feel there are ethical issues there! I work long hours too, driving, going to games, writing up reports of games and players. So, therefore, I reasoned if I am going to even try and see who might be out there then I would need to try the infamous internet dating. The modern way.

So, I did. A mate recommended a site, and I signed up.

Oh Lord, there is a whole virtual new world out there. If you've never been there, it is a place unlike any other. An unreal fake-news crazy cyber space.

Firstly, there are loads of hurdles to overcome. You have to write your profile – what are you going to say to paint a picture of yourself in a few lines? Try it – 200 words max. You then have to find a photo – I have so few of me and of course you do want to find a 'good one' and a recent one.

Well, I say a recent one. Once I got on the site, set my parameters of search – age range, area, type, interests and all that (I mean I tried putting 'I want Julie Christie as of 1968, aged late twenties, but who would be interested in a sixty-five year old three-times divorced father of seven, wedded to his demanding job – and, oh it would be handy if she will put up with my football obsession' but I couldn't fit it into the box provided) well, then you start getting photos and profiles of prospective 'matches' the algorithm throws at you. Believe me, the things you see when you don't have a gun.

How can I put this? Gorillas in drag? No, not fair. Accurate, possibly, but not fair. Then the ages and photo do not match at all. There's a woman clearly in her early seventies from the photo and the age says '51'. But then there's a photo of a woman in her late thirties, I would say, and the age given is '58'. Something is wrong here.

There's a whole different language too – 'average' build means what most of us would frankly call 'fat'. For a guy then 'height: 5'11' means barely able to see over the steering wheel.

But no, Robbo, I thought, this is a numbers game. Think of how many players you have to watch to find that one good one. OK, OK, patience is a virtue, they say, and possibly the only one I have left.

Gradually the odd interesting one emerges. Of course, you are going off looks of the photos primarily (Ok, if you are shallow like me) then you read the profile, nothing alarming like 'I believe in live and let live but don't like all the Poles over here' or 'Interest: The Lifestyle' or 'I'm a Pisces and really would really like to find a Virgo'. That ship has sailed, dear, a long time ago. But some looked ok, even pleasant.

So, then you 'Like' or even send a 'Message'. Then you never hear from them.

I did start to get people 'Liking' me and some messages. I then began to get a few where we 'Liked' each other – happy days!

Then you never hear from them.

But some you do. You message back and forth. The next big hurdle is to actually speak to them. Hearing their voice on the phone is a massive step. One woman had been messaging with me, great photos, local, right age bracket and all going well. Then we spoke on the phone, and she had this shrill, screechy voice that was like fingernails across a blackboard and that was that.

The next massive hurdle is the first date.

I have only had time for a couple, of course. I have to say they have been some of the most stressful experiences of my life. I cannot tell you of the nerves, the stress, the anticipation, the management of expectations and the sheer naked fear.

I was beginning to despair.

Then someone called 'Taylor' messaged me.

"I see you work in football. I love football!"

I looked at her photo. And looked again. Nah, this was a scam. The photo showed a beautiful woman, probably early forties at most, shoulder length blonde hair, amazing big brown eyes and a stunning smile. I immediately thought 'there's a little bald fat sweaty bloke sat at a laptop in a sleazy bedsit in Paddington having a laugh here.'

But nothing ventured, and frankly I was beginning to get to the end of my little online journey...we started messaging. She was very funny, very cheeky (can't be right, I'm thinking), local, divorced with grown up kids. Then she said, "this is my mobile number, lets message off site."

Ok, I said, and we did.

Shall I call you? No, Taylor said, I don't like talking to men I don't know.

What? Hang on. What's that about?

Anyway, I looked at the photo again and thought, what the hell. We messaged some more.

Why don't we meet tomorrow for a coffee? I messaged. (No chance, I'm thinking.)

I never meet someone for weeks and weeks, she said. But OK, let's.

Gulp!

Turns out her name is not Taylor, but Julie. OK.

She said she would have her grandson with her as she looks after him one day a week and suggested a Garden Centre café. So into bizarre-land here, I thought as I set off the next morning, to meet a woman with her grandson in a garden centre café. Those of you who know me may remark that I would have to be dragged kicking and screaming into a garden centre normally. Getting ready I had tried five different shirts on before settling on one. I can't ever remember doing that before, not even when sixteen. Mind you, I probably didn't have five shirts back then.

I sat in my car in the car park and my heart was hammering, my hands sweating, my face clammy – very attractive, I'm thinking. I just knew she could not look anything like her photos, if she was she at all! She would be fat or mad, possibly both. I was preparing myself for the inevitable disappointment - and the subsequent excruciating half hour making small talk in a fucking garden centre café with someone I would never want to see again.

She'd told me what car she drove and sure enough right on time such a car pulled in and drove past me. I saw a brief glimpse of blonde hair. She parked on the next line of cars nearer the entrance than me and got out, got a child out and they started walking towards the entrance. I got out of my car, shivering with nerves. I caught up with them just before the entrance doors.

I called out her name. "Julie".

She turned, and I was sunk. Without trace.

My first thought was "Robbo, you are punching well above your weight here."

She looked just like the photo. Her two-year-old grandson, Harry, was lovely. We politely hugged briefly, as you do, and I mumbled something, and we found our way somehow to the café. She got Harry into a high chair, and I got us two teas.

We sat at that table in the corner for about two hours until the debris Harry had made of his banana, his orange, and his drink was scattered all round us. I have no idea what we talked about. Or, rather, fortunately, what Taylor talked about because, to be honest, I just sat there gawping like a fool. Every now and then I said to myself, in a blind panic, "Robbo, for fuck's sake, say something remotely intelligent. Failing that, just say anything."

She was beautiful. Her eyes, her mouth, her skin with a slight bronze tan – she too had just come back from Tenerife, coincidentally, but clearly the sun had shone on her much more than it had on me. Well, why wouldn't it? The way she would say something funny or cheeky and then just look straight at me, a smile lighting up her face and everything in radar distance. When she held the restless Harry on her lap and stroked his hair till he fell asleep on her chest, and gently kissed his hair, I just melted.

That was Thursday morning. We arranged to meet on the Saturday. She came back on the Sunday. When she left on Sunday evening, I sorted Diego the Dog out with his last walk and collapsed on my bed, sleeping eleven hours straight.

Was it the coronavirus?

No, it was….something else.

I have tried to do the right thing as I saw it at the time. Sometimes things work out,, sometimes they don't,. With Julie I felt like all my Christmases had come together. I was very aware – and remain so – that we had been so lucky. It all seems so random. What if I had not 'Liked' Julie or she me? What if she had not messaged me or agreed to meet? It all seems so tenuous, so knife edge, so variable. I do believe you make your own luck in life. I don't believe Karma is a rigid thing but just that what you put out is what you get back. Maybe I was due some return.

I had learned that you needed to do the right thing, follow that inner voice, do what you knew to be right – not for external reasons but because you know it is right. If you do that, then I have found you get your rewards. It may not be immediate, it may not be connected, but it is just that feeling that what you give, is what you get. Do the right thing just because it is the right thing. Virtue is indeed it's own reward.

Years ago, it was a very cold winter's night in the West End in London. Late night Christmas shopping with the sales already on. It was dark and bitterly cold but the lights along Regent Street were bright and cheerful, the glitzy stores full of happy shoppers buying everything that stayed still long enough. I had bought a lovely thick warm cotton sweater, pale green as I recall. West End prices but lovely. As I walked along, I passed a young lad sat in a doorway. I looked down at him as we passed. He was skinny, with a thin nylon anorak on, his head bowed almost touching his knees as he huddled to himself, shivering. I walked on but couldn't lose the image. I walked back and gave him the designer bag with the sweater in it.

I didn't really do it for him, to be honest. I did it for me. I knew what was right and if I didn't do it then I would not be comfortable with myself. My family had been homeless in London when I was a child, not very far from where this lad sat, shivering in this miserable doorway. My Mum had brought me and my sister up to know right from wrong and once you do then you cannot escape that knowledge.

I wanted the lovely thick sweater. But he needed it.

I could not look myself in the mirror if I had known the right thing to do and just turned away and not done it. It was for my peace of mind. I was being self-centred in a way. My conscience would not let me rest if I did not do the right thing.

I have not always done the right thing in my life. I have done things, made decisions, taken actions that with the 20:20 vision of long-range hindsight still have the power to make me bow my head in embarrassment and shame. But I have always known, one way or another, what was right and what was wrong. I have learned enough about myself to know I just won't rest easy if I do the wrong thing, knowing it to be wrong.

It was the funeral of a friend of mine a while ago in March of 2020 as lockdown loomed. I decided after much agonising not to go. I so much wanted to pay my respects and show my support for his wife – also a friend – and his family. But because of the virus I did not go. I felt – and feel – bad about it but I know it was the right thing for me not to go, in my judgement. So, doing the right thing is not always comfortable, is not guaranteed to be easy to live with in real life but it is what we must do once we know it.

The Monday after we had met on the Thursday the country went into lockdown. Julie and I talked of couples held apart by wars, by one of them going off to fight a distant dangerous conflict and my family have had their share of that. In comparison this enforced separation for twenty one days and nights….yes, twenty one, count them…was nothing. It's a romantic, bitter-sweet, time-limited, painful ache. We both have had our shares of the pains of life and we know we can bear this if we had to. So, we did.

We came up with games we played while apart. Compiling our bucket list of the places we want to go together, the silly things we want to do. Talking every night, messaging through the day, sharing songs. We both had work to do, which was good, both had things to sort out, chores to fulfil, responsibilities. Time passes slowly, but it does pass. Life is short, though, and the less you have of it left, the more precious it becomes.

It's all a question of balance. Bad timing, great fortune, a price to pay, longing, duty, responsibilities, commitment, promises, the memory of a smile, the scent of 'Eternity' on a pillow.

I wrote her a letter every day during lockdown and would walk with Diego the Dog up the lane to the post box every afternoon. (Later at our first Christmas together one of her lovely presents would be a book she had got printed of all the letters. She titled it 'Love Letters from Lockdown' and it's on the book shelves behind me as I write this.)

We worked it through and have now embarked on building a life together. She is smart and funny, and keeps me on my toes. I talk to her about more things and more honestly than I ever have before in my life. I hide nothing away. She wakes up in the morning looking gorgeous and the day progresses from there. She asks me all sorts of questions about my life – why did I do this? What did I want with that? In doing so, she makes me revalue and re-assess.

When I'm not with her I feel I am waiting for my real life to begin again.

But I tell you something.

I am alive.

So, now as I write this, we are together, building a life together and I have never been happier or more in love. How did I get to be so lucky?

How did I get from that first painful sudden immersion into the world of love right through so much to this happy ending, finding the love of my life so late? How could I not have got it right before now? Or, as I am not complaining, not right enough?

To be honest, I don't know the answers. I just notice these ghosts swirling round me and hear their voices in the old songs I listen to.

Everything changes. All the time.

Me and my hungry heart.

3. Dancing in the Dark

The King's Head in Romford, then, 1972, oceans of lager, Bacardi and 'snakebites', walls of noise from the nightly rock bands, jammed with young people, bouncers at the door. City centre concrete, nameless, soul-less land but some heady, heavy music and the scents of sex, beer and fierce cheap perfume. Oh, rock and roll, pills over the counter, needles left abandoned in the little dressing room, the smell of stale beer during the dreary daylight hours, drenched in sweat and that same cheap perfume every night, mixing with the 'Old Spice' and 'Brut'. A fine place for an eighteen-year-old lost heartbroken boy to be earning a pound that long summer of 1972.

Johnny Nash, 'I Can See Clearly Now', Slade, the Stones, Alice Cooper, Johnny Johnson and the Bandwagon, The Chi-Lites 'Oh Girl', Rod Stewart 'You Wear It Well', the Temptations 'Papa Was A Rolling Stone'. The juke-box taking my wages. Getting a taste for Pernod, living large and pointless, killing time in some temporary noisy backwater, growing up. Killing time. And a few brain cells.

Walking home in the small hours, one early morning, having long missed the last bus, sleeping a while in a roadside garden, hitching a lift the last part of the way in a misty dawn light, some nightshift worker laughing at me.

Wall to wall sound each frantic night, drinkers three deep all along the long bar from seven thirty onwards. Flirting with the other bar staff, friends either side of the wooden divide. One guy wants me to front his band, be the singer.
"What do you want to do?" he asks.
"Joe Cocker type stuff?" I reply.
"Yeah, Joe Cocker, right. Let's do it. I'll get the guys together."
But the next week he gets sent down for possession. Word comes back from the Scrubs:
"There's more drugs in here than at the King's Head!"

Another guy tells me he is mates with Stevie Marriott, one of my heroes. He reckons him and Stevie used to be dating the Shrimpton girls together.
Mind you, I am learning to take any drinker's tale with a shrug.

Sharon is there in the back of my mind every day but I just fall forward, tumbling through the days and nights, swimming in a tide of drink, drugs, loud rock music and girls. Yes, the girls.

One of the girls on the scene was Lindy. She used to work behind the bar before my time but got the elbow when the landlady cottoned on that the landlord and Lindy were going at it when her back was turned. Lindy not so much played the field but rode gloriously through it waving her knickers over her head. She was totally in control of her life of pleasures and party. I knew her thin nervous fiancé, Eric, too, and pitied him, like we all did. What Lindy wanted, or whoever Lindy wanted, she just went out and took.
Lindy was a tall blue-eyed Scottish blonde, a little hard faced, maybe, on the more solid side of curvy but built for fun with fine long legs. She knew what she wanted all right.

And then, inexplicably, one night she wanted me.

"What are you doing after work?" She leant across the bar, daring me to look at her superb breasts spilling out of the strappy top, on another of those noisy hot working nights.
"Going home," I gulped, concentrating determinedly on her blue eyes.
She frowned at me and pouted.
"Come out with me. A couple of us are going to the Lacy Lady."
Me? Are you serious?
"My Mum's expecting me home….." I blurted out.
"Well, phone her," she said, an amused look on her face.
"….and I haven't got any money."
"Don't worry about money, I've got money. You've got everything you need."

I had run out of nervous excuses. What could I do?
"OK."
She winked at me.
"See you later then."

The Lacy Lady at Seven Kings, Ilford. Oh geez, I was out of my depth here. This was no pub - this was my first night club. There would be a lot of night club times. Later I would be like a fish in water but not then, no, not yet then.
Dancing to James Brown, 'Sex Machine'. Her blue eyes fixed on me, her body close, smelling sweet, a real woman, curves and smooth skin, yeah, another vodka and tonic, plenty of ice, thanks. Get up, get on up.

Soft Scottish burr in my ear, laughing at me, running her hands over my chest and teenage flat stomach, under my suddenly open black shirt, drinking me in, consuming me. And there's me, caught in the headlights. A fine pair of headlights, though, as I recall.

She and her friend were, improbably, Traffic Wardens. We went back to her friend's nearby bed-sit because Lindy shared a flat with her sister and her sister would be home. Lindy was, after all, engaged. So, in the bedsit, her friend and this other fella on one bed, me and Lindy on a mattress by the unlit fire in the darkened room. I was so nervous. Dark room, with yellow street light coming in from outside.
We somehow got naked underneath a light cover. She wrapped her arms around me and I was overwhelmed by all this soft yet firm flesh, she whispered in my ear.
"Listen, this is my bad week."
I almost cried with relief. She misread my slumping shoulders.
"Oh, don't be like that," she whispered, "we can still have some fun."
She gently pushed me back on the mattress and she headed south. Fun indeed.

Time stood still in that little bedsit. It was a long night.

A lifetime later.
"God, you turn me on," she said.
I do? How? Why?

Hours passed, morning came, not that I had any sleep. I had to go to work. She didn't. I staggered off.

Later, back at the pub, bleary eyed, with love bites on my neck and stomach like I had tangled with a particularly angry rottweiler. Towards the end of the lunchtime shift, in came Lindy, looking far better than she had a right to, surely far better than I did.
She leant across the bar again, her hand gently on my face and pulled me close and whispered in my ear.
"My sister is at work, my flat's free. I'll meet you by the cinema when you get off work and we can finish what we started."
She was clearly on a mission and there was indeed a job to finish.

At her smart flat on the edge of Romford, it seemed her bad week was over. The weekend starts here then. She took me to bed. I hadn't uttered a word since she had come into the pub.

"I love the way you tremble when you come," she said, a while later. Probably a short while later.
"That's not passion, that's fear," I thought. But I was not complaining. I was too busy trying to catch my breath.
"What do you feel?" she asked, leaning up on one elbow to look at me.
Knackered, would have been the most honest answer.
"I don't know. What about you?"
She sighed.
"Too much," she said, "I feel too much." She closed her eyes.

I walked away from the flat feeling ten feet tall. I can actually remember saying to myself:
"I am a man now."

Fool.

I looked back at the flat. I could see Lindy was stood by the window on the first floor, a thin silky robe round her, holding aside the curtain. She waved. I waved cheerily back and bounced off to work.

I am ashamed to say I avoided her after that. I am not really sure why. It was mostly fear, I think. She came to the pub from time to time, once with her equally good-looking sister, giggling together and both looking at me, so by then I guess sister was in on the story. But I slipped out the back when my shift was over, the older more experienced barmaids laughing at me. I slipped out and ran to the bus stop and went home.

There was something I never said.
Thank you, Lindy.

Listen, I am not going through the years on a blow-by-blow account, excusing the pun. I am not listing conquests or any of that shit. I am trying to mark out the route, note the landmarks, somehow check where I have come, see and recall where that route took me. Lindy is the right place to start for obvious reasons. It feels like sex has been a major influence on my life story somehow so I should note that, recognize that. More to the point, my partners have been important. The sex was maybe one place where our lives bumped up against each other but the relationships have been much more than that, often rarely that. It's just a reference point or points like a line of streetlights over a horizon, seen back over my shoulder, each lighting a place I have been, a time I have known, people who have shared a slice of my life with me, some common connecting points. A little light in the darkness.

In Sheffield, getting towards my prime, maybe, I'd been out playing football, as usual, towards the end of the season, an early summer evening game, time of joy. Back from the game with the guys, walking in the student union with that fresh showered feeling where you can still feel the odd knock or bruise from the game, a disco is on, we wander in, relaxed, a couple of pints in along the road. I stood there, talking with Roy Lindon and a couple of guys, when enter stage left suddenly a girl bursts in to our group and literally throws herself at me, arms around my neck. It was a beautiful girl from Cheshire I had been briefly dating, Helen, a while before. She was slim with short blonde hair and a very pretty face. I had not seen her for a while, we had all just got back after a term end break or something.

"I've been looking everywhere for you," she said breathlessly, dragging me to the dance floor as the guys laughed at me, shaking their heads. That Robbo, they were saying. What?

Later we went back to her room in the Halls of Residence, Tapton Hall up in Crookes on the number 52 bus route. We fell into bed, clothes being discarded.

"When I was away," she was blurting out," there was this guy…I mean, I was missing you and.."

"Ssshhh," I said, kissing her mouth, kicking off my jeans " It's OK, don't worry."

She was head over heels for me. A fine-looking girl. I took her home to London. My Dad told me later he thought she was the best looking girl I ever took home. We went to the Old Boys club, me keen to show off this lovely girl to all the crew, to all the memories. We danced to Stevie Wonder's 'Superstition', I recall.

One night back in Sheffield, as we were leaving a disco, the DJ played this haunting new song as the crowd was dispersing. As she queued for her coat, I went back to ask the DJ who it was. Lou Reed, he says, 'Walk On The Wild Side'. New song. Couldn't get it out of my mind.

Helen bought me the LP. 'Transformer'. 1973.

She went on the pill for me, put on a little weight.
I dumped her.
She then got engaged to a good mate of mine, Dave. But it did not last. By then I was already caught up with another girl, of course, and this one lasted somewhat longer. I kept the LP for a long time though and even today have that song on my i-pod.
I don't know what to say, how to make sense of any of this really, how the music lasted longer than the girl.
I hope Helen, if she ever thinks of me, smiles a bit. All of them, the Helens and the Lindys and the others over the years. Not so many really.

The summer of 1973, I went off after the exams on my own, heading down to Cornwall, worked in a night club in a huge sprawling holiday camp near Perranporth, living in a crappy little caravan back from the cliff edge by the wide yellow sandy beach. Still strung out on that first love. When I was first there, in the first week, I went running on the long sandy beach each morning. Before long I was working so many hours, for very little money, that I didn't have the energy to get up any earlier than I had to. I ended up staying on the camp on my one day a week off, drinking myself stupid, like everyone else. I was lean and sun tanned nevertheless, wearing cut off jean shorts and little else when off duty, beads around my neck, tired, somehow suntanned, scruffy, drinking too much, still strung out on that teenage love, carrying my stereo and records down to Cornwall on the train and bus. Free, Mott the Hoople, Rod Stewart, Jimi. There were plenty of girls there but my heart was not in it, really. A couple of mates came down and worked there, too, and I made new friends. There was Seamus, the daft Irishman in his late thirties I would guess, who drank too much and whose life was collapsing round him. Seamus had a woman and child in Reading where he worked in the student bar but he'd run off to Cornwall for the summer... as did all sorts of other unemployed and unemployables, students, surfers, beach bums and drifters.

Seamus and I sat on the beach one night, having been drinking right through the night, , watching the sun come up, drinking sloe gin straight from the bottle that he had grabbed out of the night club bar.
'So, young Chris, what are you going to do with your life?'
'I dunno, go back home, I suppose, then go back to university. Me sister's getting married this summer, I need to earn some proper money to buy her a present and I'm saving nothing here, just wasting my time.'
'Don't knock it,' said Seamus,' wasting time is much underrated. I should know, I've made a career of it.'
I laughed but I knew I did not want to end up like Seamus, a boozer and loser, even though a nice guy, drifting from one dead end to another, bottle in hand, living on a steadily diminishing charm. I knew, though, that I could end up like that, easily. I have always known that. But it was time to get back on the plan, back on message. I went home.

Around the student union there were a few really good looking girls. You'd see them in the café or canteen, or crossing over from the labs or arts block to the union building. The 'Union Angels' I called them. One of them had long blondish hair, cut in a layered style, good figure and nice eyes.
On night me and the football boys were out on a long session. We'd met at the Broomhill Tavern at five thirty and been drinking steadily ever since. Eventually we would be ending up at the 'Pyjama Jump' one of the big student events at the Top Rank down in the city centre with two thousand other students who all wore nightwear of some sort. Some of the lads were predictably in night dresses borrowed from girlfriends or whatever, but I had pyjama trousers and a silly t-shirt on. It was October 1973.
The Searchers were playing live, 'Needles and Pins'. It was early hours by now. I had been through drunkenness and come out the other side. Way down the track. I was stood with my mate, Stevie Johnson from Manchester, strong Manc accent, United fanatic,

excellent striker, maths genius, daft as the proverbial brush, my roommate though I was never there. I always blamed Stevie because he was the last person I talked to before I lurched over to try my luck with the Union Angel with the long blondish hair. I ended up marrying her. Disastrously. I used to kid Stevie that he should have stopped me somehow, should have seen it all coming. But, of course, as with everything else, I had no-one to blame but myself.

She was from Widnes, just along the road to Warrington from Liverpool. Undoubtedly one of the most depressing towns I have ever visited. She came from a solid Catholic working-class family there. She was a year older than me. Her schoolwork had always come easy to her but, like it sometimes worked out, by the time she was doing 'A' levels she had not developed the work habit and for the first time the level was too much of a challenge. The plan had been to train as a doctor but the 'A' levels were not good enough. She had to settle for a human physiology course at Sheffield University instead and then struggled through the course there. She was too easily distracted, mostly by me by that stage.

Within a few weeks we were effectively living together. Tumbling forwards. Suddenly at nineteen I was engaged and the whole circus of a working-class wedding was revving up and getting underway. We were to get married in 1975 when I finished my degree. I would be twenty one years old.

My mum said I was too young. I thought I knew better. As usual, she was right.

A weekend in Widnes, me throwing up in some car park – not from drink but from stomach reaction that kicked in unexplained from time to time and would haunt me for years until I found out I may have a low tolerance to gluten. But back then I think it was a reaction to impending doom. I should have seen the pattern, it was often when I was in Widnes and increased as the wedding train gathered speed. My body was maybe telling me what my brain would not consider.

But the danger to me was just not seeing at all. Of course, I was too young and too stupid.

A few years ago, my son, Nye, said one day he'd found my day by day diary from 1975 at his Mum's and had 'rescued it'. Was it alright if he read it? I said, sure, tell me what you think.
He came back a while later.
"Your whole life revolved around football, drinking, girls and discos," he laughed.
"Well, I was twenty, twenty one, what do you expect?"

But once I read it, I saw that threaded through the diary is the impending wedding as summer approaches. My fiancée's see-sawing moods and negativity comes through the pages and at times I almost seem to know I am making a mistake which is hugely frustrating now. Nevertheless, amidst me working hard for my finals and getting a 2:1 in political theory and institutions, sorting out a management trainee job in container transport (another major mistake), Chelsea getting relegated, me worrying about my eleven pound overdraft, me reporting very self-critically on each match I played, scoring twenty plus goals in the season, weighing eleven and a half stone, turning twenty one (the Bay City Rollers were on in Sheffield city centre that night – I didn't go) I walked blindly on through the traditional wedding and beyond.

On the wedding night in Widnes, at the catholic working men's club where our reception was held, the Bride's Dad said to me:
"I hope you know what you're letting yourself in for."
Talk about the writing being on the wall.

Of course, there were lots of good times too. Decorate it up and off you go. Living in Preston, me a new Catholic by now (don't ask), working in Heysham, playing crap-level football in parks with no dressing rooms because I was travelling with work too much to train often, listening to my new hero, Bruce Springsteen, I was still a long-lost London boy in foreign parts, as I would be for too long. We lived in a flat in a large terraced house in Fulwood Parade in Preston, walking through the streets now becoming full of Bangladeshi families. I was in the wrong job – a management trainee in Transport – and married to the wrong woman. One of these things I realized quickly enough. The other took a little while.

We came back to the smoke for a year, my wife teaching at an autistic school in Walthamstow, me doing a masters at the LSE while working a lot of shifts with my Dad on the docks in Millwall. We shared a flat in Walthamstow with my old mate, Griz and his lady, Jean from Sunderland till we got ourselves together enough to buy our first place, a flat in Leyton, for £8,500. Then it was off back to Preston again, coincidentally, but now I was working for the union, NALGO, and I was on a mission.

We were on the track to family and beyond so we needed a house. We found a three-bed newish bungalow we could almost afford at £16,000 in a town we had never heard of before – Bacup, in Rossendale, and another chapter in my life got underway. The years of politics, working for the union in Manchester, promoted to District Officer at twenty four or so, and getting elected to the local council in Rossendale, shaking up the local labour party, waving that red flag.

The cracks in my marriage were being well and truly papered over now and I slapped it on heavy duty style. My eldest son, Pat was born in June 1981 and Nye came along in November 1982 – just seventeen months between these lovely boys. I will talk more about my children later on. Our youngest champion Micky followed in September 1984.

Now I have to tell you that somehow, I felt back then that if you could make such beautiful children then the marriage was really OK, wasn't it? Well, no.

Inevitably or not, I don't know at this distance, with me up on those stages, traveling round on union or party business, leading, leading from the front, leading with my chin, full of fire and passion, me in my late twenties, a bit better dressed than the scruffy long-haired teenager, something was going to give.

I behaved for a long time. And then I didn't. Those many weekends away with the British Gas gang – great people, riotous times. Lager and discos, many late nights, eighties fashion, hair gel and shoulder pads, women in lycra leggings and spandex tops, big hair, out on the razzle away from homes and husbands.

My great mate in the Union then was Bill Chesworth from St Helens and he and I had many escapades together, many great times and many laughs. He told me that when he was first married, his uncle who was his mentor, told him he should get dressed up every Friday night, a smart suit – and Ches liked a smart suit – and go out down the pub so it became a matter of routine. The routine would be the dressing up and the Friday night out with the lads. His uncle had told him that he wouldn't always need to be so dressed up but one day he would need to and it would be worth it. Ches and I laughed at that. We were aware of our own failings and how ridiculous we made life seem at times.

Those times – the seventies and eighties – were a very different time and a different world than now, obviously. Values and norms were different. You could say I was lucky to have been a teenage just as the pill became widely available and have finished my carousing days before Aids hit us all. Certainly, attitudes towards women have changed, to an extent, at least, and even more certainly I get the feeling young women today are (hopefully) much more in control of their destinies and their appearance and their own morals. To be fair to myself I was always brought up to be respectful of everyone and certainly I was taught the old fashioned 'gentlemanly' virtues of the time and this was added to by the developing, burgeoning feminism of the sixties and onwards. So, although I am a product of my times as much as anyone, and accept my times featured too much of what we would dismiss as sexism today, in everyday life, I don't think I can honestly be accused of disrespecting women. When I reflect on these relationships I am looking at them from my angle – like all of this book – and telling you how it feels to me and how I recall things and people and places. I am not reverse engineering. I am not painting the unconstructed past in a new modern wash of correctness. This is what I recall. That is it.

Have I treated women badly along the way? Yes, there have been a few broken hearts and a few broken promises. I have left some women crying. But, to be fair, I have left some smiling too.

Anyway, back in the late seventies and early eighties I was still out there, every day, working for the union, working for the party, slogging round, meeting to meeting, campaigning, speaking, arguing – and then partying hard, too. Life in the fast lane, I guess.

Around that time, I recall going back to Sheffield for a weekend, to play in a football game and to meet up with some old mates and hit the town, too. I walked into a night club in Sheffield called 'Josephine's' and stood watching the dancers. I was back in that great city playing football, as I say, and feeling no pain at all. Or so I thought or would have said if asked.
I said to my mate, Pete Bartlett, "she's the one". He followed my gaze to a beautiful blonde, slim, white trousers (well, it was the 80s). "Is she the best looking girl in the place?" I asked. Maybe I had had a few drinks by then.
"Yes," he said, "no doubt."
So off I went.

Later, we stood in a shadowed corner of the club, and as she gazed into my eyes and told me her story, reaching out and holding my hand as I listened, Pete walked by. He smiled and shook his head.
"I bet you've always done this," he laughed.
"No," I said, and it occurred briefly to me that I maybe should have done and had never thought of it. I perhaps should have picked the best girl in the club and gone for her, tried every Saturday night, set my sights so high, and not got tied up so young, but then this girl stepped closer and I could smell her hair, and her eyes were clear and blue and her breath was on my lips and everything fell away. Her name was Jill, from Oughtibridge just outside Sheffield, as I recall.
"I bet your wife would hate me if she could see me now," she said later, whispering in my ear almost in wonder. A sweet girl with a cheating lost boy. I never saw her again. She was well out of it.

I look back over that occasion, that night club, that girl and barely recognise myself let alone her. Of course, at the time I can remember that following week thinking about Jill from Oughtibridge a lot and wondering if we might have got on well beyond that hour we had together. Now, of course, I look back and realise I was looking for something. I did not know what it was then. It was not sex; I can tell you that. Sex was a by-product, an incidental along the way, pleasant and alluring as it may well be. I can look back now and over the years and the ups and downs it seems I was seeking that feeling I had in my first love. I craved that depth of feeling. I was in love with love. Now, too, from this vantage point of having finally after all these intervening years found what I was looking for it is a lot clearer than it's been along the way.

I could try and rationalize it all now, from the distance of these many years. I could say how my first wife and I grew apart, how she constantly told me how unhappy she was and consistently complained; her wildly varying moods wore me down. But I don't know, I have to take responsibility and always have. I was slipping into my lost years and did not know it. Everything was slipping away from underneath me and I had no idea, no foresight of it at all.

I would lose an election, a marriage, a home, nearly my children, my livelihood, another marriage, my direction, my money, and finally my health.

Again, there was no-one to blame but me. But hey, that's down the line a bit, there's more ghosts here yet, they have some more to say.

I will say this. When I look back, I trace my mistakes and own them all. I blame no-one else for the decisions I made. However, that doesn't mean I don't recognize I have made some bad ones. I think getting married in the first place, way too young was the start of a series of consequences. Of course, you can look back and say "well if I hadn't got married then to that person, I wouldn't have these particular children" – and of course, they trump everything. However, it does not help to gloss over the initial bad choices or decisions because of that. I married too young and I married the wrong person. It set me off on a path and led me to more crossroads and some decisions that were good and some that decidedly were not.

I have had some great successes – in personal and in work terms. As my close friends tell me, I have led some interesting lives. I certainly walked myself down a rabbit hole of dead ends at one time but then, with help, I did find my way back out.

Years later, when I was on my way back out, when I was finding myself again, I had a very public relationship crash in full view which I will tell you about later when we visit those lost years properly. But the ghost that is whispering in my ear now is the ghost that rescued me then and pointed me back along the path to myself. Another woman I probably did not thank, or certainly not enough, if

I did. Another woman who for some reason reached out and held me and lifted me clear. A beautiful, warm ghost.

Carol Coombes and I had worked together for a few years. This was in Birmingham in the early nineties. I was working for Co-Enterprise, helping set up community businesses. Carol was full of life and fire with a throaty, dusky laugh that drove me nuts. The first day I met her, my boss Mike Dalzell took me over to see the inner-city project she was working on. She was having trouble with her boss, it seemed, and Mike wanted to see if we could help. Mike and I walked into this community centre office. Carol was there, white t-shirt, jeans and boots, slim with short black hair, big brown eyes. Fuck me, I thought, what's Demi Moore doing here in Birmingham?
"Have I got c-u-n-t written across my forehead?" she asked me straight off, eyes blazing, brummie edge in her husky voice.
"Not that I can see," I said, holding my hands up.
"Good, cos I was beginning to wonder."
Mike laughed at her, "Carol, this is Chris. Chris, meet Carol."

A year or so later, she came and worked in the community development project we worked in. I was managing semi-pro football part-time and building my career but trying to do some good in the day job, helping community businesses in inner-city Birmingham. Carol and I sat next to each other. We seemed to spend a lot of time giggling and laughing. She was a single mum with four beautiful kids and nothing in life got her down. She had been there, seen it, done it, and she had a healthy cynicism about men in general. She was bright, clever, funny, independent, sharp and gorgeous. What was not to like?

She had a tattoo of an owl on her bicep, dark against her tawny skin.
"Why an owl?" I asked.
"Because it's a tough bird," she said and punched me on the arm. She cracked me up.

One day I had arranged to meet Karen, the woman I was living with, at my office, we were going out somewhere. Carol and I had been out at a project and we came up the stairs and into the office, laughing at something as usual. Karen was sat there at my desk talking to Mike and the others. They all looked up at me and Carol when we came rolling in. Karen's eyes narrowed.

As Karen and I left the office soon after, she suddenly turned and hit me, punching me on the arm.
"What?" I said, jumping back.
"You never told me she looked like that," she hissed. What the fuck?

But for all that, there was nothing more than friendship between me and Carol in those days. She was in a relationship and so was I. She was clear thinking on such things and had better standards than me, or than those I'd had before, at least. To be fair, I was already a reformed character by then. My Viking days, as a good mate would later term them, were already behind me.

One time, in the office, Christmas time, staff party sort of thing, I recall I had my guitar in the office for some reason, for something we were doing, some parody song me and one of the other guys had worked out for fun. We all then played some guessing game based on a montage of photos. Somehow someone mentioned that as Carol was second guessing my answers so easily anyone would think she was my girlfriend.
"No," Carol looked away, "I'm not blonde enough."
I opened my mouth to disagree or at least say something but I was just surprised and trying to work out what she meant and the moment passed.

So, time goes on and I left the set-up there to go full-time in football and our paths drifted away. We would generally keep in touch but I had not actually seen her for quite a while. Then the shit hits the proverbial and I am in the middle of this huge break-up with

Karen being played out in the newspapers – of which, more later. I was managing Cheltenham Town by now, it was near the end of the season in April 1996 or thereabouts. I was in a daze, stumbling through the days. I needed someone to talk to. I phoned Carol, as we had been promising to meet up for a while.

We arranged to meet in a café bar one lunchtime in Birmingham city centre on Digbeth just down from the office where she still worked, where we had worked together. The break-up had hit me hard and I had not been eating much, I was training hard though, working out almost every day with my mate, Pete Cohen, training me at the Chapel Rock Gym in Cheltenham. So, I was at a decent fighting weight, in jeans and denim shirt, waiting on Carol in this trendy city centre café bar one sunny April midweek day. In she walks, looking good as usual.

Drinking coffee, telling my tale, and Carol made me laugh - again, as usual. She was kind and sympathetic but could just raise an eyebrow when I got too maudlin. It turns out she is single now, too, as it happens, well, more or less. I needed to get out, cheer up, she says. I agreed though I didn't feel like it. We arranged to meet up one evening, have a meal, maybe catch a movie, just chill out, just friends.

Yeah, right. Somewhere a clock is ticking, a countdown has begun.

We went to Chinatown on a cool early summer night as the city centre shadows got moodier. We went to the cinema nearby and watched 'The Birdcage' starring Robin Williams. I have always really liked the film ever since but had to see it again because I missed most of it the first time round.

The way it happened was about fifteen minutes in, I turned to Carol and kissed her. She sat back and reached out for my hand.
"Good," she said, "now I know what we're doing."
We kissed a lot more.

Back in the front room of her council house in Ladywood that night with the babysitter gone and her kids upstairs, we reinvented sex (or so it seemed to me). She was sensational. She was warm, affectionate, generous and exciting. She had class, a natural, can't buy, can't lose, class.

But it was a strange time for me. Overall, I was a mess, reeling from the sudden, spectacular break-up with Karen, so public, so painful. Not knowing where it was all going, getting mixed messages from Karen. Would we get back together?

Meanwhile, I would escape from my stressful life in Cheltenham with the season ending and drive up the M5 once a week and Carol and I would exist in a different world. It was a world where there was just me and her. In a comedy club in Birmingham, on a night away – bizarrely – in Nottingham, in a small hotel. Then I would return, often in the early hours as the sun was coming up, driving south back to my frantic goldfish bowl life.

I sat in a pub in Birmingham with Mike, still Carol's boss and a friend to both of us. Carol went to the bar.
"Are you sure this is a good idea?" Mike asked.
"What?"
"You and Carol. Seems to me she can get hurt here. You don't know what is going to happen with Karen yet. You're all over the place."
"Yes," I agreed, "but Carol knows that is how it is. We are just having a good time when we can. No strings. That's what we've said."
"I hope so," sighed Mike.

The end of the season came and I had three weeks booked in Italy, my usual escape of choice (and it still is). Karen and I had rented this old mill up in the Ligurian mountains off a doctor in London. I had the flights booked to Pisa and a rental car waiting. I wasn't sure if

Karen was going to come but as it transpired, she wasn't. That's how up and down it was, how uncertain everything was.

Late one night I got a coach from Cheltenham bus station to Gatwick. I stayed in an airport hotel and took my early flight to Pisa. Alone.

I drove up into the hills, following the instructions I had been given. I turned off the mountain road down a track. There was a river in front of me. I could see the village up on the hill above. I checked the instructions again. 'Drive across the ford'. I got out of the car. The river did not look too deep but I could not really tell. There were mountains all around me, overlooking me in this little green valley with the clear, cold river dashing by. I looked back at my bright yellow rented Twingo. I was tired and wanted to find the mill. Fuck it, I thought, it's not my car. I got back in and with a deep breath drove into the river, across the ford and out the other side. Around a corner of the track, amongst the trees, was the old mill, set into the hillside with the village road and small village above. It was old grey stone, with a lower separate floor which housed a bedroom with four bunks and a bathroom. Upstairs on the level of the small garden was the main house with an open plan lounge and kitchen, with wooden floors, and on by the bathroom and main bedroom with just enough room for a double bed. It was simple and beautiful. In the garden was the old mill race which I eventually discovered could be filled with water by opening a lever whereby the lower stone pool would fill up to make a small swimming pool about waist high in cool water.

Just along the track, through the trees, ran the river, tumbling over the stones. I unpacked my clothes and walked along the path which opened out along the river with the high stony mountain behind. There was me, the mill, the mountains, the river, the trees, the birdsong – and little else. Occasionally a car would go by on the village road above. The sun shone hard and bright every day. I was lonely as hell in this paradise.

I had books, of course. I was reading Nick Hornby's 'High Fidelity', I recall. There was the radio with the local 'Punta Radio' station. I got food from the village, and cheap harsh local white wine which I drank to take the edge off the lonely evenings.

At night I could hear the river, still tumbling along, and now and then the buzzy little motorbikes the local kids drove, but mostly, in the still of the night, I could hear the scratching of mice or whatever on the roof above, and beyond that the slow beating of my battered old heart.

I dropped a bottle of after-shave on the stone floor of the bathroom and it shattered. Even after I cleared it up the smell of Paco Rabanne lingered for days. I felt miserable and lost.

During the days, when I wasn't lying in the garden, taking occasional refuge in the cool mill race as the day heated up, I drove around the mountain villages or down to the coast which was just forty minutes away. I wandered around the magical seaside villages of Portovenere and Lerici, practicing my wonky Italian. Evenings I would eat at the local restaurant on the side of the hill with great views, sitting outside, working my way through 'La Gazzetta della Sporta' slowly. But I was always thinking how nice it would be to share this with someone else.

I would drive to the next village and park at the bottom of the steep cobbled street. I would then walk slowly up to the café where in the dark back room, once I had revived with an espresso, black and thick, from the smart old woman that ran the café, I would use the payphone and phone Carol. It was the highlight of my days. I would try and convey to the café owner that I was phoning my woman, who I missed. She seemed to understand or maybe she just indulged me, I don't know.

The dialling was laborious and precarious but when I heard Carol's voice, I was still and calm and no longer alone.

"Come out and spend the last week with me," I begged, "just get a flight and I'll meet you at Pisa airport." Amazingly, she did. She made arrangements to pack the kids off to their Dad's and got herself a flight. I could not believe it. I drove down to Pisa and waited in the airport, an hour early.

So, we had a week together in Italy that June of 1996. I took her to Lerici and we swam in the sea together then lay on the beach scoring the local beauties out of ten and laughing together. We went to Pisa and Portovenere, climbing up the back streets. I took her up to the café in the mountain village so she could phone home to her kids. I smiled at the old woman in the café as Carol phoned from the back room. Now, at least, she understood, if not before.

We ate in the local restaurant which clung to the side of the hill, looking out over the valley. "No Gazzetta now?" the proprietor said in Italian and laughed at me and made a fuss of Carol.

Back at the mill, what had been a lonely vigil became an idyll. There are so many images and fragments of conversation I recall from those few days when all my troubles were left a long way away and there was nothing but Carol and the sunshine, and the cool nights, and my beautiful Italy. As usual, the memories make me smile.

I know, looking back, you can say it was all in that first full flush of a relationship when you can't get enough of each other. That's all it was. It would have passed. Maybe so. Fact is we never got past that point because I fucked it up. So, all I can recall is those passionate times in the garden, in the mill race, in the bedroom with the high beamed ceiling with Punta Radio playing low in the background. Because, as it turned out, that is all we had.

In the quiet of our last night, in the early hours, I lay awake with Carol's head on my shoulder and my arm around her, her smooth thigh across my body. Each night we slept intertwined in some way, connected, together. This night we had been asleep a while, or so I thought.
"I love you," I heard her say quietly in the dark, almost a whisper, speaking into my chest.
"I know," I said.
"Bastard," she dug me in the ribs, "I thought you were asleep."

Carol was smart, she had booked her return on the flight before mine. She was not sure if I would have arranged for Karen to meet me at the airport in some big reconciliation. I was so mixed up maybe I tried that, I don't recall. As it worked out, she waited at Gatwick and we drove back to Birmingham together with her again ridiculing my taste in music.
"Hootie and his fucking Blowfish? Let's get some Mary J on!"

Back to England, Cheltenham, pre-season, reality. I was rested, suntanned and still as mixed up as ever. For some reason that completely escapes me now, I felt a compulsion to try and rescue the relationship with Karen, doomed as it was, or at least see it through to some sort of conclusion. It felt still up in the air. Anyway, the point is where did that leave Carol? I had no idea.

Back in Cheltenham, I met up with Karen again and that stumbled on, off and on, still some painful throes, still stinging. I was getting back on the swing of football pre-season, planning, training.

A week or so later, I phoned Carol and we arranged to go out in Birmingham again, to a Billie Holiday competition bizarrely. In Italy I had been telling Carol what great legs she had – which was very true - though she never wore short skirts, invariably jeans or longer wrap-around dresses. I parked up outside her house and she came out to meet me. The gold patterned mini dress showed off her tan and certainly her legs. She looked sensational. She told me later it was her teenage daughter's dress. Either way, she looked great and I was delighted I had maybe played a part in giving her the encouragement and the confidence.

It was a bit awkward at first. The question of why I had left it a week or so was hanging there. Carol as usual had too much class to ask me. Or maybe too much self-preservation, I don't know.

But then she put me at ease as she always did. She used to call me 'Sharky' because she said I was a killer. Though she also said I was so full of it, too. She had no trouble putting me in my place but she would reach out and hold my arm, or touch my face, or punch me in the ribs or run her hand up my back under my loose shirt. How did I let her fall through my hands?

I drove back down the M5 that night in my usual daze. I didn't see her again for many years. I didn't get back with Karen. Within a week I had met someone else who I soon was living with and later married. Another real time limited love, but that's a later story.

Over the years, Carol and I kept in distant touch. The occasional email, a text to tell me she is a grandmother now, which is the most bizarre thing of all in a way.

As I have said before, given the wonderful life I have enjoyed these last years, I have no basis of complaint at all. Anyway, who would listen? No, I have been so lucky. But the point is I am trying to understand what has happened in my life and at points I really struggle.

When I read that old diary of 1975 that Nye found, the fact that my first wife and I were not compatible was so obvious even in the months leading up to the wedding. We were too young, too unformed, and there was no way her moods and me could last. OK, we were together about eleven years and of course we had three beautiful boys – of whom more later – but that does not change the facts. My bafflement comes from why I could not see it at the time. It is so bloody stark-staringly obvious now and I think it was back then to my Mum, and maybe her Dad, too, with his wedding day warning.

The same with Carol. How did I get it so wrong? Looking back, she and I were so compatible. We were friends long before we were lovers. We had both been around the block but come out smiling. She had me weighed up, judged, categorised and sussed – yet she still held her arms out to me. I know at the time I was so mixed up and battered from the public break-up with Karen, that I handled it all so badly. Is that a reasonable excuse? I don't think so. It wasn't that I was not ready for another relationship because within a few weeks I had met someone I would marry and be together with for over twenty years, having two more lovely sons. I have pondered this over the years and have no answers.

Did I have in the back of my mind that I still wanted to do the family thing and have kids that I actually brought up? Not yet, I don't think. Did I sense that Carol with her lovely four kids had finished that road? Maybe, I don't know. I think, though, that maybe that is justifying myself way down the line, after the event. Maybe we were just not right enough for each other as much as I always thought so much of her. Maybe we were better friends than lovers. Or better lovers than partners. Maybe it was just never the right time, right place for both of us.

Bottom line? I just fucked up.

We stayed in touch, as I say. Carol would phone me from time to time, usually starting to speak as if in the middle of a conversation and it would take me a while to catch up. She always had a cause, a campaign. We would talk about our children, and then in time, grandchildren and as ever, she would make me smile and leave me feeling a better person.

About eight or so years ago Carol asked me to come along and speak to a group of women she was working with – she ran training courses based on personal development for women. I was flattered. I went along and it was lovely to see her. She looked much the same of course, ageless. I did my bit and we were then sat with the group of women in the bar at the Radisson Hotel in Birmingham City Centre having a coffee and it was time for me to go, to drive back to Surrey. I said my goodbyes to the group and Carol walked me from the bar to the revolving front doors of the hotel. She was making me laugh as usual about something. I turned to her to say goodbye. I was wearing a pale grey Ted Baker suit and with an open necked black Boss polo shirt beneath it. She put her hand on my arm and then straightened my suit jacket.
"Sharky," she said softly, with a smile. She looked back over at her group of women then pulled me close and kissed me briefly, fiercely on the lips.
"You don't change," she said, laughing.

It seems so churlish to complain and I am not. Things worked out so bloody well for me. That is not my point. I made some really bad decisions along the way which I don't understand. That is all I am saying.

I remember Carol saying to me once 'life is like a jam doughnut', she said in that lovely husky voice. "You can try and be neat and eat it and you still get covered in sugar. Or you can just dive in and go for the jam."

Then, about three years ago Carol phoned and she said:
"Listen, Sharky, I've got something to tell you. It's shit news, really, but I want you to hear it from me. I've got cancer. In my throat."
"Fucking hell," I murmured.
"Yes, you could say that and in fact, I did, but there you go. Going to fight it of course, not having that chemo crap, going natural. Doctors don't like it but I've started this campaign".

And she was off. The Doctors had given her about eight months to live.
"but then they know fuck all," she said, cheerily.

I said I would come and see her and a couple of days later we met in a café in Birmingham town centre. She looked terrific and I told her so.
"I know!" she said with the usual laugh," I'm on a vegan diet, no shit food at all, taking vitamins and all sorts. I've never been so fucking healthy!"

We sat and talked for two hours which flew by in seconds, talking about our kids and our grandchildren and everything else. And of course, about cancer and death and time. Then suddenly she realised she was late for her next meeting and we went outside. We hugged and said our goodbyes. As I walked away, I heard her say:
"Hey, Sharky.."
I turned round. She was stood on the street facing me. For the first time I saw a little hesitation in her eyes, a little glimmer of fear.
"No, it's OK," she smiled, the moment passing," I will... I will see you again."
I smiled too and we each went our separate ways.

But she never did. That was the last time we would see each other.

A few months later her family contacted me to say she had died. I drove up to Birmingham on a wet and rainy day for the funeral. I have never seen so many people at a crematorium. Carol had been one of the original punks back in the day and all the aging punks of the Birmingham scene were there with now grey Mohicans, lined faces and battered leather coats. And so were people from just about every group, age, class and background you can think of. As we all slowly filed in, I listened to people talking about her and it was clear she had touched the lives of every one of them, made them all feel special even if just for a little moment, as she had me.

From Lindy to Carol and beyond. It's been a hell of a ride, though. I have had the great fortune to meet some wonderful people along the way and I celebrate their gifts to me every day.

4. Downbound Train

So, let's go back a bit again first.
I'd lost the General Election battle in Rossendale in June 1983. Not surprising, really, Labour got hammered just about everywhere. I was losing my first marriage – again, also, in hindsight, not a great surprise as I have said. My wife was unhappy. I was unhappy.
By now we had three boys as Micky had been born in September 1984. This is where I begin to lose it big style. OK, I was unhappy and I had had a few affairs and I knew in my heart that my wife and I could not be happy. I stumbled to a decision that meant I left my wife. I rationalized it as I was not leaving the boys, of course, as we all do. I argued that I deserved some happiness, too. It wasn't good for them to be growing up in a household where their parents were obviously so unhappy with each other. Yeah, yeah.

I had an affair with a young woman who I worked with. The oldest cliché of screwing your secretary. Yep, I know. Oh, she was young, slim, affectionate and so on and so on. When it all came out just before Christmas that year, I was genuinely unsure what to do. I took myself off to London to Griz's for a week, trying to make some sense of the mess I was in. I don't know what Griz and his wife, Jayne made of it, though. They gave me shelter from the storm.

In the end, I made the wrong decision (again). I decided to leave my first wife and set up house with the new girl. At first, we lived nearby in Stacksteads in a crappy little back-to-back house we rented. Then in time we moved further to Ramsbottom and then Blackburn and eventually the Lakes. Oh, I kept in close contact with the boys, at some considerable emotional cost to us all, I guess, but that is not the point. I should have been closer.
Years later, when Nye and I were talking about this, he said how when he was growing up, he would have loved to have just been able to call round, maybe after school, and have a chat, just hang out, maybe share a problem or a triumph. But, no, it all had to be arranged access and hard work.

But let me be clear. To have stayed with my first wife would have been wrong, too – that would have been a further mistake. I could have tried to grit my teeth and bear it for the boys and that would have been noble and maybe honourable but I doubt I could have done it long term. No, what I should have done is to have moved out, but stayed nearby and lived alone – and not taken up with anyone else and started the same mistakes all over again so quickly and predictably. I should have given myself some breathing space. I should have built an independent life for me – and the boys. I should have stayed nearby for them.
You know, from the age of nineteen when I started living with the girl who became my first wife back in Sheffield, I have only spent a couple of months not living with one woman or another over all these years. I think that is a sign of some sort of weakness, to be honest. The spell I had recently of living on my own before I met Julie was instructive to be sure and well overdue.
So, this frying pan to the fire mistake was the start then of a downward spiral for me. I lost my way completely because, I understand now, I lost my moral compass, my sense of myself. Deep down what I was doing was not me, was not right by my own standards. I did not know in what way then and I did not understand this was what was happening but it was and it scrambled me.

It was the eighties; people were making money. Once again, I had very little. I thought maybe I should try this money lark. I swooped drunkenly (yet dryly sober) from one wrong turn job to another ending up selling insurance and commercial finance for Commercial Union. I was chasing the fluttering banknotes falling occasionally from the sky on the wet cold streets of Rossendale, Bolton, Blackburn and then up to the Lakes. I wore sharp suits, drove a foreign car that was long and sleek. I ran three branches of financial consultants and started specializing in the hotel businesses of the Lakes – mainly because no-one else was. I would cold call hotels on the phone basically asking if they wanted to re-mortgage their hotel

or expand it. I would go visit and set it up, working with the building societies and banks. I worked hard and pretty smart. I had business interests, too. A share in an awful Italian restaurant outside Burnley that no-one knew was there. I was a consultant to a computer company called Orbit owned by a City fan and good guy called Tony Booth. Tony sent me over to Holland to look at their business there. I would go one day a week to the offices in Manchester, checking through accounts and reports. I had no idea what I was doing really but I looked the part. When I asked Tony why he asked me to help him when there were all sorts of finance people coming through the doors of growing businesses then, selling money and services.
'You were the only one who gave me straight answers I could understand', he said. I was trading on myself.

We'd bought a huge old house in Blackburn somehow, called 'Garth'. Endless rambling rooms in need of investment we did not have. We had debts. I sold the house one Christmas Eve, having only owned it about nine months, and made enough money to get straight and do it all over again, as everyone in that situation does.

I had always written things. A couple of novels, a screenplay, a stage play and radio play. But I didn't do anything with them. I always had this hankering if I could not be a footballer then I would be a writer.

I was also quite a boxing fan. My Dad had boxed in the navy and I did a little at the Crown & Manor youth club in Hoxton growing up. I had this idea of writing a book about John Conteh, the former world champion light heavyweight. It would be a life story but he and I would go back and visit some of the key places in his life so it would also be about the present time. I even had a name for it – 'Between Today and Yesterday; The John Conteh Story' – after an Alan Price song I liked. John had won the world title which he held from 1974 to 1978, then become a real celebrity with his Liverpool charm (he was even on the cover of Paul McCartney's 'Band on the Run' album in 1973, and then hit the skids a bit with well-publicised alcoholism including one drink driving incident when he allegedly drove down a street in Mayfair in his Rolls Royce and hit every single parked car along the street. He was a couple of years older than me, a good all-round sportsman and had been sober a few years by then.

How could I contact him? This was pre-internet of course. I contacted the 'Boxing News' and through them was referred to an East End 'businessman' involved with the boxing world who knew John and could introduce us. I rang this guy and we arranged to meet in a drinking club in Whitechapel. I told this guy what I had in mind and I must have seemed kosher because he went out and made a phone call and ten minutes later John Conteh walked in.

I got on well with John. He was funny, bright and very sociable. I outlined my plans and he was keen. We agreed we would split any income 50/50. He had a new agent and would need to speak to him. Over the next few weeks, we had a few telephone conversations and then he said his new agent was not up for it. The agent was trying to help promote John's new acting career and felt that 'dragging up the past' would harm his prospects. I felt that given John's past was so well known, putting him back in the public eye would be a positive but I understood he had to go with his agent's advice so the idea was shelved.

I still think it would have been a good book. Maybe someday I will write it.

Meanwhile I had the financial consultancy business to attend to. I hated the work – I just could not get excited about the ins and outs of money - but it was bringing money in to me and my family. I persevered though it was at great cost to my mental wellbeing and eventually my physical health too.

Most of my clients were in the Lakes. Another company – Milldon International – poached me to come and run three branches of financial consultants for them. Time to move to the Lakes then, rent a house up there, be in amongst it, nothing to keep us here, finally get a dog maybe, be good for the boys to come up there.

I found an old farmhouse called Soulby Fell Farm, near Dacre, up above the hills at the north end of Ullswater, my favourite lake. It was cheap and available, owned by some landed family with a stately home nearby. The rough drive down from the farm was about a mile long before you hit the narrow lane that led you to Dacre then on to Penrith. Way up and out there.

I made some shit decisions in these years, lost all direction, all purpose and identity. But Soulby Fell itself was a joy every day I stepped out of the old white farmhouse and looked around the hills and sucked in the fresh strong air. It was a way station along the road to hell but what a fine place to be coming apart in.

I loved the Lakes and looking back I am glad I got to spend a little time there - even at an awful period in my life.

One morning, turning out of the gate on the lane at the farm, I turned to go down to Ullswater and there on the road in front of me on this spring morning were two beautiful hares, dancing and playing in the weak morning sunshine.

I criss-crossed the Lakes going to hotels, arranging finance. The work was mind-numbing and so far from who I ever thought I was. I just have no comprehension what I thought I was doing. Anyway, the setting for this steady fall into desolation, illness and loss was at least beautiful.

But I did get the dog. One of my best ever decisions. I went up to Carlisle and bought the last of a litter. A brawny, square headed yellow lab. He was Charley. He was a total nightmare, eating anything he could reach, chasing off over the fells after sheep or deer, real hard work. He became my best friend. We loved each other unreservedly and unconditionally from the off. He was so attentive to me.

We would walk off across the fells together and he never strayed far from me then, always half an eye on where I was, just wanting to be together. He was great with the kids who when toddlers would climb over him, pulling his whiskers, sticking fingers into his mouth or eyes and he would put up with it all, ever affectionate and protective towards them, though not adverse at all from nicking a biscuit off them.

To this day nearly all my passwords for any account are or have been 'charley'. He was with me every step of the way through the next fourteen years of hell, recovery and return. He is with me still though he died some years ago.

Two out of three weekends I would have the boys. I would drive down to Bacup on Friday afternoons, pick them up in my old battered Range Rover or the speedy Saab. We would roar up the M6 full of spirit. I loved having them around and they loved Soulby Fell as I did. We would go wandering in the woods, playing in the barns, cricket in the farmyard, football everywhere, Cumberland sausages from the butchers in Penrith, fires in the front room grate, snow on the hills, Charley bouncing along with us of course, the kitchen warm from the temperamental oil-fired range. But Sundays were awful for me, their departure looming closer by the second. Eventually I could put it off no more and would pack them into the car and drive back south with such a heavy heart. Paying the price on every one of those Sundays and the awful drive back up the M6 alone, returning to Soulby Fell.

One weekend the boys had gone off down the track with Charley. My eldest son, Pat, then about nine or so, came puffing back panicking, tears on his face.
'Dad! Dad! We've lost Charley' he sobbed. They'd been in the woods and he'd seen a deer and that was it, he was off. I grabbed a

jacket, pulled on my boots and me and Pat ran back down the track to find Nye and Micky, similarly distraught. We searched the woods, calling his name. How awful that must have been for the boys. How tough deciding 'we'd better go and tell Dad'. Then a long run up the track to the farmhouse for Pat, the eldest. We hurriedly made our way along the track to the forest. Anyway, suddenly there he was again, wagging his tail, big brown eyes, happy as a lark, coming back to us, what's up guys? Panic over.

So it was by no means all bad. We discovered the Sharrow Bay Hotel, just across the lake from us, the first of the classic country house hotels. Wonderful food, great setting.

My second wife and I had two children now – Danny and Rachel. Danny had health problems from the off, struggling with one chest infection after another. There was only about seventeen months between them – similar to Pat and Nye (and later on, down the track, Keir and Oscar). When my wife told me she was pregnant with Rachel, I sighed, it was too soon for another baby, too quick. She took that sigh and blew it into a storm. She got the notion I didn't want Rachel and in the post-natal depression that hit her after Rachel was born, kept returning to that over and over. I had not wanted another child so quickly but every child is a blessing and Rachel certainly was and still is. Besides, I had a daughter! A whole new ball game.

But something was gone, something slipping away from then on. My wife got deeper into her depression and further from me and it seemed there was nothing I could do about it. I tried though.

Three of the four women I have lived with for any serious length of time have ended up seriously depressed. Even I can see the connecting point! Each have had two children within seventeen months or so, too, so there are other factors to consider. I understand medical research points to a propensity towards depression as a key not just the triggering factors and for different reasons I can see that in each of them.

And I was on the road, working, working, smiling, charming, sign these papers, recruit more bodies, on the phone, sell, sell, working, digging deeper holes, running myself ragged, five kids now, up and down the M6, long hours, fighting in the courts whenever my ex-wife stopped the access which was often, the alarm goes in the dark, get up, auto-pilot, get showered, cold, coffee, suit, car keys and away again, working till dark, tired, back, kids in bed, wife grumpy, tired, tired, go to bed, got to sleep, early start tomorrow. I was in my mid-thirties and killing myself.

I know a lot of people get in the same boat and are maybe there now. I know, too, that when you are out of work with a family to feed that's another kind of stress – been there, too, as we shall see. It's the hard side of life.

If you have love, though, someone with you, someone just to hold your hand now and then, someone whispering in your ear that it will be OK, then a lot more is possible. A look across a room, a sudden smile, something nice said about you when in company with others, a compliment, arms round you at night, someone holding you close, making you feel wanted – hell, then I can take on the world, and have done. I have held someone in my arms and literally felt the tension and pain draining out of my chest into their embrace. Maybe it's just me, I can't say.

I have fought my way every step, lived on my wits and hard work, been down blind alleys and dead-ends, stood in a green field on my own and cried, sat on a balcony in the soft night of Dubai, looking out over the sea, and felt the certainty of coming sadness, I have been fooled, lost, found, read my wife's infidelity off a page, burnt bridges chasing an illusory woman, reached out and touched when I should have turned and walked away, been battered, bruised, hospitalized, seen my personal life spread cross a newspaper with grainy photos, seen an old grizzled stranger looking vaguely like my father appear in my mirror some mornings, and yet still, even yet, bizarrely, crazily, a look across a crowded tube, a glimpse of a promise, a possibility of love and fire, a touch of a hand on my arm, that too long held gaze, could make me catch my breath.

OK, it was not happening so much those days, and only in its passing did I look back and notice its former presence and regular occurrence.

Like all of us I have been made of the whole sum of experiences, from beginning to now, for good and bad, every little thing counts and affects, moulds and chips, refashions and styles. The lost years count, too. Every day is worth the same. Some you notice more than others. Some you remember clearer. But they all count, they all have created you as you stand in the only moment that exists. Now.

But this was then and I blundered on. My main office was in Kendal, a really nice town. Through my business I met a guy called Peter Cavendish, a bit younger than me, early thirties maybe, this was 1989, I think, so I was thirty-five. Peter had a printing company called Pandect ('P and etc.'?) He had worked in advertising, in Paris on major Renault accounts for an agency there, now looking to get his own business going, designing advertising for local businesses. I helped him and his girlfriend, a doe-eyed, pretty girl, get a mortgage on a flat in town from the Yorkshire Building Society whose manager I knew and did a lot of business with. Peter was a good talker, a chancer with ideas and talent, he knew his stuff on advertising and Pandect was growing.

In amongst the blur of my life, with the three branches, the businesses, Orbit the computer company in Manchester, the crap restaurant in Burnley, somehow Peter and I got to sit down and talk about his business. He needed bank finance to expand, the work was there, he needed my help and contacts. I became a Director

with him, a partner, and set up the credit facilities at the Nat West and all was well and we were on the happy road to being rich, nice cars, big houses, champagne, smarter suits, bright ties and all that shit.
Time rolls on, Kendal high street, there's the tall slim redhead who sold me my first mobile phone. I'm walking along with one of my financial consultants and the redhead comes out of the florist with an armful of flowers.
"Not buying yourself flowers now, Jenny?"
"Yes, I've given up on you buying me any."
Laughing and onwards, smart suits, still the patter, out on the road, round the hotels, setting up business mortgages, advising, dealing, home exhausted up that long track to the farmhouse, Susie working with me in the office, Danny and Rachel in the nursery, picking the kids up, paying the bills, down to Manchester for Orbit, la-la land, talking at regional meetings, work, sleep, work. And no joy.

Peter tells me the work is getting him down, it's tough to really make money, the work is there, about a dozen people working in the company now, it's a slog and that ain't what we had in mind. I don't have the time to do more, time for me to step back. We agree that I will step away as a Director, I even sign the forms, but he needs to get the overdraft finished off first as I am a co-signer and the bank won't let him go on his own.
He talks about flying the coop, running out, leaving it all. I don't think he's serious but say 'well, sort the overdraft out first, and get me out of it'. He agrees, assures me he would never leave me in the lurch, has plans to settle up, no problem, Chris, don't worry.

Just before Christmas, must have been Christmas 1990, I get really ill. It starts as a cold, then it's flu and then I am really laid low, aching head, tired, can't breathe. I go to see the Doctor. Flu bug, run down, take some time off, take it easy.
Back up at the farm, lying on the sofa, feeling like I am at death's door but my wife is not impressed or helpful. Peter drives up, brings some more medical supplies, cold and flu tablets.

"Jesus, you look like shit, man," he whispers to me. Weirdly, my left eye is beginning to swell up and close. "You gotta get that Doctor out," Peter says. My wife stays silent.
We get the Doctor out. He looks at me and frowns.
"I have never seen someone get so bad so quickly," he says. He phones the hospital, Carlisle General. Go straight away. Do I need an ambulance? No, my wife can drive me, I say.
My wife drops me off outside the hospital and drives off – we did have two children to factor in - , I walk in, unable to see out of my now closed, swollen left eye, full of flu and cold.
I don't remember too much about the next couple of days. Isolation ward, a drip, a nurse in white taking my temperature, and covering me up with a sheet, Doctor looking at my eye, sleep, medication, sleep.
It seems my flu turned into infected sinuses and then an infected eye socket, hence the displacement of the eye and so on. But there is something else worrying them – my liver function scores are rock bottom, barely alive.
Comes time for me to leave, a lot better, though still seeing double. Consultant wants to see me first. My wife waits in corridor, impatient to drive me home.
"You need to stop your drinking," he says firmly. What?
"I don't drink," I said, "well, not much."
He clearly does not believe me, has heard it all before. I have to get my wife in from the corridor to convince him. He sits and thinks.
"Well, then, you have clearly had significant liver damage. We need to do some more tests."
They do, they find I have had viral hepatitis. I never found out which sort. The Doctor says: "This will take a long time to get over. You need to rest and take care of yourself." He smiles at my wife, "or get someone else to."

Back home, my wife barely speaks to me. I can barely move. A few days later, when watching football on TV, my eye settles back into place and the double vision goes. I am weak as a kitten but I need to get back out there. Soon as I shift position, Charley sits up and looks at me. He stays close. But I know the score here. No sick pay scheme for me, I need to keep the wheel turning.

I get up next morning, shower, get the suit on and drive out into the beautiful Soulby Fell winter landscape, down that track, and I am back on the road. Ain't no-one going to do this for me, I am on my own.

My wife and I are obviously on the rocks. I can't believe I went through the illness with barely a kind word from her. I cannot connect with her. We are far, far apart. She is locked deep into some sort of distant place that I cannot reach. I urge her to get help but she won't. I am the problem, not her. Looking back, I am not sure what I could have done different, to be really honest.

I arrange for us to have a night away at a hotel, like we often used to do. Her Dad comes up to babysit. It was her Dad, in fact, who lent us the £2k to invest in the restaurant, so I tell him that is struggling. Away at the lovely country hotel, wooden paneled rooms, thick carpets. We go down to the restaurant to eat. She is refusing to speak to me. We order. After a while, she just gets up and leaves the table, goes up to the room. The waitress looks confused. Her and me both. I apologise. On the way out of the dining room, back to the bedroom I pass the telephone booths in the lobby. I make a decision. I am getting out. I make some calls.

I took my wife back home and told her I had had enough, I was going away for a couple of days and we would take things from there. I go and stay with a friend. The sort of friend who holds me in her arms and tells me "you can always stay here." That sort of friend.
I get a flat at Grange-over-Sands. I rarely stay there. Before long I am with Karen, who I used to know from my trade union days, a feisty curvy blonde from Wigan with a big laugh and warm arms. Another shelter from the storm. Another chapter. Another life.

Karen has her own house in Whittle-le-Woods just outside Chorley, half way through being redecorated and rebuilt. She has three dogs – which is a bit of a problem because before long I have my Charley with me, of course, but we sort it out. Love me, love my dog.

Although I have someone looking after me now – and Karen does that very well – there were two big challenges just round the corner, but for now it was hard enough to keep my businesses going, start the whole awful divorce process, fighting again for access, and just get up every day and roll on.

My solicitor is Mark Gosnell, an old football mate, now a judge in Bolton, bizarrely, I believe. Mark had dealt with my first divorce and though this was not his area of speciality he sorted me through this one.
He phoned me one day.
"You do have a problem now, mate."
"Go on, make my day."
"Well, you now have first wife getting together with second wife – yes, I know, former sworn enemies – and sharing notes. You have the Unholy Alliance against you, mate."
Unholy Alliance indeed. For some reason, which still escapes me, some sort of weird solidarity perhaps, first wife, on hearing I was split up from the second wife, immediately stopped me from having access to the boys. Needless to say, second wife was preventing me from seeing Danny and Rachel. They apparently got together and, as Mark said, starting comparing notes and plotting.

I just sigh. I have fought so much to see the boys – fighting through the courts to get access, then back to the courts when first wife ignored the court orders and so on. This actually went on until the boys were old enough to sort it themselves really. One Christmas when I had yet again been denied access despite a court order, first wife phoned me up and said "You might as well come and pick them up, they are refusing to do anything." I knew we had turned a corner. I tried to play it cool as I picked them up but their big smiles made it hard. Once in the car we all laughed and cheered. We had made it.

Anyway, back then, I just knew I had yet another fight on my hands, and now for Danny and Rachel, too. But more of that later.

For now, I had all that to contend with but the two big challenges were coming. Firstly, I was finding it physically hard to keep going. This was a couple of months after my initial illness and spell in Carlisle Hospital by now, maybe March 1991, but I was struggling. My mate, Tony Carter, who used to work for me running the Lancaster office, said that I would just close the office door each afternoon about three and sit at my desk and put my head on my arms and sleep for an hour. They would leave me alone. Then I would get up and go again. It could not continue. There was something wrong.
I was just so bone tired.

However, the other bomb then hit first while the illness was still ticking. I was in the Kendal office early one morning and a guy who ran the print shop for Peter at Pandect phoned me.
"Hi – do you know where Peter is?"
"No, mate, no idea. You tried the flat?"
"Yeah, no answer. Thing is we're all here at work and the place is all locked up."
That was the beginning of the nightmare.
Peter had done a runner. The awful picture emerged slowly. He had run up the overdraft and credit facilities to the maximum and disappeared. Even his girlfriend didn't know where he was. She was left with the flat and that mortgage. Pandect collapsed. We were all chasing the now elusive Peter Cavendish.
I worked with the bank. Credit card receipts showed him in Italy and then in Paris in France. Maybe he'd gone back to the agency he used to work for there? I knew their name and found the address. I went over. No, they had not heard from Peter in years. I believed them, they seemed genuine enough, I had no way of knowing.

People would phone me chasing his debts, or Pandect's debts. I would explain what I had lost more than anyone. We kept looking but no trace.

I went in for another meeting with the bank. The branch manager we had dealt with looked ashen, the regional manager was there, too. They were owed about forty grand, as I recall, which was a lot of money in 1991, and still is, come to that. They wanted me to pay. I couldn't. I had no assets – Soulby Fell was rented, anyway. Besides, I wouldn't. Why should I pay for someone else's criminal act? I had been ripped off and so had the bank.

I had a great accountant, Nick and a great solicitor, Greg. Two real good guys. We got together. We were at an impasse.
"There is one way out," said Greg and looked at Nick. Nick nodded.
"You can declare yourself bankrupt," said Greg. "Because you are basically. You have liabilities. Not just the bank but the inland revenue. Some other smaller debts. But it's the bank that's the big one. What's more, you are not going to be able to pay this off because you are ill. You can't do it."

For the first time someone else was laying it out before me. They could all see it clearly. It was obvious to them if not to me. Nick and Greg both agreed.

In September 1991 I walked into the court at Preston and signed the forms to declare myself bankrupt. I went back to Karen's and went to bed. Other than to meet with the official receiver a couple of times – once he had got the lay of the land and knew I was bankrupt because of someone else's criminal act and did not have money stashed away anywhere, he was fine and helpful, and finally told me I would get an automatic discharge in time - I stayed in bed for three months.

Three months. I would sleep eighteen hours a day. I had no energy and no strength.

The GP surgery was just over the road. I would drag myself over there every couple of weeks. He was great. He pinpointed it early on. I had M.E. – myalgic encephalomyeltis – probably brought on by the hepatitis. Good news, it wouldn't kill me and would get better. Bad news, he couldn't say when. This was before M.E. was widely recognized. It was great that here was a clued-up GP and there was a definite cause identified. I had something to work on.

I had to let everything go. I had no choice, I had nothing. No house, no car, no money, no job. I just had a few clothes – very few – and, of course, a dog. Karen took me under her wing and looked after me. Even amidst all the shit, I knew I was still lucky. I kept in touch with the boys best I could. Keeping in touch with Danny and Rachel was harder.

Karen had a great big Wigan family who, though startled at first, who wouldn't be – I mean, with five kids and two divorces, and a bankruptcy, I was hardly every mother's dream – they took me to heart. Karen's brother-in-law was David Lowe, a great character who made his money from dealing high value cars in the trade, and worked himself up from nothing to being a millionaire and was a top guy and became a good friend. 'Lowey' was renowned for being tight with his money and had his image to think of. Nevertheless, when the time was right, he said, 'listen, you ever need a car to go and see your lads, just let me know' and later, when we got to be mates, 'you need anything, money, anything, you let me know.' It was great to have such support but I wasn't going to start borrowing off mates.

I had to find something to do, to try and occupy myself for the few hours I was awake each day. I started writing. A bad novel, I am sure, but I was doing something. Karen had an old nylon-stringed cheapo acoustic guitar lying round. I got a book from Chorley Library and started plunking away, fortunately when the house was empty. Over the months I finished the novel and learnt to play the guitar reasonably well. I got stronger. Not a straight line of progress but fits and starts. I meditated when I could, most days – but again, more of that later.

I needed to get out into the world as much as I could, anyway. First, I decided I would try a bit of taxi-driving in Chorley. I just sat down and read the A-Z over and over and went out on my bike and then got a job driving day-times. It was a crap job but it was a job. I experimented with what was the best music to be playing to get maximum tips. I tried all sorts – country, rock, pop and so on. There was a hand-down winner – opera. Pavarotti won easily. Old biddies would ask for the 'driver who plays opera' when they booked their taxis down to the shops.

Karen's parents had an antiques business. I started doing a bit to help out. I put a few bob together and bought a really knackered old diesel van which farted acrid blue smoke wherever we went. I started doing the antique markets – Preston, Halifax and so on – buying and selling, starting with selling gear for Karen's parents and then my own, particularly old musical instruments. I enjoyed it and read up on it. Other market stall-holders would bring me pieces to have a look at and give a verdict on. But I never had the capital to do it properly and I knew it was a stop gap.

I got stronger. I saw the boys as much as I could. Karen and I went on a week holiday with her family to Lanzarote and I began to feel like I had something of a life back again. We all went to see Eric Clapton a few times at the Albert Hall, drinking champagne in a box, paid for by Lowey. My hair had got long enough one time for a pony-tail but I cut it off after a while.

I was coming up for air. It was time to make a new start, make a new life.

I guess it tells the story again of my upbringing that coming through all this my response was – OK, what next? I never stopped believing that I could re-invent myself. I was down the trusty Library – this was before the internet, of course – looking at what I should do. Should I retrain to become a psychologist? Or lawyer even? I did not really fancy going back to University for another degree even if I could afford it – which I couldn't. What did I really want to do? If I could do anything, what would I want to be?

One day at Karen's I was watching football on TV. No surprise there, then. Kenny Dalglish was managing Blackburn Rovers at that time. He stood on the side-lines in a long brown overcoat urging his team on. I sat up and stared.
"That's it," I said aloud. "I'm going to be a football manager."

And I was.

5. Roulette

Sierra Leone is the second poorest country in the world. Some years ago, I was driving through the back country going towards Makeni, where not long before the civil war had raged bitterly. The rough road took us through little collections of huts, hardly even villages and across rivers on fragile bridges. One reason for Sierra Leone's poverty is that there is very little regular electricity. After dusk commerce even in Freetown would be restricted by the light shed by little generators or paraffin lanterns, or even candles. Out in the bush there was even less.

We drove through one small hamlet, another collection of dusty, fragile huts with corrugated iron roofs if they were lucky, mostly mud and branches. As was often the case there was one hut, not dissimilar to the others, maybe a bit bigger, that was the local store, tavern, gathering place, whatever and sometimes they had a generator and maybe a satellite tv dish. As we drove by in a dusty blur, I saw a blackboard outside the place. It had an announcement in chalk – 'Today: Live at 4 – Premier League: Blackburn vs Bolton.'

They say there are upwards of six billion people in the world. When we have a big Premier League game – Chelsea vs United, say – then one billion of those will watch it. Is it any wonder then that in post-war Britain, on the streets of North London, in the working –class culture of the day that football was king? I have seen it being played in ragged games of joy in the inland of Ghana, the stony desert of Egypt, the wastelands of the townships outside Johannesburg, the mountains of Nepal and the beaches of Rio. My starting place for playing was King Square off Central Street in Islington. That patch of tarmac in between the blocks of flats was my Wembley, my Stamford Bridge. Every night if the weather allowed, nearly every day, I was there.

But I was already hooked by then, already a football man. You have to go back even further. I went to my first game at age four. My Dad was an Arsenal fan and their Highbury was probably the nearest ground. At my first game Dad's Arsenal in the usual red were playing a team in blue. It shows what a contrary little sod I must have been at that age because I said I would support the other team. Who are they? They're called Chelsea.

And that was that.

We went to see them that season, too, at the old run-down expanse of Stamford Bridge with the dog track round the outside of it between you and the pitch. I loved it all. I was actually more of a Jimmy Greaves fan than even a Chelsea fan. Later when he left for AC Milan, I was heartbroken but stayed loyal to the Blues. The idea that I would ever actually meet players was bizarre. No-one thought that back then. We didn't wear replica shirts either. We had woolly scarves and bob-hats and wooden rattles – we really did! The smell of Bovril at half-time, the large crowds – invariably male and invariably white.

I did however meet Jimmy Greaves some years later when I was about ten. My Dad was playing in a charity game and Jimmy was on the other side – playing in goal with Ron Springett's yellow England jersey on! I don't remember anything about the game but I remember sitting outside the (inevitable) pub and Jimmy coming out and signing an autograph for me which I was ecstatic about.

But again, this was all just part of the process. The love of the game was in my blood because it was in the air. I just breathed it in. My Mum was from Tottenham so her family were Spurs fans. Everyone had their team. It was the religion of the working class. The beautiful game. Such a simple game, something for a ball and you go from there. You can play on your own or twenty a side. Any surface vaguely flat will do, anything for goal posts and you got a game. That's why you see it all over the world.

But back then I didn't need to know any of this background. Family story has it that I got a football for my first Christmas present and kicked it through my Grandad's paper as he sat reading it before I could walk. Who knows? It doesn't matter. Like so many other kids, football was in my soul, in my blood, to stay.

My Dad would take me to Hackney Marshes and I was in heaven – football as far as the eye could see, football games everywhere, a sea of players and colour and football posts. What more could a boy want?

I have said before that when I weigh up what things I have done right and what I have done wrong over my life, there are some activities that always come out well. I don't regret a single second of ever playing with my children or caring for them, or even of travelling if I am honest, or meditating or certainly of reading books or playing my guitar – these are the things hand on heart that are what make my world go round. But above all, I can never regret a single moment playing, watching or living football. Or even talking about it, come to that, or reading about it.

Maybe that's a poor limited life. I don't know. It's how it is. It is how it has been.

When I was primary school age, I would go to school early so I could play football in the playground, such as it was at Moreland Street Primary School back then. I would play every second I could in break and dinner times come rain or shine. I would stay behind after school if anyone else would stay with me to play. After my tea I would go out to King Square and the tarmac pitch and play there till it was time for me to go home to bed. In the dark London winter, I would play those endless football games between my toy soldiers, writing out the programmes and match reports. I read about 'Roy of the Rovers' in my comics, watched whatever football there was on TV – very little then - had a battered dog-eared chart showing every team in the four divisions which I moved after every Saturday to show their league positions till the little cardboard team names got torn and repaired, torn and repaired again and again. I would play for my school team and my Dad and I would go and see a game somewhere in London each weekend. We visited all the London league grounds by the time I was eleven. Every year we would go and see the Amateur Cup Final and the England Schoolboys games at Wembley.

Sometimes I got to watch my Dad play, he was strong and stocky and equally home as a two-footed fast running centre forward or a brave and agile goal keeper. He could head the ball harder than I could kick it. Like so many of his generation the war interrupted what may have been a great career. When I was a kid, he was getting paid to play in 'amateur' football or starring in works football like the great BRS road transport national cup competition. He was an instinctive footballer himself so no great coach.

My first proper game was for Moreland Street Primary School on the shale pitch at Coram's Fields. I was eight years old so this would be 1962 and the team was the one school team so had lads of eleven years old in it. The fearsome Mr. Hodgkinson organised the school football. He threw me a tatty black and red quartered school shirt with a number eight on the back.
'Robinson – inside right'.
And that was that.

We played eleven-a-side on big pitches with big goals because that is all there was. I have no idea what I was like. I know I was keen, that's for sure.

I can still remember the names of the kids I played with at Moreland Street. My mate Philip Oxlade – who I remember one teacher saying to another looked less like a footballer than me but was a better player, (thanks, mate) – Steven Thompson, Andy Wilson, Kim Maynard, Dennis Shirley, Joey Hume, Danny Rix, Robert

Holton and Richard Weaver and so on. I can tell you their positions and what they were like as players.

My wife once said to me 'how come you can remember the name of any football player you ever saw even if you just saw him for ten minutes in a park game yet you can't remember what I asked you to pick up from the shops this morning?'

Ah, yes, that old chestnut.

We won things at school. We won the local cup and so on, I can remember going to Finsbury Town Hall and getting presented with a little gold medal that I kept for years.

I didn't play a competitive game on grass until I went to secondary school. Up to then it was all street football, tarmac, school playground and the shale pitch at Coram's Field. Oh, we went to Highbury Fields or Parliament Hill Fields occasionally for a kick about but not a proper game.

In my first week at Owens, we took the trip out to the school playing fields in Chandos Avenue in Totteridge. It was to become a second home to me – the school playing fields just down from the Old Boys playing fields where they had the club discos that would become a major scene for me in teenage lovelorn days as I have said. But the school playing fields with the old wooden pavilion were new to me that week in September 1965.

Some mornings going out to work I get a smell of wet grass and I am back there that day – as simple as that. I can remember the smell and feel of the grass, my black woolly socks and new boots. All the kids were divided up into several smaller trial games. The teacher taking mine was Mr. Paul, the music teacher. Don't know how much of a judge he was but I found myself straight into the school team and I was flying.

I have to get this picture right. Clearly, I was a decent player, I played representative football later on. Clearly, I love the game, too. I came to understand it well in time. But here's the thing – I was never as good a player as I thought I should be. Amazingly I suffered most of all from lack of confidence. I could play and occasionally showed it very well. But I think I often watched games go by. I have often said that the player I was at 12 needed the coach I was at 50 and then I could have done a lot better. I would have encouraged and guided. I did not have any coaching really until I went to Sheffield. But then neither did anyone else really back then.

I got dropped from the school team once when I was 13 and ran all the way down City Road to where my Mum worked at Jaeger down by Old Street. When she came out of work I burst into tears. I got back in the team but my confidence was shot. Later – and we had a really strong 1st XI – I played probably half in the firsts and half in the seconds. The history teacher, Geoff Clark was a really good footballer and cricketer. I can remember him saying to me when I was 17 or so, having watched me play in the seconds – "you run the game for about fifteen minutes then you stop". I thought it was a fitness thing so did do extra training – on my own in the gym at dinner times, striking a ball against one wall, controlling it, running down the other end and doing the same. But now looking back it was a confidence thing.

We had moved out of London to a council estate in South Ockendon, Essex when I was just coming up for my 'O Levels,' though I kept traveling in and out every day – commuting to school. At 16 I decided to play some more football locally and went and had a trial for my local club Aveley FC, then managed by a guy called Terry Matthews. I went and trained with them and he said I was a good player and recommended me to their Under-18 youth team which ran under the name Aveley Youth Club. I played for them, got into district trials for Thurrock and did well.

The first trial game for Thurrock, in front of West Ham and Spurs scouts, was probably the best game I ever played as a boy. I was in midfield and I just fizzed around, putting everything to rights. After

about ten minutes one of the guys with clipboards asked me my name as I waited for a throw-in. I told him and wondered why he wanted to know. At half-time my dad, usually quite dour, was almost hopping from foot to foot.
"You're doing really well; they've already got your name." I almost fell over with shock. My Dad never said I did well! What was going on?

I went out for the second half on a high and more than anything else that makes my point. I was given confidence and like most players it brought the best out of me. I ran the game. I scored from about thirty yards, the ball sailing over the keeper off the underside of the bar. Everyone cheered, I just smiled and shrugged like it happened every game.

At the end of the game the officials were very excited because I was a year younger than anyone else so it would mean I could have two years with the Under 18 team.

If that first game for Thurrock Under-18s was my best ever, the next was probably my worst. I injured my knee somehow in the warm-up (and bizarrely, I remember ripping my shorts on a nail as I was helping put the nets up – keen to the last) and foolishly decided to play on. I was limping, and therefore struggled and therefore lost that confidence again. I was poor and was dropped and that was the end of that. They forgot the first game quick enough and there should have been a bitter lesson in that.

I went up to Sheffield University which was a hot-bed of football and absolutely loved it. They had four or five teams plus a 'Freshers' team just for first years playing every Wednesday and Saturday and two training sessions a week. But first I had to get in the team. I went to the trials. There were lots of midfielders so I played up front. There was a lad from Durham on my side called David Armstrong. At the end of the game, I wasn't picked. He came up to me and said he couldn't understand it as I was obviously a good player. It was nice of him. He got in. We had history classes together and became mates. The next week he played for the Freshers and they got beat. He told me it was crazy, that I was way better than the lad who did play up front.

That week there was a 'sign up' game on the notice board. These were random friendlies arranged on Thursday afternoons and it was first come first served. You could sign your name up on the list on the football Club notice board in the Student Union and you were in. Davie and I played. It was against a local hotel side, a team of Italian waiters and kitchen hands. We won 8-0 and I scored six. I was in the Freshers team the next week. By the Xmas I was in the first team and had scored 25 goals already.

Again, I did well but not as well as I felt I should have. I scored goals for fun and that meant I kept getting picked as a striker. However, I was neither six foot plus or super quick and at some stage when you get to a certain level, as a striker, you need to be one or the other – or you did then. I should have played in midfield and knew that but there were so many midfield players. I taught myself to be a back to goal striker, good in the air, good touch, receiving the ball to feet, shielding it, playing others in, holding defenders off – what you might call a Teddy Sheringham type later down the road. I got that act off to a tee and scored goals. But in doing so I think I limited how far I would go in the game as a player. Who knows?

Whatever else, I loved playing football at Sheffield. For the University we travelled all over the North West – Newcastle, York, Durham, Lancaster, Liverpool (where I made my first team debut), Manchester. Many great games, trips and nights out. The social side of the whole thing was just wonderful. I had doubted if I would find lads like me at University – I was in that first working-class wave remember. But I did.

They say football in the UK is mired in a drinking culture and that was certainly true back then. We were students, after all! We had many awful drinking-based games and conventions.

On the way back we would sing. All sorts of songs, everyone took part. It was another world for me and wonderful. One time we all went on a night out to a strip club in Chorlton in Manchester. The strippers were awful and we were soon shouting 'Put your clothes back on!" But they had a German Oompah band and soon we were all up on the tables singing.

For some reason the Drifters' 'Saturday Night at the Movies' was our theme song and we would sing it loudly and enthusiastically given any opportunity.

The whole setting of the football was a joy to me. After training we would go to the Broomhill Tavern in Crookes where a lot of the student halls of residence were. The 'Tav' was the centre of our world. You could go in there any night and there were people you knew. I had never really had that before at all, that sense of community and it was not lost on me that it came through football.

We had some good players, too. In my first year we had the immaculate Roy Linden at the back – our Laurent Blanc – and Tony Windsor in midfield who ran the club. Tony was a great guy who had stayed on at Sheffield to do a Ph D in metallurgy and so managed to have six years of university football. In my year were Bobby Hopley from Devon who had played at Plymouth Argyle, an athletic all-round midfielder and Pete Williams from the Gower who had played for Swansea City reserves when he was at school – and was a centre-forward! My mate Stevie Johnson from Manchester was a deadly finisher who had the unhealthiest diet of anyone I ever knew and was as skinny as a rake – but he could score for fun. Stevie was a die-hard United fan from Collyhurst, with a very strong Manc accent. He was football through and through, too. Oh, yeah, he got a first in Maths and went on to design guided missiles or something ("it's all the stuff you protest about," he said later.)

My mate Davie Armstrong who I met at the trials was from Tow Law in County Durham. Dave was a midfielder but like me he had to change position and ended up a really cultured left back. I went up to Durham with David and met his lovely family and learnt about the working-class life in the north east, too.

Great times with great people, all with football as the common connector. I went back to Sheffield a few years ago when I had some work to do up there. I re-visited the Tav. It had inevitably been redesigned and opened up instead of the collection of small rooms I remembered.

I also played for Hallam in the Yorkshire Amateur League, at one time, traveling all over Yorkshire with them to places like Oughtibridge and Frickley, a teenager with my long hair and cockney accent, getting kicked all over by hairy-arsed Yorkshire centre halves but I loved it. We went to Barcelona with the University team in my first year for an international tournament which we won thanks mostly to a lad called John Ridley, who I roomed with. John was in his last year at university and went on to sign for Port Vale, his home town club and later sign for Leicester City for good money and play for Chesterfield for years. Two or three of the team at Sheffield I was in turned pro – the standard was that good – but I didn't make it.

I went back to Sheffield a few times to play in the game they had against the Old Boys and always enjoyed that. We would have a meal and end up in a night club. One year John Ridley and I were in a club. He was playing regularly for Leicester City then. I asked him what it was like being a pro. He frowned and thought about it.
"It's really hard," he said, "I mean it's good, but the pressure...but when you win, fucking hell, that's great."
A few years later I would know what he meant, but not then.

So back in the summer of 1975 and I had got married and we moved to Preston and I am on that Management Training course with the National Freight Corporation, learning to be a transport manager, time as a trainee up at Heysham interspersed with courses away at Aldermaston. I was 21 years old. How many mistakes can I put into one sentence? I was too young to get married, I was ill-suited to being a transport manager, bored witless by it in fact, the time at Heysham was tedious and pointless and I learnt little on the courses. At least there was a good bunch of people on the courses, young graduates mostly like me, working with the various companies in the NFC group. We had some adventures – I recall taking a dare to break the thick ice on the lake in the grounds of the old house at Aldermaston which was the training centre and diving in, all for a bottle of vodka – and we formed a football team to take part in the very same company football cup that my Dad had played in years before. Truth is, I didn't know what I wanted to do and going into transport management seemed as good as anything else. I had some notion I had been a student long enough and I should get a paid job. I started in the September and by the Christmas was applying for Masters courses at university which eventually led to me going to the LSE.

Meanwhile, though, crazily piling up the mistakes, I was traveling too much for work to play football at anything like a reasonable level. I played for a local Preston team called Ribbleton Avenue Old Boys in a local parks league when I was around. Awful pitches, awful football. I tried to do a bit when I played and got kicked all over as ever, too dumb to lie down.

I got one of my worst ever injuries playing then. I went up for a ball on the edge of the area, chesting it around a big knobhead of a Centre half and into the area. He thought little of it, though, as he launched himself at me and his big bony knee landed with his full weight in the small of my back. Penalty, and I am in agony. On comes whoever carried the magic sponge for us.

'You've got to get up, lad' he hissed in my ear,' you take the penalties.'

I somehow got up, took the penalty, scored, collapsed and got carted off to hospital. Four weeks off work with crushed ligaments in my back.

It was about this time I was offered the short-term contract at Granada TV and made yet another howler by turning it down. What was I thinking? Was I thinking at all? More of that later.

Back down to London and September 1976 I start at the LSE whilst working full-time on the docks with my Dad, somehow fitting it all in. But then there was the football. I come along with a big rep from being at Sheffield who are world-beaters. Within a couple of weeks, I am 1st XI captain and coach, playing probably the best football of my career. I have to be really inventive on my first foray into coaching. We have just a small gym to work in. I invent all sorts of silly games like crab football to make the space work but the trouble is lads from other University clubs like rugby come along because they have heard about it and love it. I take the whole squad out in the winter London night and run them around Lincoln's Inn Field in a figure of eight in the dimly lit park. All fine until someone runs into an iron fence at shin height and gashes himself badly. Oh well, let's try something else.

I am as fit as I ever was, running, strong, doing a couple of hundred keepy-ups each time of asking, leading from the front. I get the team playing well, we have an ex-pro called Barry Diamond from Coventry City, a Geordie though, at the back and me up front. After the first week Barry comes up to me and says "from the first time I saw you at the trial I reckoned you were an ex-pro, too." We settle a good side down and I build the team spirit. Each week when I put up the team sheet I just scrawl 'Super Team' across the team sheet and they know who I mean. They all love it and we go on a long unbeaten run with me and Nicky Hammond scoring goals up front, scouser Jimmy Wignall dancing down the left wing, Ian Morgan and Stuart Seagal in midfield and Barry sweeping up behind a tall Manc called Micky Gee. We had a very talented lad called Reggie Davis in the squad but no-one can work out his best position. I put him at left back and he stars. I begin to like this coaching lark.

One ref after a midweek game says I should go to Crystal Palace for a trial, another guy who comes to watch says he can get me in at Barnet. I do go to Ilford on trial – they later became part of Dagenham & Redbridge, I think, but they are having a hard time as it happens and have just lost badly. They have a scouse boss called John Evans and we spend all the training session running as they are being punished, his insults echoing round their rainswept corrugated iron stadium. Me and a black lad are on trial, we both pack it in after a couple of weeks. No-one seems at all interested in us.
"I could be George Fucking Best and they wouldn't ever know it," he says which is true, as we leave the ground together after one of the sessions. I make mental notes all the time. If I was coaching here, I would do this different. If I was manager, I wouldn't do that.

Then we are off to the north west and I am in my labour movement career – local politics and the trade union world. Yet again there was no time for regular football. If you want to play at a decent semi-pro level you have to be available – usually two games most weeks and some traveling involved, one or often two training sessions. I was earning a living with a growing family to support and could not commit to that. I regret that now, of course, though I would make the same decision in the same circumstances. All about priorities I guess, that pyramid of needs. This time in the north west, living in Bacup in the bleak Rossendale valley was when I was 24 to when I was about 30 – my prime playing years. And they passed by with me playing in a 'chip shop league'.

Oh, I did play whenever I could and I enjoyed it. I used to go in the Joiners Arms in Bacup for our Labour Party meetings and they had a team. The landlord, Bill Murray, encouraged me to turn out for them in the local Bacup League – which I discovered was locally called the 'chip shop league' for some reason. It was pub teams, working men's club teams on scruffy, muddy uneven pitches but real football. The home pitch at Bacup Rec was perched on the side of a steep hill. I played there on Thursday 3rd May 1979, the day Thatcher got elected and the sleety rain was coming in horizontally off the moors and fells. But it was football, I was playing.

There were no changing rooms at Bacup Rec. I got on the local council and started creating hell. I discovered the local council had contributed towards a local golf club having a new access road – and they reckoned they couldn't afford changing rooms for the hundreds of local people playing up on the Rec. On the day that the council was to finally vote, I put the word around and a horde of local players mobbed the meeting. It came to the vote, I did my bit, the lads cheered and the council could not for shame vote against it. One of the lads called out;
"Is that it, Robbo?"
"Yeah," I called back, laughing, "it's sorted."

They all filed out and left us to the rest of the council's boring business and shouts of 'Well done, Robbo!' echoed back down the corridors as they all departed – probably for the nearest pub. I felt I had actually achieved something. The changing rooms are still there; I doubt whether the pitches are any better, though. Rossendale is all hills so it's not easy to find a flat pitch, or wasn't then.

A local journalist, Nigel Wareing, played in goal for the Joiners Arms and he was a decent keeper. He told me he was starting playing for Goodshaw United in a much better league and they were interested in me going there, too. I went and joined Goodshaw and played about four seasons for them and enjoyed it. They had some good players – my solicitor, Mark Gosnell was at centre half, we had the Nuttall brothers, Alan and Dave, and a sharp skilful lad called Peter Barnes played up front with me. Our home pitch was pretty awful, just along the Burnley Road at Crawshawbooth coming out of Rawtenstall. It was behind a pub but the changing rooms and very basic showers were tucked underneath a butcher's shop. The butcher would periodically complain about the language coming up from his cellar. We often had to clear the sheep off the pitch to play. Again, I scored a lot of goals. The manager, a good lad called Andy Nuttall, who had been a fair player himself, got my game worked out. "Just play it to Robbo's feet," he would say, "no good anywhere else." I was likened to the old comic book character 'Gorgeous Gus' who would only walk through a game but if you played it to him would usually score. It was all part of the usual banter of a dressing room.

We had a lad called Hubert who played for us now and then in midfield. Daft as a brush. Being a local councilor had its twists and turns when I was playing. Every time Hubert saw me he would shout 'what about our roof?' as he reckoned the council were not repairing his family's council house. Eventually I made some enquiries and it transpired that Hubert had not paid rent for some considerable time and the council wanted some movement there first. Next time Hubert saw me I got the usual shout:
"What about our roof?"
"What about our rent?" I shouted back and Hubert never raised it again.

Goodshaw United represented the best level I could play at without having to commit to regular training or travelling which I could not do. Andy was happy for me to turn up and play and that meant I at least got some football. I was often asked if I would be interested in playing at Bacup Borough, Rossendale United or Clitheroe – the better local semi-pro teams – but as much as I wanted to, I could not commit the time so regretfully turned each advance down.

We played in the cup away over near Todmorden. We got changed in a pub called "The Swan with Two Necks' all in one small bar. The ground was over the back, very heavy and muddy. We won a scrappy game and when we trudged up the back lane to the pub I was moaning about there being no showers again.

In the little bar we had changed in there were eleven buckets of hot water and we all groaned. But then the landlady brought in trays with eleven pints and eleven pie and peas and the world seemed a brighter place.

I played in one game and my first wife turned up when there was about half hour to go. The ball ran off the field and I went to pick it up and she was nearby.

"Hi," I said cheerfully, "we're five-nil up and I've got three of 'em."

"Lovely," she said, "does that mean you can come home now?"

Well, OK, not everyone felt the magic.

After home games for Goodshaw – and even some away games – we would go down the lane to a little working men's club tucked away where an old mill had been. We would have a couple of pints before the married lads would go off to their wives and the single lads would start their Saturday nights out. The club had hardly any trade. There were always a couple of old fellas sat in the snooker room. These 'old gimmers' as local lingo would say were not short of a cutting remark when our lads played snooker.

Alan Nuttall was just lining up a tricky long shot, taking his time, cue gently back and forth. Just before he took his stroke, as everyone held their breath, one old gimmer said loudly to the older.

"A good man would pot this."

Alan looked up exasperated as we all fell about.

Goodshaw was typical of the heart of football around the country. Working men enjoying their sport, enjoying the banter and competition, some good, some not so, mostly very keen, then a shower, if you were lucky, a couple of pints and away. Most of the lads at Goodshaw played Sunday morning football, too, for another side that Andy Nuttall ran. It was the game, it was the magic of that ball, the smells of football dressing rooms, the Ralgex (or further back, the 'white horse liniment'), the sweat, the steam from the shower (if you were lucky), the nasty deodorants. And the banter, the 'crack'.

I miss it every day.

Then my marriage imploded, I had all the upset and turmoil of the lost years. One of the things I lost was football. I was so busy working and driving myself on I had not time to play football. I never got to watch it either other than occasionally on tv.

I can remember one Saturday, driving out of the lane at Soulby Fell in my old Range Rover, going off working yet again and I realized suddenly it was a Saturday and I had no idea who Chelsea were playing. It hit me how far I had fallen away from what was close to me, how far I had drifted. But I knew I was locked in and committed to that hamster wheel right at that time. I just had to forget about the day's football. I can remember telling myself as I drove along, "just let it go, don't stress about who Chelsea are playing, you can't take that on as well" and I did. I let it go.

And I lost myself in the process.

So, when I began to put myself back together, it was perhaps no surprise that it was to football that I would turn. But how would I make the leap from my sick bed to being a professional football manager? You've seen the background. I was a decent player but no pro. I loved the game passionately but then so did millions of others. It was a chasm in front of me.

But then, what had Mum told me every day when I was growing up?

"You can be anything you want to be if you work hard enough".

And Mum was always right, wasn't she?

I had to make a start somewhere if I was going to be a football manager. So, in May 1991 I started the road back to fitness and on to wherever the football bug might take me. I did my first level coaching course with the local FA. In those days it was the FA Preliminary Certificate in Coaching – or the 'Prelim' as it was known. My venue was Bolton Lads Club which was not too far as I was still living outside Chorley with Karen and still off sick. I just was not sure I could physically last.

As on most coaching courses the tutor shows you what to do and you, the participants, are the players he uses. Then you all have a go and eventually you all do some assessed coaching. This means it's a lot of physical work. I was barely out of bed at that stage.

Nervousness about my physical state added to my usual periodic low confidence on the football front but I was determined to give it a go. It was fine. As usual the motley crew of would-be coaches soon bond as you have that common ground of football. Over the next couple of weekends, I got there early and gave everything. It was pretty basic stuff but for me it was just a joy to be out kicking a football. The tutor was a taciturn Oldham guy called Alan Keeley.
At the end of the course, we were each told how we had done.
"Right," he said, peering at his clipboard, "you got straight 'A's, well done. What you doing next week?"
I explained I was just coming off the sick and getting back on my feet and so on.
"Do you fancy a week's coaching? I'm running a kids' course for Bobby Charlton at Matlock and could do with a hand. Do you fancy it?"
Did I ever. It was a long trek up and down to Matlock every day but I loved it. On the second day I met the legend himself. At the end of the week, I got a cheque signed by Bobby himself – now 'Sir' Bobby, of course, but not back then. I had been paid to coach football. I was off and running.

I ended up working for Bobby off and on for two years. I started doing more kids courses with Alan including working for Manchester City on community courses, then met the people running the Bobby Charlton Sports company – John Shiels (who now runs the Manchester United Foundation) and Alan Parker, two great lads, and other coaches like Ian Bateman (now a senior coach with the FA) and a big bony lad from Tipton who was destined to be a great mate, John 'Eado' Eades. I was soon running courses myself. It was mostly school holiday stuff but it was fine with me. I was gathering pace.

I was asked if I would be interested in going to Saudi with Bobby and a group of coaches to do some skills coaching and demonstrations. Off we went with a couple of ex-United and ex-City apprentices along for good measure. There are very few places in Saudi where you can legally drink of course. One of them is the British Embassy in Riyadh. Within hours of landing in Saudi we were at the embassy compound ready to play an exhibition game against a team picked from the British servicemen there on the neat Astroturf pitch with its own little stadium in the compound. For some reason I was asked to play at centre half and happily did so with big Eado alongside me. Of course, the kick was that in midfield we had the man himself – Sir Bobby Charlton. Bobby was in his early fifties then but still very fit and as keen and enthusiastic as ever. I could not believe I was playing in the same team as Bobby Charlton but there we are.

Once the game got underway, though, it was a game and you get involved in it. That's my excuse anyway. After about fifteen minutes I intercepted a pass, chested it down and looked up. Bobby was in midfield and, as ever, wanted the ball, but I saw that little John Cooper from Port Vale, the winger, had made a run behind his full back. I hit it long. Bobby wasn't happy.
"Play it to my feet," he said.
"Fuck off," I snapped back, "he's nearer the goal than you." He just turned and got on with the game. As we moved up field –

fortunately Coops had got on the end of my long pass – it suddenly hit me. I had just told one of the greatest footballers England has ever seen, winner of a World Cup and 106 caps, to 'fuck off'.
Oh, yes, and he was my boss, too.
It didn't seem to affect Bobby, though. We went on to win 5-1 and he scored a hat-trick – one right foot, one left and one rare header. He was terrific and didn't seem at all upset or miffed at me. We walked off together.
"Well played, Robbo", he muttered as we trooped off. I was in football heaven. Knackered, but in heaven.
I found Saudi Arabia a strange place. Firstly, there was the heat. We mostly did our coaching in late afternoon or evening out of the heat of the day, in theory. I still, at first, found it almost unbearable. The concrete stadiums were real hot spots, breathless, humid. I then remembered what we had been told at the British Embassy and found some salt tablets – an old-fashioned remedy – and started taking them and almost instantly felt better.

The idea was that we would go around the whole country doing these skill tests and demonstrations. The winner would be invited back to the UK to attend the big Bobby Charlton Summer Soccer School. As we went around, as I usually do, I tried to pick up a few words of the local language – in this case, of course, Arabic. I have found that, as I get older, I am more interested in languages than I was at school. But this was just half a dozen words to say 'stop, go, quicker, hello, thanks' and so on.

Anyway, the local religious people began to get less and less happy. We were just a normal bunch of British football coaches. As we got used to the heat we would often coach in just shorts. That was the first complaint, we had to wear t-shirts. At a certain time, every evening, the call for prayer would go up and all the local kids would line up and be led in prayer for fifteen minutes or so. This was fine with us. We would take the chance to have a cold drink and sit in a group together in the shade waiting for the break to be over. The mutterings from some of the locals began to get louder each place we would go. Apparently, some thought we were an unhealthy western influence.

The other noticeable thing was that each place we went we were attracting bigger crowds to watch us. We reckoned as we went from town to town that maybe there was not a lot else to do in these towns at that time because thousands began turning up to watch the tests and demos. This seemed to aggravate the religious people even more. Finally in one stadium, when the call for prayer went up, we all wandered back to the dressing room for some cold drinks and a rest. We were all sat there and there was more and more of a commotion outside. It turned out the local religious people were telling the crowd that we were protesting at the prayers and refusing to come out and do the second half of the evening's coaching. The crowd – several thousand – had invaded the pitch and were mobbing the dressing room.

It became clear we would have to do something. Ray Whelan, who was the boss of Bobby Charlton Sports then, conferred with Bobby then looked anxiously round the dressing room.
"OK, lads, " he said, "Bobby is going to have to go out there and tell the crowd we are not refusing to coach." His eyes alighted on big John Parker, a rugby player really, built like the side of a house. "Right, Parks, you go with him." Then he saw me.
"And you'd better go, too, Robbo - as you speak the lingo."
I was spluttering about my five words wouldn't be much bloody good, my mate Eado was rolling on the floor with laughter and I find me and Parks flanking Bobby, ready to brave the mob. As we pushed our way out the other lads decided we would all go and they came with us. Amidst the confusion the sight of all of us coming back out seemed in itself to placate the crowd and we shooed them back to the stands and finished the gig. I hardly got to use my five words of Arabic in the melee. I am sure me shouting "it's a corner!" would have sorted things out.

Chris Robinson – Over, Under or Through

When we were back in Riyadh one of the big clubs there was discussing with Bobby and the management about a longer-term link-up. Part of the deal was that they wanted someone to be Director of Youth Development. Bobby and his guys recommended me. Was I interested? I talked to the lads. If I would be paid enough to be able to bring a big chunk home after a year and if I got to manage the youth team, too, and they sorted out house, car and so on, then yes, I was up for it. I looked round their facilities which were excellent – good stadium, training ground, gym, swimming pool.

The discussions dragged on. My involvement was just part of a much bigger deal and partnership.

Meanwhile we went on touring. Out in the desert one evening the buses to pick us up were late. We crammed into a couple of cars. Bobby said he would sit on the back of the truck from Pepsi Cola, the sponsors, that went everywhere with us, carrying crates of their wares to give out. We were sat in traffic and our car was just next to the Pepsi pick-up truck. I happened to look at the next car which was a taxi. Inside the back was a westerner. As we waited in the traffic, I watched as he idly looked round and then he caught sight of the Pepsi truck – with Bobby Charlton sitting on the back! He literally shook his head in disbelief and clutched his chest. He must have thought he was going crazy in the heat. The middle of nowhere in deepest Saudi Arabia and there is one of the most recognizable sporting faces in the world sat on the back of a pick-up truck next to him.

The politics of it all were getting tricky and eventually we cut short the tour and came home a few days early. The overall deal with the club in Riyadh didn't materialize so my bit of it fell by the wayside, too, eventually.

As we waited in the Intercontinental Hotel in Riyadh, which was our base, for our taxis to the airport, a group of Irish air hostesses came in, dressed in the long all-covering black. As they got into the air-conditioned luxury of the hotel, they took off their burkha covering and looked very smart and curvy in their uniforms. I realized another reason Saudi Arabia had been strange. In the time we were there, other than in the big western hotels and at the British Embassy, we never even met or talked to any females. It was only when we back at the Intercontinental, looking at the Irish girls, that we realized what we had been missing!

I enjoyed working for Bobby. It wasn't a regular job as such but it was football, I was learning and I was getting paid. He was a great enthusiast for the game and still a wonderfully gifted player. He was one of the few players I ever came into contact with who seemed genuinely two footed. He could do anything – but seemed bemused when others couldn't. That was maybe why he wasn't a great coach.

Once at the summer school, I was coaching my group of 11-year-olds. Bobby would wander round from group to group and loved to get involved and play some football. We were working on volleying.
"Right, Robbo," said Bobby, "I can help here. You go out to the wing and cross the ball to me about waist high and I'll show them how to volley."
"OK, Bobby." Out to the wing I go with a few balls. I start clipping crosses in. I thought I was doing OK. I was getting about 50% right at waist high. It's not easy. You try it. After a while Bobby came over and said:
"Can't you get them all at waist high for me?"
"Bobby," I said, "if I could I'd have won 100 caps for England like you did."
He seemed to get the point.

I did some work for the FA, too, and then Manchester City. Alan Keeley, my old tutor, was running some courses for the FA in their 'Soccer Skills' programme and he got me involved in that. We ran some of the courses for Manchester City, too, and Alan introduced me to Steve Fleet and the guys at City's Centre of Excellence in Platt Lane, Moss Side. I really fancied this. I knew I would love to be working in a centre, taking a year group, working and developing the young talent. Trouble was, so would everyone else and there were quite a few in the queue ahead of me including some ex-players and quite a few better qualified coaches than me.

I did get one gig, though. Manchester Polytechnic – a huge college with 18,000 students – were taking their football seriously and approached City to hire some time at the Centre. They also wanted someone to coach their first team and were ready to pay. I got the gig. It was ideal for me. The standard was decent, I knew University football and I could work with a team. I tried to get to as many of their games as I could, too. The first game I went to, ironically, was away at Liverpool University, on the same pitch within the running track that I had made my debut for Sheffield University's first team about 19 years previously. I got on well with the Poly lads and really learned a lot and built my coaching experience.

I had weighed up the situation and reckoned that my route forward was to go via non-league. I didn't reckon I was going to have much chance of getting taken on by a pro club even at the Centre of Excellence level. I didn't have the name or the qualifications, or the network at that time. But I reckoned I did know non-league football. My target was to be professional manager anywhere or if not a coach at Conference level.

I wrote to eleven local non-league clubs offering my services, ready to coach at any level for them, unpaid, just to build my experience and networks. I did not get a single reply.
I was living with Karen near Chorley. Her employers wanted to move her down the midlands and were offering her a good deal. We decided we would go. Karen bought a house just outside Evesham, an ancient, dusty, quirky cottage called Dream Cottage in Harvington and me and Charley up sticks and went along.

Now in the Midlands my quest for a start in non-league management had a major advantage – the *Sports Argus*. This was a special Saturday edition of the Birmingham Evening News. The 'Argus' was the bible of non-league soccer in the Midlands, covering all the games, the teams, the gossip. It was – and probably still is – wonderful. All over the Midlands the football world waited on that edition out around 6pm on a Saturday night. The non-league news was read avidly, pored over on Sundays by all the managers and the phones would start ringing and the rumours flying. The non-league news was led by Colin Stoner and I would get to know him very well over the years. We spoke once a twice a week on the phone for years once I got into the game and he was a really nice guy and very helpful – and I guess I helped him, too – although we never actually met!

But that was to come. For now, I read the reports and waited on a chance. There it was! Willenhall Town in the West Midlands League had sacked their manager. This was in the February 1993. Time for an application – but would I do any better than I had in the north west where I had been carefully, consistently ignored?

I did my homework. Willenhall Town had seen better times and had got to the final of the FA Vase at Wembley about ten years before when they were managed by ex-Wolves and Villa player, Barry Stobart. They had been up in the heights of the Southern League then just off the conference but ran into huge trouble with the Inland Revenue and over the years had dropped down.

I drove up to see their ground. Willenhall is a poor industrial area just outside Wolverhampton in the heart of the 'Black Country'. It is most known for being the lock and key making centre of the UK. As I drove up there it seemed to me most notable for scruffy, semi-derelict industrial units, rough car parks with crisp packets blowing across them and old-fashioned chippies and corner shops. I was searching for the ground in the wonderfully inviting 'Noose Lane'. I found it; it was a normal pretty run-down non-league club with a social club. But I got a chance to slip inside and the pitch was superb – a big wide flat beauty. I fancied this!

Incredibly I got a phone call from Gordon Mills, the club secretary. They were interested. Over various meetings, discussions, phone calls I seemed to be getting closer. But still no decision. I phoned up Gordon up to find out what was going on. He said a number of the committee, including him, really liked me but others were wary because I had not managed before and didn't know the league. However, he said they were close to a decision and I was frontrunner. Finally, the puff of white smoke emerged. I had got the job!
There were just six games to go in the season. The transfer deadline was over. I could not sign anyone but at least whatever happened we would not get relegated. We were down near the bottom but safe. I took my first training session.

Whatever a manager says or whatever reputation he comes with, players basically make their minds up about him in the first ten minutes of the first training session. Does he know the game? I had confidence in my coaching so just sailed in and it seemed to work. We didn't have much to work with - a useful if then slightly overweight ex-Wolves and Wrexham player called Darren Wright and a couple of useful younger lads, like Adie Smith and David Butler, and a very raw but interesting forward called Lee Eades who everyone called 'Bully' as he was the spitting image of his idol, Steve Bull from Wolves.

My biggest problem was understanding what the hell anyone was saying! The Black Country accent was a nightmare for me. I was introduced to the physio, a Black Country legend called John Porter, who had the strongest Black Country accent I ever came across. It took me all of those first five weeks to understand a single bloody word he said – and only then did I realize he indeed knew what he was talking about!

The first game for me was at home against Oldbury Town who were on their way to winning the league under a good manager called Jeff Allard who I would get to know well. They were a strong, well organised team and we were not! Most times when you go to a club as a new manager it's because they are struggling so it's not unusual to still be in the mire early on; that's often why they have sacked the last fella!

I got changed in the little manager's office, basically just a cupboard with a desk and no room for anything else. There was some sort of season chart on the wall which I never used. In fact, after that first game, I hardly ever used the office. I would get changed in the dressing room with the lads most times. However, that first game, I was sat there, hearing the crowd arriving outside, bricking it. What the hell had I talked myself into? What was I going to say to the players? I hardly knew all their names let alone what they were like. I walked out and around the pitch. Jeff Allard was kind enough to say hello – "Welcome to the league," he said pleasantly. They were 3-0 up in fifteen minutes and I was shell shocked. Somehow my rag bag team rallied a bit and we held it at that right through. I could tell we were going to struggle but as we were safe from relegation and I couldn't sign anyone else, I just had to ride it out.

The last match of the season was away at Stourport. Two remarkable things happened. Firstly, we won. At last. Two, Barry Stobart, Willenhall Town's most successful ever manager who by then I had met a few times and was a really nice guy, agreed to become my assistant Manager for the next season. I don't know where I got the nerve to ask him, an experienced tried and tested manager and ex-pro, to come and help me, a rookie from nowhere but somehow I did and, even more miraculously, he did.
I was planning for the next season. I had Barry as assistant and John Porter as physio (more of him later) – they both knew a lot of players locally and said they could get some in. I was soon into the non-league routine, that wonderful little world. We trained Monday and Thursday nights and played Saturdays. Once the season got

under way we would play most Tuesdays too so dropped Monday training then. I would go and watch local games on any Monday, Tuesday or Wednesday nights I could all over the midlands. I watched anything and everything, I got to know people, I collected phone numbers, I asked questions, I read that Argus from front to back.

I was obsessed. Karen, who I was living with, understandably complained.
"To be good, you have to be obsessed,' I said.
"Yes, but just because you're obsessed doesn't mean you're good,' she replied. Fair point. But I believed. And I worked hard.
Port found me Gary Piggott, an ex-West Brom striker from Dudley now playing park football and still only about 23, who would score 42 goals in 44 games, and then Matt Nelson, another ex-West Brom, ex-England youth winger. Barry enlisted Steve Mullings, former Dudley Town winger. These three were all black and were our strike force. Port used to call them 'The Three Degrees', three excellent lads who could play and score goals. Barry's son, Loy, former Notts Forest midfielder came and we already had Darren Wright, ex-Wolves and Wrexham and still only 25 and he got fit and firing on all cylinders. We also had a young defender called Ade Smith who was on the edge of the team but I kept telling him he was the best defender in the league because he was. He went on to really blossom and have a long career with Bromsgrove Rovers and then Kidderminster Harriers. So, you can see, we built something of a side. It began to come together. We improved and gradually found our style, our voice. I played a 3-4-3 system with Daz Wright as sweeper when everyone else was playing 4-4-2.

I was immersed in it; I loved the non-league scene in the midlands. The little grounds tucked away in the back streets, the small bands of fanatics at each club who went everywhere, the loyal servants and clubmen who ran the clubs.

But I learnt it was hard to keep a team together at that level. Lads moved for work, or bigger clubs came in offering more money when we had very little and hardly any players on contract. We finished in the top half so made progress – enough to get elevated to the new Midlands Alliance when the leagues were reformed. But Gary Piggott got offered a job as a forklift driver if he would sign for Dudley Town so we let him go – even after Preston North End had agreed to buy him off us and offered Gary a contract. Their manager was the unusual John Beck who played a very rigid long ball game with very strange methods. Gary was there two weeks on trial and they offered him the deal and us a few grand. He said he wanted to come back and talk to me about it.

'They don't play football like we do,' he said, shaking his head. He decided not to sign. A few weeks later the season ended and he ended up going to Dudley Town and we let him go for nothing because of his job offer. Such was non-league football. Another cracking young local striker, Lee Eades who I mentioned before, our 'Bully', gave up because he wanted to watch his beloved Wolves.

It was there at Willenhall, back at my very first training session, that I met the famous 'Port'. John Porter, the 'physio' at Willenhall Town, local legend from nearby Tipton. I had no idea who he was. Worse than that, I couldn't understand a bloody word he said.

Now you have to understand that the Black Country has its own very strong local dialect. It's like Brummie on steroids. Locals are notoriously called 'yam yams. I couldn't work any of this out. Maybe it's because as I discovered 'you are' is pronounced 'yo'am' and 'are you?' is 'amya'. I could go on. As a Londoner I was adrift in a foreign country.

The other thing I soon discovered about the Black Country was it was football heaven. There were non-league clubs everywhere! I started straight out getting to as many games as I could and was delighted to discover the delights of Wednesfield, Bilston, Darlaston, Gornal..I could go on. Every little industrial town around

Dudley and Tipton had a non-league ground. It was just great. Real football country.

Now Port was a product of this environment. At first, I just thought he was an old-fashioned bucket and sponge man and made a mental note that I might need to find a 'proper' physio in summer along with some new players. How wrong I was.

He had the strongest Black Country accent I ever encountered. By the time I began to understand what he was saying I had realised he knew what he was doing and he knew the game. As a physio he was top although he had his own homespun strapping techniques and remedies. At training midweek, I would often ask him if a particular player would be fit for Saturday. He would look at the player then look up at me and just either nod or shake his head. He was never ever wrong. Not once.

I discovered he was a warm, funny man underneath his tough exterior. Then the stories began to emerge.

Port and his lovely wife Kath always seemed to have very good sun tans. They were always back and to from Spain although he never missed a game. The story on that was that he was working as part of a gang digging the channel tunnel. They had it all worked out. Half of the gang would work and sign the other half in. That meant the other half were getting paid real good money but off work. They took it in turns. This ruse worked really well, allowing many opportunities for quick sun breaks in Spain. However, one day, lying on a sun bed beside a hotel Spain, Port rolled over to see his boss walking purposefully towards him. As far as the boss knew Port was working under the channel. The game was up.

There were many stories but I didn't know truth from fiction and Port would just laugh when I asked him.
However, one story I can verify because I was there. We played a team called Knypersley Victoria up near Stoke in a midweek night

game in one cup or other. We had a young quick clever team by then. We gave Knypersley the run around and they started to respond in industrial fashion. They were scything down our young players right left and centre. Port as physio was continuously on and off the pitch. I was complaining bitterly to the ref (surely not?) and the vociferous local crowd were going increasingly barmy.

One more time one of our young players – maybe Russ Brown or Lee Elliott – was laid out. We were in the last few seconds; we were winning but getting absolutely battered. On goes Port yet again, we are all up in arms. But now Port has had enough. He used to go on with a medical bag in one hand and a sponge and water bag in the other. As he gets up from attending to the injured player, he picks up his two bags turns round and puts the nut on the offending Knypersley player who goes down poleaxed. There is bedlam.

All their team seem to be chasing Port, carrying his two bags, as he runs off with a whole line of them following him. I can remember laughing because it was so bizarre and so much like a scene from Benny Hill. I could hear the music in my head. The crowd are going frantic. The ref wisely blows for time. However, the crowd invade the pitch. We are all legging it for the dressing rooms, or trying to – their big manager Rob Horton has hold of both lapels of my overcoat (very stylish as a manager, I was) and is lifting me off the ground, shouting something I can't hear in my face. We all finally get into the dressing room, and lock the door while there is banging and shouting outside as the crowd try to get in. Our players are battered and bleeding, I'm shaken from my encounter with their manager.

Port sits in a corner, one legged calmly crossed over the other, smoking a cigarette.

A couple of weeks later Port comes up to me at training.
"Gaffer, I've been charged by the FA for that Knypersley game. Can you get me off?"

I think the odds are against us somehow because Port's headbutt is the talk of non-league football but look at the document. The ref said "The Willenhall physio *appeared* to headbutt a Knypersley player."

"There you go, Port", I said, "it says 'appeared to' – he didn't really see it. Tell them you just leant in to talk to him." Port seems happy with this and went off.

He got off the charge.

Port knew the game and he knew a lot of players. He brought in a whole series of top players as I have said. I inherited some real talent and went out and found some more like Adie Fitzhugh, Loy Stobart and Nick Birch. We had a great young team and we had a great time on that lovely big flat pitch.

Port had a great sense of humour and was much loved by the staff and players. We had a big local derby FA Cup game at Halesowen Town who were then a league above us. It was a very significant game for us and a lot of tension around. When I arrived at their ground Port asked me if he could speak to the team in the dressing room before they went out. This was very unusual but by then I absolutely trusted Port so said yes. He had a big sack with him. At the right moment in the strained atmosphere of the dressing room I said ' right, lads, Port wants to say a few words'. Eyebrows were raised. Port took centre stage with his sack. He reached inside and pulled out a huge four foot long Swan Vesta.

"This is it, lads. The Big Match."

He went on. He took an apple out the sack. Took a bite.

"You only get one bite of the apple in the cup." He threw the apple in the bin. By the time he'd finished we are all in tears of laughter. He completely defused the situation. The lads went out with smiles on their faces and we won.

Time moved on and I went up the leagues ending up as manager of Cheltenham Town. Port and I worked together again some years later at Evesham United and stayed in touch.

A couple years ago I got a phone call one day and it was Kath, Port's wife.
"He wants to speak to you, Chris, but he's not so good. He's got throat cancer bad. But he wanted me to call you."
Port came on the line, his voice strained and hoarse but still unmistakably Port. We talked for a good while, reminiscing, saying how we both wished we could have worked together again and talking football, as you do. We finished as he was tiring and I said I would come up and see him soon.
He died a week later.
Thanks, Port, for your friendship and all the great memories. You were a great football man.
See you on the far post.

But back then, after eighteen months or so at Willenhall I had got around and people had begun to notice my team could play. I applied for the manager's job at Nuneaton Borough, two leagues above and they decided in the end not to give it me and go for a more experienced manager as they were in relegation trouble. I then applied for the job at Atherstone United in the same league as Borough and also in the same relegation trouble. I got that and kept them up. Borough went down - which was quite sweet, of course, I must admit.

Atherstone United was a great little club, a village team really up in the Southern League Premier division with the big boys of Cheltenham Town, Rushden & Diamonds and so on. They had very little money but great character exemplified by two great very experienced centre halves: Steve Jackson and Malcolm Randle who were terrific pros and great lads. I called them 'Hinge and Brackett'.
We lost the first three games there including the last one 7-1 at home to the wealthy Rushden & Diamonds. We had even gone 1-0 up! I made a big mistake by playing three at the back and wing backs against a team with excellent full backs and wingers. I was

worried about being without Jacko and Malc at the back – one injured and one suspended – and got it wrong. But I learnt.

I thought long and hard. I had to do something because we were right down in the drop-zone. I was reading everything I could as usual. I remembered reading Jack Charlton's autobiography including the chapter when he explained how he set up his Newcastle team playing a simple long ball game. I dug the book out. This was the answer. We didn't have the players to play my preferred passing game. We would play it long from the full backs and miss out midfield. I put two young hard-working defenders, Robbie Burke and David Butler, in midfield and worked in training at the new method. We went away to Dorchester Town, a long trip with lunch in a hotel in Weymouth beforehand.

I came out with the lads to warm up. They had a new ground then, courtesy of some re-development involving Tesco I think, but it was impressive and they had a decent side. One of the great things about non-league is that every club, no matter how small, has its group of die-hard supporters who would be there come what may wherever their team went to. Now at that level the chances were you would know them because there were not that many!

Anyway, there were the usual knot of our fans in the away end and two of them were holding up a sign. It said 'Robinson Out'. I thought 'fucking hell, that's a bit harsh!'. I'd only been there about two weeks! And it was not like they were suddenly losing because they had been losing for weeks – which is why the previous guy got the bullet!

I tried to act nonchalant and ignore it and get the lads going on their warm up. Out of the corner of my eye I spot the lovely Keith Allen, secretary at the Atherstone (and later club secretary at Wycombe Wanderers amongst others) bustling around the side of the pitch. He stops in front of the small knot of our supporters and focuses on one of the lads holding up the sign – 'Joe! Take that sign down! Right now!' And bizarrely, they did! Can you imagine that at Old Trafford?

Well, we won that day, away at Dorchester and turned the corner. I had found a system that worked for us and got results. We went on an exhilarating run and the lads ran their hearts for us. We overcame injuries and any problem that came our way. We had some help though.

One of the stalwart supporters of the club was the local vicar. He was a lovely slightly built middle aged guy called Brian and he was a real fan. He used to ask his parishioners to pray for us every Sunday from the pulpit. I would take any help on offer at that stage.
Our main striker was a well-built lad called Robbie Ellison, a strong hard running lad who was a hod carrier as his day job. Well, Robbie got injured – a bad stomach muscle injury and the medics said he would be out for six weeks – well, by this stage we only had a few vital weeks to go in the season as we fought to stay up. This was disastrous news.

Brian the Vicar came up to me as I came into the ground for a training session.
"I've heard about Robbie," he said, looking worried.
"Yeah, looks like he's out for the season."
"Well, "Brian said, as we walked together into the little ground." I don't know if you know but my wife, Betty, is a faith healer. She's quite well known actually. She says she can help."
Now I did not want to offend Brian the Vicar – or Betty, who I had never met – but I had no faith in faith healers! However, like I say, we were desperate.
"Look, Brian, I'll tell you what. I'll have a word with Robbie. If he's up for it then fine."
"Splendid," said Brian happily. 'It really will work."
Yeah, right. So, I went into the little scruffy treatment room where Port was working on a player. A disconsolate Robbie sat in a chair by the side, still in work clothes as there was no training for him.

"Rob – a word."
We walked out on the pitch. I told him about Brian's suggestion.
"Look, "I said, "if it's not for you then that's no problem. To be honest I don't believe in this sort of thing myself."
"No," he said, "no, I'll do it. We'll give it a go. Can't do any harm, can it? I'll try anything.'
I was surprised.
'OK, fair enough, I'll fix it up with Brian and Betty."
"One thing, Gaffer, "said Rob, a bit embarrassed. "Will you come with me?"

The next Thursday night Rob and I drew up outside Brian and Betty's council house on the small estate in Atherstone. I don't know what I was expecting. It was a very ordinary house. Rob and I looked at each other. We had come round early evening as I had training to take that evening.
"Come on, "I said, "let's get this over with."
Brian met us at the door and took us in to the living room where Betty sat in an armchair. She was an ordinary looking middle-aged woman, quite plump with glasses and a ready smile. Brian did the introductions. Betty stood up, not without a little difficulty as I recall.
'Right," she said, "let's get started. Rob, stand here in front of me. Chris – you stand behind him, just in case he – well, just in case. Brian, you sit there."
I stood up awkwardly behind Robbie, feeling very embarrassed. How long would this take? I had training to take.
Betty stepped closer to Robbie, looking up into his eyes, then touched him lightly on the forehead. Robbie collapsed backwards. I managed to grab on and hold him – six foot of meaty striker.
'Just lay him down there on the rug," said Betty, calm as you like. I staggered around and managed to get Robbie laid out with Brian's help. Robbie was out cold.
Fucking hell, I thought, she's killed me centre forward! How am I going to explain this to the Chairman?

Betty hovered her hands over Robbie's stomach and seemed to be muttering something to herself but I couldn't catch what she was saying. I looked at Brian. He sat beaming on the sofa.

Gradually Robbie came round and we helped him to sit up next to Brian. I was still standing there in the little front room in that council house in the back streets of Atherstone one spring evening, trying to make sense of what had happened.
"So, "said Betty, "that's sorted Robbie out, now, how about you, Chris?"
Well, we were out of there and back in my car in about three seconds flat. I mumbled something about training and we were off. In the car I turned to Robbie.
"What the fuck was that all about?" I asked.
Robbie shook his head. "I dunno, she just touched me head and that's all I can remember."
"So, how do you feel now?"
He shrugged.
"Allright, I suppose. No different really."
Be that as it may. Two weeks later he came off the bench in our away game at Cambridge, fully fit.

Chapter Six – Wrecking Ball

We got out of the relegation zone in some style. The long ball system worked well and frustrated better teams, pinning them back. I recall us beating promotion contenders Gloucester City at home too along the way. It was great fun.

Sat the end of season celebration, two young supporters shuffled over to me where I stood with Karen.
"Robbo," they mumbled.
"All right, lads?"
"Yeah…well, we just wanted to, like.. just say thanks." One of them thrust a bottle of cheap white wine into my hands. I thanked them. They ambled off. I couldn't help but laugh.
"What are you laughing at?" asked Karen, "that was a lovely thing for them to do."
"Yes, I know," I said, "but they are the same two lads who were holding up the 'Robinson Out' banner three weeks at Dorchester!"

At least, as a football manager, I learnt not to take supporters' praise or criticism to heart.

Over summer we worked hard, I brought a couple of new players in and we were able to start playing the sort of football I wanted us to play. We started really well and after a couple of weeks we were in fourth position, up with the big boys. So when I read in the trusty Argus that Cheltenham Town, one of those big boys, was looking for a new manager after having come second in the league for each of the previous couple of seasons and just missed out on promotion back to Conference each time, then my mind started whirling. I threw my hat in the ring.

I drove down to Cheltenham to look at their ground at Whaddon Road. I was still living near Evesham at the time, in Harvington. It was only about twenty minutes from Cheltenham. I drove into the big car park by the ground and looked around. It was a proper football ground – a real step up from Willenhall or Atherstone. It was also a full-time job. My target, my goal – to be a full-time manager. But why would they back an outsider like me?

The Argus and other papers were full of possible big names, ex-pros and experienced Conference and League Managers coming in to take the reins. I knew I would be a real long shot but had nothing to lose. You had to take these opportunities when they came up. I had learned that already. You could not afford to wait for the ideal timing if you were ambitious and I certainly was that. I would have liked to stay longer at Atherstone ideally. We had a good young squad together plus a couple of the older heads still around and engaged and they were good people to work for. Ah, why worry? Send the letter in. I would probably not hear from them anyway – just like those eleven clubs I applied to back in the north-west when I was trying to get a start as a manager.

For all that though I had this little sneaky sliver of confidence that said if I could just get an interview, I knew I could put myself over well. There was just a slim chance.

I got an interview. At the Queens Hotel in Cheltenham, away from the ground as apparently, they were trying to keep the process low profile. I turned up a week early – I was that keen. Yes, I did, I was waiting in the lobby for ages before re-checking the invite letter. Exactly a week early.

A week later the interview went well, I thought. The usual middle-aged white men in club blazers. They were pleasant enough though and I liked the Chairman, Arthur Hayward. There were the usual predictable questions.
"What makes you think you can come from a smaller club and be successful at a bigger club like us?"
"Well, "I said, with what I hoped was a winning smile "that smaller club is three places above you in the league right now for starters."

A couple of days later I was driving on the M6 with the boys, bringing them down for a visit when I got a call from my old mate, John Eades from Bobby Charlton days.
"Hey – I've just had a phone call from a Director of Cheltenham Town asking about you!"
I had put Eado down as one of my character references.
"What did you say?"
"I told them you were a shite manager and a worse coach!"
"Fair enough."
"No, I actually said you could be anything you wanted to be and you choose to be successful."
'Oh, I like that!"
"Yes, you owe me a fucking pint!"

Funnily enough, as I put the phone away, I noticed we were just driving past the turn-off for Willenhall. It seemed some sort of omen. They must be interested if they were taking up references?

They were. I got the job. I certainly was not tempted away by the riches of the Beautiful Game. At that level the money is crap, especially when you take the insecurity into account. Not for the last time, as it would turn out, I actually took a pay cut to go full-time in football. I had been working for the community enterprise outfit in Birmingham and had a part-time contract with Atherstone United. But this was full-time, all my eggs in one basket. This was what I had worked so hard and so obsessively for over the preceding years. This was the target. When I sat in that armchair in Whittle-le-Woods, still recovering from my illness, my life in shreds, watching Kenny Dalglish on TV, that is what I had set as my target. When I got started at Willenhall I even bought a big brown overcoat like the one he had been wearing that day on TV. It was a sort of joke against myself. I called it my 'Kenny Coat.'

Anyway, I was now a full-time football manager. I had done it in about five years.

What do they say? Be careful for what you wish for?

Maybe so and maybe it did turn out a bit that way. But I don't regret it. I achieved what I had set out to achieve. Now I had to kick on and be more successful. It was another start. That was all. Not an end.

Here we go then, fasten your seat belts!

So, where to start? Well, there were press conferences to start with, which were new to me in a football context. I loved all that though, I could sail through them too, falling back on my old Trade Union media training.

I had to get to grips with the squad – sort out what I had and what we needed. I had seen them play a pre-season game so had the beginnings of an idea or two. I knew they had a good squad and had so narrowly missed out on promotion the previous two years. The Directors had said they felt they didn't need much change. Problem was, as I soon discovered, the players had other ideas. The experienced goalkeeper, Martin Thomas, was offered a goalkeeping coach job at a pro club and announced his retirement and good goalkeepers then, as now, were hard to find. The best player in creative terms, Lee 'Archie' Howells, had a persistent injury which kept troubling him until he had eventually to have a double hernia operation. This was a bit of a bugger because I had planned to build my team round him. Another player believed the club had promised him he could move to Gillingham with the previous manager and was effectively downing tools. The bright young centre half Steve Jones was attracting league attention and would soon be sold to Swansea. And so on. So it turned out I did have a re-building job to do after all though I at least did inherit some good players like Chris Banks, Bob Bloomer (though he had not long broken his leg and was on the long road back) Jimmy Smith, Jimmy Wring and Jason Eaton.

There was no scouting set up. The club wanted me to revive their youth trainee scheme – then termed 'YTS' – to develop some sellable talent but there was not much of a youth set-up to start with. The assistant manager, Pete Atkins, had been the favourite to get the manager job and I was persuaded by the Board to offer him the job as my assistant as he knew the players etc. I did and he turned it down and left, which of course he had every right to do. So, I had no assistant or coach.

There was little real talent in the youth team as it stood and the reserves lacked lustre.

But at least I could get on with coaching and working with the players. I knew from my own experience as a player that they just wanted you to get to work. They would make their own minds up then as to whether you knew what you were doing, never mind what the media said. I cracked on with that.

It was really full on, a 24-hour a day job with no let up, the phone always going, always more to do, games to watch, people to talk to, training, games, meetings.

I loved it all.

I would get it about nine, and go to the little office I had up in the stands next door to 'Jasper' Cook, the Commercial Manager. I would be on the phone. Then once I got the youth scheme going, I was coaching the YTS lads from around 10, then a bit of lunch and back to the phone. In the evenings there would be games if we were playing, or training or games to watch to scout players, which I really enjoyed. I was rarely home till gone eleven every night. Friday nights were usually off – though again the phone wouldn't stop – and there was a bit of a break on Sundays though I would be impossible to be with if we had lost – which fortunately did not happen much.

The Directors said they wanted me to raise the profile of the club. I would go and do talks at business network meetings, or radio interviews and was soon writing a weekly column for the local daily paper, the 'Echo'.

I won't go over it blow by blow. The season records are there to be seen if that is your thing. The Board had given me a two-year contract. The idea was to regroup in year one and then go for it in year two and win promotion. That is what I did – although the re-group was more of a re-build, as I've said.
I set up the youth scheme – signing a leggy skinny lad called Michael Duff as one of the trainees along the way.
I raised the profile as requested – though I am not sure the Directors got exactly what they had in mind on that score. I remember doing one business breakfast meeting at the Queens Hotel, funnily enough, where I had been for my interview. I did my usual presentation and tried to make it entertaining. It was going down well as it did, to be honest. And I got to the bit where I introduced a slide titled – 'What Directors Know About Football'. Now nicking a little from Tommy Docherty's book, this slide was blank and that always brought a laugh. As the crowd jeered happily, I noticed three stone faced individuals glowering in the front row – three of the Club Directors were there! Gulp! Oh well..

We made money by buying and selling players. We had a good FA Cup run with a lucrative televised sell out replay against Barry Fry's Peterborough along the way. We were never out of the top six even when re-building and as we headed into the second season we were soon right on course for promotion. Many of the young youth products like Christy Fenwick and David Parker – and the afore-mentioned Michael Duff – got their first team debuts along the way, too.

I made it clear to the Directors right from the start that whilst I was always ready to discuss team selection with them, it was my decision and mine only. This was more of a problem than it should have been. After each game I would have to get changed, go out and do the local media interviews then go up to the Directors Lounge to show my face. I would only stay briefly but it had to be done. I soon discovered that at least some of the Directors did not have a clue about football. We might have played really well but just failed to win and I would be greeted with 'what went wrong there then?' Conversely, we could have played awful but nicked a win and I would invariably be slapped on the back with a 'well done, Robbo!' on my appearance up in the Board room where the Directors would be hitting the booze with the opposition counterparts. I learnt to be cynical about them mostly. Ultimately in that situation as a football manager you are a professional ruled by amateurs and that is not healthy.

Only after my appearance there could I go down to the Players' Lounge and join the players and my guests and relax a bit. If we won, I would be ready to go out for a meal with friends in Cheltenham and enjoy. If we lost, I would not want to speak to anyone or read a paper or anything until I could get back to training on Monday and begin to put things right.

Early on I knew I had to get an Assistant Manager. I needed to spread the load a bit. When the Board had suggested I appoint Pete Higgins I had agreed and said I was not one of those managers that needed their own people around him. I could work with anyone, I said airily. I was making a mistake and did not know it. It was only afterwards looking back on my time at Cheltenham that I understood the importance of having a team around you as staff that you knew and could trust.

However, initially that was not a problem. Pete Higgins said no and went off and I was looking for someone to take the role. My mate Tim Harris who was managing Cinderford Town at the time recommended Chris Price to me as Chris was at the end of his playing career and looking to get into management. Pricey had had a top career with Aston Villa, Blackburn Rovers and Portsmouth amongst others. He was a Hereford lad and when at his best he was one of the top right backs around. We met up and got along really well and I offered him the job.

Pricey was not a coach as such but that was not an issue because I was happy leading on that aspect anyway. But he was great at 1:1 with the players, with a lot of good advice and encouragement based on his excellent playing experience and the lads took to him straight away. He particularly worked a lot with Jimmy Wring who had always been a winger but now as we settled into a 3-4-1-2 formation, because I thought that best suited the players we had, we needed Jimmy to adapt to the role of right wing back. Pricey was always on at Jimmy but in a good way and Jimmy developed into the best right wing back in the league.

If Pricey had one drawback it was that he had a fiery temper although looking back maybe that complimented my more laidback style really well. Pricey could have an argument in an empty phone box. We once went to Baldock Town which was a long trek and when we got there, we found a small ground with hardly any fans there at all. It was being run by the Stein brothers who had made their name at nearby Luton but had yet to find an audience, shall we say. Behind our dug out there was no one except for an old guy and his dog. Yes, literally one man and his dog. Anyway, we were winning comfortably and the ball went over the wall by the dugout. Pricey jumped over after it and threw it back and I turned and got on with the game. I was absorbed in the game but after a bit I thought 'Where's Pricey?'. I turned round and he was still over the wall on the terraces – arguing with the old guy with the dog!

So more by luck than judgement it worked out really well with Pricey. He would often stay behind in the bar after a game and that is when a small group of the Directors used to sit and plot. Pricey would be with his own guests or players or whatever but he could keep an eye on what was going on and an ear out for what was being said. He was a good link between me and the players too.

However, before too long he got offered the manager's job at Newport County and when he came and talked to me about it, I said it was too good an opportunity for him to miss though I very much did not want to lose him. Newport was relatively local for him and they had plans to rebuild the club and it all fitted. He had been straight with me about it and I appreciated that. He took the job. As usually the case, football throws you a curve ball and within a couple of weeks we were playing Newport. We beat them about 5-1 I think and Jimmy Smith – a very gifted crafty goal scorer who Pricey used to be on at for not working hard enough – had a field day and scored four, I think. The players loved it, of course, and gave Pricey a lot of stick but he took it all on the chin.

We had rebuilt. I brought in Darren Wright who had played for me at Willenhall and Atherstone United and was a player and person I trusted absolutely. He was a very talented player, ex-Wolves and Wrexham, but had been forced to quit the full-time game because of a knee problem. He was someone who gave you a hundred per cent every game but could really play too, off either foot. The first name on the team sheet for me and he soon became a fans' favourite too. Archie Howells was still struggling with his injury and I needed someone to play that '10' role so signed Paul Chenoweth from Bath City – another classy clever player and top lad. Jason Eaton was on fire up front – I particularly remember his hat-trick away at rivals Gloucester City. It was all coming together.

I signed Jamie Victory for nothing and he went on to be a real stalwart for Cheltenham Town. I had first seen him playing against our reserves for Bournemouth Reserves when he was on loan there from West Ham. I tried to get him on loan to us later but West Ham said they had plans for him but Jamie and I stayed in touch and spoke when I heard he had actually left West Ham several months later. He told me he was going abroad to a Finnish club, I think. Anyway, a week later he phoned me to say that the Finland deal had fallen through and he was happy to come and sign for us if I was still interested. He played his first game that week in a pre-season game at Cinderford Town on an awful pitch. Before the game one particular Director came up to me and said "What's this I hear from the Chairman? You've signed this Victory lad and are paying him a bloody fortune? Who is he?"

I told him and said Jamie was travelling from East London and in fact was on no more than most first team players.

"But I've never heard of him!" he exclaimed.

"He is – as of now - the best player we have" I said and pushed past him to go to the dressing room.

A few weeks later in a Board meeting – I used to attend them to discuss football matters then leave the meeting for their other business stuff - the Chairman was complimenting me on signing Jamie who had shown he was a top player already. The Directors agreed and banged the table. I looked at the Director who had cornered me at Cinderford before Jamie's first game but he wouldn't look at me. Amateurs.

I needed a good centre back to play alongside the club captain Chris Banks and I needed a top goalkeeper. At that time, I was asked by Tony Jennings the manager of the England 'C' team – the national semi pro side – if I would select and manage an FA XI made up of the best non-league talent in the South West. I was flattered to do so. Graham Allner, the experienced Kidderminster Harriers manager (and years later another Cheltenham Town manager) told me he'd done that before and took it as an opportunity to try out players that he was thinking of signing. This seemed a great idea.

Gloucester City – our closest rivals – were also promotion contenders and their flamboyant and controversial Chairman was Keith Gardner. Funnily enough Keith would often phone me for a chat on a Friday nights and we got on well. Gloucester had Mark 'Boka' Freeman at centre back who they had paid good money for. I liked Boka – he was originally a Willenhall lad, though before my time – he was a big tough no-nonsense centre back who attacked the ball and anything else that got in the way. He was all heart though he could also play a bit, as it happened. He was one to go to war with. So I picked Boka to play alongside our Chris Banks for the FA XI to see how that worked.

Our FA XI played the Combined Services at Mangotsfield and I think we drew 1-1. Jason Eaton went on to go into the national squad and we all really enjoyed the event. More importantly I could see Banksy and Boka would work well together. It took me a few months but with the hard work of our Chairman Arthur Hayward, we managed to get Boka into a Cheltenham shirt and get him transferred from Gloucester City.

The goalkeeper issue was more difficult and I tried a whole list of them before finally settling on Kevin Malloy who did a decent job for us.

I was doing a lot of the scouting myself. I really enjoyed this but looking back it is clear now I needed a better structure to help. My mate Martyn McNulty did some local scouting and my old friend John Ruck helped out when he wasn't busy scouting for Martin O'Neill at Leicester City. We signed some good players, and some not so good.

With Pricey now gone to Newport I had sense enough to know by now I needed help. I asked experienced managers Pete Amos and Bobby Hope but both declined with regret. In fact, both of these really top guys told me later that came to feel they had made a mistake in not coming on board and I would have loved to work with either of them. In the end Bob Bloomer took the role combining with his playing duties. Bob was a top pro and good guy but he was still playing and it was difficult for anyone to fulfil what I needed and be a player still too. Overall, in hindsight, not replacing Pricey in the right way was another major mistake. I had always disparaged those managers who wanted to bring an entourage of coaches and assistants with them but I came round to understanding, by bitter experience, that you needed your own team of staff you could trust too – particularly if you were under pressure for quick results.

So as the first season came to an end we had rebuilt and done well. The very wealthy Rushden & Diamonds backed by the Doctor Marten's millionaire Max Griggs won the League but we came a very creditable third, crucially ahead of rivals Gloucester City by three points.

I had set up the youth trainee scheme and that was working well and we had some good talent on board. However, the scheme indirectly caused me a major personal problem. Karen and I were living in Harvington, near Evesham. I was working all hours and completely absorbed in the job. However, Karen would come along and enjoyed the games and the buzz of the role. I worked hard with the trainees - coaching them myself and encouraging where I could. We signed one local lad called Simon Goodwin who had been a YTS at Southampton but had left there after some personal issues. We agreed with Southampton he could join us as he looked a promising centre back, around six foot tall, and a decent player. He was one of those youth players that got their chance in the County Cup for the first team. He always seemed to have personal issues and problems and he even came and stayed with us for a while as he fell out with his family.

I had a strict behaviour policy with the trainees – all aged 16 or 17. They were not allowed in pubs or clubs for example, other than with family. I was trying to get them to focus on their football opportunity.

Anyway, Karen was around thirty-two at this time and worked in HR for British Gas. Then it transpired that Karen had been seen in a Cheltenham night club with Simon Goodwin, amongst others. Unbeknown to me this news was just going to spread round the town and around the club. This became apparent to Karen – and presumably the lad Goodwin. She decided to spill the beans with me and fess up. She told me they had been seeing each other and were having an affair. He was 16 and she was 32. He was a YTS at the club, and she was the live-in partner of the club manager.

As soon as I heard this from her, I packed my bags and walked out. A club Director, Wayne Allen, phoned me to let me know these rumours were circulating just as Karen finished confessing to me. He immediately invited me to stay with him and his wife, Liz, while we sorted out what would happen next.

So, the circus really came to town. I had immediately told the Chairman what was going on and he was supportive. The club made moves to sack Goodwin for the breach of rules – he had been in the night club on several occasions apparently and the other couple of trainees who were also breaking the curfew were disciplined too.

However, within days the local daily paper – the 'Echo' – got the story and ran it front page. 'The YTS and the Boss' Girl' I think the headline was. That really started the frenzy. News agencies were on to me and national papers. The problem was I had to keep my phone on for work stuff.

One agency was very persistent. The story was going to be in the 'New of the World' apparently so I should tell my side while I could, so they said. Karen was hounded, photographed coming out of the Harvington house and offered several thousand of pounds to sell her story. To be fair she – like me – stuck with 'no comment.' The persistent agency would not give up though. I said to them I'm only talking about football matters, nothing else, and I hung up yet again. Five minutes later the phone went again. It was the same agency.
"Don't hang up!" said the reporter, "this is a football question."
"OK," I said warily. "Go on then."
"Is this lad Goodwin any good as a player?"
"Fuck off," I said but had to laugh.

I asked one journalist why there was so much interest. This was only Cheltenham Town after all not Arsenal or Man United.
"It doesn't matter," he said frankly, "it's football."

In the event it was the Daily Star that ran with the story nationally with a similar headline to the Echo and a vague photo of Karen leaving the house. "Curvy blonde Karen left their luxury Cotswolds cottage in her gold Porsche refusing to comment." Well, she was blonde and did happen to have a sort of bronze coloured Porsche, I suppose!

The night that the story really broke in the media I was due to attend a local football league's end of season awards night which was being held in the social club at the ground to present the prizes – a normal sort of duty. My mate Martyn McNulty phoned me:
"Look, Robbo, you don't have to go. I'll tell them you've got to cancel. They'll understand."
"No fucking way, "I said, "I've done nothing wrong. I'm not hiding. I'll continue to do my job".

Brave words but of course it was all very embarrassing. Martyn arranged to meet me in the club car park and said we would go in together. I really did not know what to expect. We went in the social club. It was heaving. As I came in the door behind Martyn, they all got up and applauded. A standing ovation. There is no working people out, is there?

I had always got on well with the supporters. Back in my Willenhall days in my first job the lovely Barry Stobart, who kindly agreed to be my first Assistant Manager, had advised me:
"After every game – win, lose or draw – go and sit with the hard-core supporters in the bar. It will pay dividends."
I did. After a game - certainly if we drew or lost, not always when we had won – I would go and sit down with the main core of supporters in the club bar. I started that at Willenhall Town as advised by Barry, and went on the same at Atherstone United. My

first game at Cheltenham Town – it was a night game against Ilkeston, I think, and we won 3-0 as I recall – I walked into the supporters' bar with a pint of lager in my hand and looked round. There was a bit if a hush and a lot of elbows nudging people. I spotted the largest, noisiest group of hardened fans and walked over.
"Right, lads, shift up, find us a seat."
They did, struck dumb, and I squeezed in and sat down.
"Come on, then, "I said, "what did you think?"
And so it began. They soon found their tongues. I would go in often then and they would tell me in no uncertain terms where they thought I was going wrong but more often than not they just asked sensible questions – "Why do you play that system? Why was so-and-so not playing? Why did you sub Jimmy off – he was our best player?"
I answered honestly and if I had got it wrong, I would say so but often the explanations would be giving them info they did not know and they then understood.

Anyway, walking into that club that night and getting that reception was a little pay back for my open and honest approach, I felt. Now I had to front up to the players!

Our next game was our last of the season – away at Rugby Town. The players had arranged an end of season players' do in Nottingham afterwards.
So, I walked into the away dressing room at Rugby before the game. "Ok, lads, listen up." I told them what I knew about what had happened. I knew they would have heard all the gossip and read the stuff in the media. I told them my side of things and was concise and honest. I put it all out there.
"Look," I concluded," that's it then. Out in the open. You don't need to tiptoe on eggshells around me."
There were a lot of nodding heads and straight forward eye contact around the dressing room. Then Martin Boyle, our striker from Bristol spoke up.

"So, gaffer – out on the pull with us in Notts tonight then?"
A lot of laughter, a lot more banter but the atmosphere was cleared. Several of the lads spoke to me over the following couple of days and said all the lads "admired my balls for fronting up like that" and agreed it was the best thing to have done. Ever onwards.

When the story had hit the media, I had phoned the Chairman and offered to resign as the club could do without all this crap. He would not hear of it, making it clear I had not done anything wrong and they were all behind me. I am sure he was sincere personally in saying that but I did have a sneaking suspicion some of the Directors would use it against me down the line.

It was strange to read about myself in the national media and be the subject of people looking at me and whispering and nudging each other. Cheltenham Town were big fishes in a little pool so everything about them was news in that lovely old town. But for my private life to be of any interest to anyone outside the local area just bemused me. Of course, as is often the case, when you get a story about you in the papers for the first time you realise how many inaccuracies there are and that makes you wonder about every other story!

I went off to Italy for three weeks and with help from Carol and others I put myself back together and came back for the next season raring to go.

We got underway and were doing well. It became apparent we needed a striker because Jason Eaton, our star striker from the previous season, had a persistent back injury and Martin Boyle had broken his collar bone against Rushden & Diamonds and was on the long slow road back. That left us just with Jimmy Smith – a great finisher but not a target man or one to lead the line. I made all this clear to the Board – we needed a striker to be sure of promotion.

The one I wanted was Gary Piggott, now doing very well at Dudley Town, who had been with me at Willenhall Town. I took one of the key Directors along to watch him with the Chairman and he had scored yet again and as ever looked a really good all-round striker. There would need to be a fee and Gary would have to be paid good wages to make up for leaving his forklift job.

I sat in the bar with the Director and the Chairman.

"So, what you're saying is that if we sign Piggott we will get promoted?" asked the Director.

"Yes," I said, "I would bet my mortgage on it."

"Oh, you are, son, you are."

Twat.

We didn't sign Gary or any all-out striker that cost us anything of a fee. The Board hovered and dallied. My mate Tim Harris recommended that I meanwhile sign Steve Cotterill. Cotts had played at Cheltenham Town, being a local lad, and then gone on to play for Wimbledon and others. He was at the end of his career, having been player-manager at Sligo in Ireland but was back looking for a club. Tim brought him to meet me at an FA Cup game against Bath. It was clear he could not train much, and could not play twice a week because of his dodgy knee but could do a job when needed, said Tim. Tim had steered me right with Pricey when I was looking for an Assistant. He knew his stuff. I had a conversation with Steve and he was keen to help and sign. I made some enquiries with people I knew. I was told he was close to a couple of the Directors including those less well inclined to me. I was also told he was looking for a manager's job really. But I was desperate. An experienced striker who could fill in as needed, maybe come off the bench, might just work, and another pair of eyes to help. I took a gamble.

As it turned out Cotts hardly played for us. I asked his opinion on things as a senior experienced player – as I did the other experienced pros. I was never frightened of other people's opinions. I even asked him to watch a game or two from the stands and come in the dressing room at halftime and have a say too, along with me. I did the same with Chris Banks, our skipper, when he was injured and had to miss a game. We were all in it together, as far as I was concerned. No-one would win unless we all won.

I looked back on these things after the event and went over them all and debated with myself what I could or should have done differently. I am more philosophical now. I played the cards as I saw them at the time. That's all I can say.

After Christmas that second season the Chairman took me aside and spoke to me about my contract. I had commented in the local paper that I knew if I didn't win promotion this second season I would be sacked. That had been the deal. He assured me I was doing well – the league table showed that – and it would not necessarily be the case that I would get sacked if we didn't win promotion. He asked what I wanted in a new contract.

I talked to some friends and went back to him on it. I didn't even ask for a raise in salary for a new two-year contract – even though I was on poor money - just a reasonable bonus if we did get promoted or had another good lucrative cup run. It was not about the money for me after all.

"I can't see any problem" he assured me and I was happy to leave it at that.

I had an enquiry from another local big club but turned them down. I was happy at Cheltenham, we were on track to win promotion and I was not getting side-tracked by anything else.

Gresley were on top of the league but couldn't get promoted because of their ground. So, second place was the one promotion place. We were third, two points behind the second placed team but had a game in hand. We were on course for promotion.

I won the Manager of the Month trophy for the League in December 1997. It was presented to me on the pitch before a game in January.

I would be sacked two weeks later.

After the event, I had a lot of friends in the game contact me with explanations or rumours about what had gone on – because on the face of it, it was strange as we were so close to promotion. I was told a lot about the late-night sessions after games in the Players Bar where certain Directors, including those who had never liked me or wanted me from the start, were in close conversation with Steve Cotterill and so on. These are the sort of rumours you always get after the event. (I might add that Cotts flatly denied being party to any such intrigue when I asked him about it later).

There was one other weird context too. We had one Director – Wayne Allen – who was a keen runner. He had barber shop in Cheltenham. Anyway, he kept on at me that it would be good for the YTSs to do a long cross country once a week and he took me over the suggested course, across Cleeve Hill, high above the racecourse on one occasion. It was not a bad idea and although I did the run with Wayne on that first occasion the idea was that he would lead them off on the run and that would give me a precious hour or two on a Tuesday morning to do some more club work – there was never enough time and I did not have enough staff. I had misgivings about it, I must say. A Director in the dressing room with the lads – not from a safeguarding point of view, there were adults around – but from what might be said. However, I let it go - and regretted it.

After a few weeks – when the training runs had been going well – there was a disagreement in the dressing room after a run and one trainee – a lad from Middlesborough called Steven Murphy – told the Director to 'fuck off'.

Wayne Allen came straight to me to complain. I said I would look into it and get back to him. I spoke to the lad in my office. 'Murph' was a good honest lad. He said there had been some criticism and banter going round and Wayne had got onto him about his running – I don't think Murph was a fan of the long runs. Anyway, it got a bit heated and Murph had told him to fuck off.

"It was just, like, dressing room stuff, Gaffer!" pleaded Murph. I knew then I should have followed my first instinct and not gone with a Director taking part of their training. I felt this was my fault.

I went back to Wayne Allen. I explained things had obviously got heated and it was dressing room banter and if you are in that then you take what comes out as long as it's not racist or whatever.

"This trainee told a Director of this club to fuck off! He should be sacked immediately!" he complained.

I said I had spoken to Murph and explained I understood the context of it. I had made it clear it was not wise, he would apologise but that was it. Wayne was still fuming.

"OK," he said through gritted teeth. "I'll remember this."

I was kicking myself about the whole thing but life went on. I was too busy to dwell on it. I had dealt with it and that was it. Or so I thought. Wayne had been a good friend to me actually – it was him that called me when the whole Karen thing was just about to hit the papers and he had invited me to stay with him and his wife straight away. I had done so for a couple of weeks and really appreciated their help. So we were quite close and I thought it would blow over.

In football there is always a next match. You live day to day. In the heat of the season it is an unforgiving schedule. We plough on.

We lost a couple of cup matches, both 1-0 as I recall – to Forest Green Rovers and then in the Trophy to Dulwich Hamlet. However, we were still on track and winning in the league and that was everyone's priority. We were now in February with only several weeks to go and we were one point off where we needed to be and we still had a game in hand.

I got a call one morning from the Chairman.
"Can you call in to my office on your way in to training?"

This in itself was not unusual. The Chairman had a factory unit at Tewkesbury and I would often call in for a coffee and a chat enroute from Hereford where I was then living in to Cheltenham.

I walked into his office. He was stood up.

"I don't know how to say this, "he started, and he looked nervous. "We had a Board meeting last night.."

Straight away, alarm bells went off for me. As mentioned, I usually attended Board meetings, so if they had met without me, it did not look good.

"..and they decided that they do not want to renew your contract next season. So, that being the case, they feel you might as well go now."

He went on about how the remainder of my contract – which was just a couple of months anyway – would of course be paid to me. (As it turned out, it wasn't and I had to take them to court to get it. The court said the contract was clear. They then bizarrely appealed and the next level court just took them apart – all just for a couple of grand! It became a bizarre scenario. Throughout which, I might add, I never went to the papers about it and kept a dignified silence publicly.)

Anyway, that was yet to come. As it was, there in the Chairman's office I was stunned but calm even if he was not.

"Well," I said. "We are on track for promotion, as agreed. And that has always been the target. We've made a lot of money from the Cup run. So it isn't for football reasons. I haven't slept with anyone's wife. So, what's the reason?"

He could not answer and could not even look me in the eye.

"I don't know what to say," he said. "It was just the majority view. I argued for you, of course." I later found out only one other Director – a real gentleman called Brian Sandland – voted for me. All the others were against me by then for whatever reasons.

As I have said, there were many theories advanced to me as to what actually happened. I never got a clear answer from the club – not even later down the road in court when they were trying to get out of paying me what they owed me. They couldn't give a straight answer to the judge even. I know some Directors just lost their nerve that close to the finish line. I know one or two never wanted me in the first place and I had upset some along the way.

In fact, the Chairman did say 'what have you done to upset Wayne Allen, by the way? He was dead against you."

This was weeks and weeks after the incident with the trainee Murphy and I had almost forgotten it. Presumably Wayne had not.

Anyway, back then in the Chairman's office the basic unpleasant arrangements were made as to when I would clear my desk and when I would give the club car back and so on. Steve Cotterill was going to take over as manager in the short term, apparently – no surprise there.

In fact when I went to the ground and got my stuff, I was driving out of the car park and met Steve walking over to the park opposite to train the YTS lads. There is a photo that I have, taken by a press photographer who was there, of me in my car talking to Cotts. He told me that he had not been involved in any discussion with Directors prior to the sacking. I walked over to say my goodbyes to the YTSs and can remember saying to a young 17-year-old Michael Duff who I had signed as a trainee and just put into the first team – "Don't let go of that shirt now!" as we shook hands. As I write this Michael has had four successful years manager of Cheltenham Town and just left for Barnsley and has had a very good playing career and is clearly going to have a good managerial one too and I am not at all surprised.

The team stuttered a bit after my sacking, losing away to Sittingbourne in the first game I think but hung on. On the last day Cheltenham Town drew away at Burton when rivals Gloucester City were playing Salisbury Town at home – a game Gloucester should have won easily. If Gloucester City had won it, as expected, they would have gone up and Cheltenham would have again missed out. As it was Gloucester inexplicably got beat at home and Cheltenham went up almost by default.

Cotts went on to have a great spell at Cheltenham Town as manager with great success and has gone on to good management work elsewhere.

Looking back on this time it is hard to really know exactly what happened of course. I have long resigned myself to accepting that I never will know the full story. I have heard and read of many different explanations or theories. It does not matter now.

I went off on holiday and tried to gather my thoughts and plan for the future. I was always reserved and limited in what I said to the media about it – I had too much respect for the supporters and players to slag anyone off publicly. I had a great response from many of the players and a lot of supporters. I had a load of letters and phone calls which were really heartening. Apparently, the Cheltenham fans were chanting 'Where's our Robbo gone?" at the next game. But matches come and go and that endless churn of the season overtakes everyone and Cheltenham Town were in the middle of a promotion race after all and you all get on with it.

I decided I wanted to keep going in football management at that stage. I was on the lookout for any suitable vacancy that came up but nothing popped up that suited at all. It was just one of those things. The season ended, time rolled on, the summer break was there and nothing came up I could go for.

I was offered the chance to buy a local club of similar size to Cheltenham Town in fact. I met a guy who had been Chairman of this club in a pub and after our discussion he nodded at his brief case and said:
"Look, I've got the controlling shares in that bag. If we can agree you can have them now."
He wanted basically nothing for them and I was tempted but the club was struggling though had great potential and I did not then have the investment it really needed, though I knew I could put some investment together if I wanted to. It was just not the right time. I passed.

In the summer I was approached by someone I knew from a smaller local club – Evesham United – and was told of their big plans to sell their ground, get a new one and really go for it. I was not sure of them but they were local, I had nothing else on the horizon and I had good mates in football asking me where was I going as they wanted to play for me or work with me.

"One thing I can promise", said the Chairman. "Once we agree a budget that is it for the season. We never go back on it."

We discussed plans to build a youth system like I had at Cheltenham Town. I decided to give it a go. That was August. The first budget cut was October. I should have left then but hung on as I had players and staff committed to me then.

We had an incredible run of injuries, including two of the three contract players we had, tying up the funding. I had never seen a run of misfortunes like it – some of the injuries were football related, some though were even work or accident related. It was just extraordinary and a continual struggle. I think we used 44 players that first season.

Overall Evesham United was not a good move for me. We managed to avoid relegation but it was a battle.

The good thing was that I managed to work with some really good people. Firstly, I got Martin Bewell, my mate from Atherstone United in as Assistant and realised I should have done that at Cheltenham Town. Then John Porter came in as physio – another great overdue decision for me. We signed some really good players like Paul West, Eric Smith, Adie Fitzhugh, Nick Birch, Jason Percival and Paul O'Brien. If we could have kept everyone fit, we would have done really well! I did set up the youth programme and got Geoff "Sammy" Salmon in from Cheltenham to run it.

But it was so uphill. The budget was so poor it was costing lads to travel and play for us. And those injuries kept coming. I was down amongst the dead men and floundering most of the time.

Then out of the blue I got a phone call that gave me the chance for a change in direction. Back in the day when I was part-time as a football manager I was also working at Co-Enterprise Birmingham (where I met Carol) helping community businesses get going and thrive. One of my main areas of work had been childcare related projects, particularly community nurseries, I had developed a simple financial management system for them and trained their staff on how to operate it. It went down well. One of the people I trained – Elaine Thomson – had then been a manager of a local community nursery in Birmingham. She was now running community childcare projects for Sheffield City Council. She phoned one day out of the blue.
"You remember that financial management training you used to do in Birmingham?"
"Yes, sure."
"Could you come and train some projects here in Sheffield in the same thing?"
I said I could. I went and did a couple. It went down well. Elaine then said the City Council wanted to contract me to deliver this training to a whole series of projects there over the next twelve months. The money was very good.
I looked at what I was doing at Evesham United. I was working with some good mates but working for people who did not keep their word. We were struggling and I was earning a pittance and still had a big family to support. It was time to man up and leave full time football and go and earn some proper money for my family.
I left Evesham United and left full-time football – for a while at least.

I had set myself a target back in early 1993 to work at being a football manager and plotted a route through non-league that would take me to a full-time job. I got there in about five years and had some wonderful times along the way. It was now 1999 and time for me to move on to the next chapter. I knew I would want to come back to full-time football at some stage – it was my real passion after all – but a path had opened up before me taking me into charity and community work. It was work I could believe in and where I could earn a good living for my family.

Looking back now, being in my eleventh year at Chelsea, having gone back into football properly in 2012, I know I would be so much a better manager now than I was then. Being a football manager was probably the most exacting and challenging job I ever had in many ways. It was a dream of a job, so engrossing and so engaging. I loved being a manager. However, at that level the financial returns in no way compensate for the raging insecurity. There were no big pay offs a la Jose Mourinho down at this level! In fact, just getting my little contract paid up for the last couple of months I was owed was a real battle, as I have said, which required me to go through two courts. Getting sacked at Cheltenham Town did break my heart to an extent. It was simply unfair. But that's football. I was at least intelligent enough to realise that this was how it was, that was the world I had worked so hard to get into.

Football is a small world. I can meet anyone who has been a pro player, scout and coach and we will have someone in common that we know at least. It is a crazy world though with its own rules and sometimes ridiculous culture. I was not finished with football. That was something I was clear about. But it was time to walk away from the full-time game for a while.

Chapter Seven – Brothers Under The Bridge

If I meet someone and they speak to me I look them in the eye and answer politely. That is what I was brought up to do. If that someone is sitting in a doorway, evidently begging, then that does not change that basic requirement of good manners. If I have money to spare, I give it to them. I do not really do it for them but for me, to be honest. I have learnt that giving is good for my soul, good for how I feel about myself and the world. I actually feel a bit grateful to them, in fact, because they have given me that chance to be a little generous. I don't question or even consider what they might do with the money – no-one asks me what I am going to do with the money when I get it in the first place. I just feel it's not for me to judge them.

Now I don't say that is what you should do. Again, it's not for me to tell anyone what to do. I am not preaching here. I have adopted this attitude because of what I was taught was good manners as a child in the first place and then what I learnt in my years working in the homeless world. I met real people, with real lives and got to feel that over all everyone I met who was homeless, including those on the streets, had their own stories, their backgrounds and their pathway just like you and me. They did not deserve any less than you and me in terms of politeness and that starting point of an open hand and open mind.

I found my way into the homeless world by good luck, as it happens. That old Robinson luck. And, yes, of course, like everyone, I have found the harder I worked, the luckier I got.

I enjoyed going back to Sheffield and working for the excellent City Council there. I worked with people running nurseries, childcare cooperatives and community projects and tried to be of use. It was good to see the City again where I had spent such happy times as a student. It's a fine city – big enough to have a variety of shops and places and yet small enough for you to be out of it and in some really good countryside of the Pennines or Dales in no time at all.

I saw in a newspaper that the Central London TEC – which was called 'Focus' – were advertising contracts to support childcare projects so I applied and got a contract there too. I had a good little consultancy business going in no time at all, with minimal overheads and doing good useful work. It soon became apparent there was a lot of work for me back down in London.

Initially I worked on childcare projects. There was a new funding programme out and projects were being assessed as to whether they could qualify to provide nursery places and so on. The work I had done back in Birmingham and then in Sheffield got me the gig. Then I was told there was a partnership of homeless projects coming together to make a joint bid for training and employment funding. Would I be interested in helping get the partnership going and help develop the partnership into an independent charity?

There was enough work in London stretching forward now that it was worth us renting a house and we moved to Sudbury Hill near Harrow for a year.

The homeless project fascinated me and I began on a steep learning curve about the homeless scene. It was actually very competitive as the way funding worked it usually meant the providers were competing against each other for money. So the prospect of trying to get them all to work together and to try and connect up training and employment services to make it something like a seamless service was quite a challenge. The big providers like Centrepoint, St Mungo's and so on were on board. Or in theory they were at least.

As I began to get out around the homeless providers and started to get to know the day centres, the hostels and the training centres the issues became a lot clearer. Firstly, I learnt that every homeless person is an individual with their own story. There were patterns –

a lot of homeless people were ex-service people with drinking issues, for example – but each person in a doorway, or a hostel bed or visiting a day centre trying to get some food and get warm had their own story. Secondly, all the issues were joined up in those individuals – they were a mix of personal issues, mental health, drugs and alcohol, unemployment, no housing and all sorts of other things. It was just their lives where many of these elements came together and ebbed and flowed. However, the provision of services to help with all these issues and the funding behind them, were not joined up. Project A got Funding B to provide Service C but not services D. E or F. For the homeless person, their needs around C, D, E and F were just their mixed up, often chaotic lives. Where training and employment were concerned, the project was trying to bring things together and then 'hide the wiring' managing the funding and the reporting requirements and all that bureaucratic stuff.

I began to try and avoid the childcare work because I was so engaged with this homeless partnership idea. There were two great talented young people working on the project too – Carole Coulon, a lovely French young woman who was a whizz with the contract details and monitoring stuff – an absolute key to providing funded projects, and Vince Murphy, a clever sharp creative young guy from a working-class background in Camden Town who worked on the partnership stuff. We were advised and guided by clever experienced funding people like Linda Butcher and John Raynes from the TEC.

We worked well. When the charity was established and ready to launch the new Trustees asked if I wanted to be the first CEO – an easy decision. Carole and Vince came on board too and we set sail. The charity was called 'Off The Streets And Into Work' or 'OSW'.

As I went out and about the centre of London meeting with the key players in the London Homeless scene- people like Victor Adebowale at Centrepoint, Colin Glover at London Connection,

Charles Fraser at St Mungo's, Mick Clarke at the De Paul Trust and so on, I was on a steep learning curve.

In every town or city there is a homeless scene or circuit featuring hostels, rough sleeping areas, day centres and so on. In a big city like London then, in the late nineties and early noughties there were various circuits. When I listened to people who were rough sleeping many explained that the hostels were often dangerous places and they actually felt safer on the streets. Some of the old hostels were dismal and gloomy places but they were being improved.

I got to known a guy called Brian who then was in his early forties. He was a well built guy with dark hair and a beard who had been in the army and had had his issues with alcohol along the way. He was sleeping 'at the BP' which meant in the walkways near the BP Offices near Waterloo which was something of a community. He got connected up by an outreach worker to one of our training programmes and I sat talking at a day centre over a cup of tea. He had a family, two daughters and a wife. Where are they? I asked.
"Don't know. Back in Dunstable, last I heard," he said, looking down at his tea on the formica topped table in the noisy, lively day centre near Trafalgar Square.
"When did you last see them?"
He sighed and looked away across the busy day centre.
"About three years ago." He shrugged then looked at me." They are better off without me, mate. The drink.."
There was a world of stories in that shrug, those words.
He didn't care much for the hostels on offer.
"Full of nutters," he said, "nothing's safe there. Better off at the BP. I know people there, see? We look out for each other."
I looked out the window, high up on the wall. It was pouring down outside and it was cold. It must be bloody rough in those hostels to be worse than outside, even in the walkways and passages near Waterloo.

The project got Brian into a flat after a few weeks. I kept in touch with the key worker. It felt great to think we had assisted a bit with someone getting on with their life and getting things back together. A few weeks later I heard Brian had only lasted a week in the flat and some time later I was at another day centre for a meeting and in the café area I saw Brian sat with some others waiting on lunch time.

I went over.

"How you doing?" I asked.

"Hello, mate!" he said cheerily enough." I'm all right, how about you?"

We talked a while. His companions drifted off.

"So, what happened with the flat?" I asked.

Again, that shrug.

"Oh, I don't know, I just couldn't hack it, mate. I didn't know what I was supposed to do. Just…..didn't know.."

"Where are you now?"

"Back at the BP," he said with a grin.

We said our goodbyes after a while and I went off. Brian was on my mind. He was clearly drinking still. Back on the streets. A lifetime of dependency and institutional life in the army plus his demons made it hard to cope. So the cold, echoing passage ways were better than a flat.

Though Brian and many others I learned that we can help and we can make a difference but usually these real lives lived by real people are multi-layered and there is not just one switch that needs throwing.

Further on down the road, I was speaking at a meeting and after someone came up and introduced themselves to me. It was Brian's key worker from a year or so before.

"I remember you took an interest in Brian and he always spoke well of you, "the guy, a slim bearded guy in his thirties from the Midlands, said. 'Just thought you'd like to know. Don't know if you'd heard?"

"What – about Brian? No."

"Oh, he died. Got some sort of liver failure and was gone. All really quick, a couple of weeks."
"Shit," I said, "that's awful".
The guy turned to walk away.
I called after him.
"Hey – did his family come and see him? His wife and daughters?"
'No. There wasn't time really, I don't think. I don't think he wanted them to know anyway."
"Did they go to his funeral?"
"No, there wasn't one." He walked away.

In summer of 2000, not long before I left Off the Streets, I discovered a scheme which offers you a paid trip to just about anywhere in the world for free. I think I read about it in a paper, maybe even 'The Big Issue'. I had never heard of it before. I sent off for the application form, filled it out and sent it off – and forgot about it.

The Churchill Fellowships -, as it is now called - were set up after old Winston's death and each year awards about 150 grants to people who come up with some travel idea that captures their imagination. It can be just about anything but often work related. My proposal was to travel round the United States visiting homeless projects to see if anyone else did what we were trying to do in Off the Streets and bring providers together to create a pathway to training and jobs for homeless people. However, really it was just an excuse to get to travel a bit in the States.

The Churchill aspect was quite ironic, as it happens. Although most often recalled as the war time leader, his history in the dock communities goes further back. In 1911 he was the Secretary of the Board of Trade when there was dock strike on and sent a navy gunboat down the Thames with its guns trained on the dockers family homes in Wapping in an attempt to pressurise them back to work. It didn't work. However, Churchill's name was mud.

So, I was amused at the irony of it – me applying for something developed in the old bastard's name.

When I got a letter inviting me for an interview, I could not even remember what I had applied to do but managed to recreate the idea. Anyway, I jumped through the hoops and got the gig. They would pay all my travel and living costs for a three-week trip to the States. The money was good enough that it meant my wife could fly out for a few days at the end to join me in New York. The thing about homelessness was it exists in just about every city. I was spoilt for choice.

I mapped out my journey. I wanted to try different modes of travel too if I could. I would go to New York for a week, then get a greyhound bus down through New Jersey to Cape May and have a couple of days there on the coast. Then I would get a ferry across the Delaware Bay to Lewes in Delaware. Then, according to the thick paperback travel book I was working off (this was pre-internet) if I walked up to the Ace Hardware Store, I could catch a bus to Washington DC.

In DC I was going to talk at a homeless conference but then I would fly, via Chicago to Memphis – I wanted to see Elvis' Graceland and walk down Beale Street and so on. Then I would fly to LA and hire a car to drive to San Diego then back to LA. Finally, a plane back across the States for a final few days in New York before flying home.

What a trip - and all paid for! I did visit some homeless projects along the way and wrote a report at the end but it was really for me a journey I had been wanting to do since I was a teenage reading Kerouac and Kesey.

I had been to New York once before but not for long. It was as ever just as it seems in the movies and on TV. It was so familiar a landscape for anyone growing up in the TV and cinema generation of the fifties and onwards in the UK.

The blue and white police cars, the yellow cabs, the steam rising from the vents on the street. It was summer when I was there and I walked down the Hudson River one evening and watched the 4th July fireworks display. They were so much more impressive than the little sparklers I had been used to back in the UK. If these were fireworks, I can remember thinking, what had we all been watching for years?

I did learn about the many homeless people who had been living in the subway tunnels and met a guy who had done that. I crossed over on the Staten Island ferry. I visited the World Trade Centre too, having a coffee in a bookstore at the foot of one of these, just down from where I was staying in Washington Square – just over a year before they would be brought crashing down.

Then I went down to the Port Authority building and caught the Greyhound Bus down to Cape May in New Jersey, right at the southern tip. The bus took me along the Jersey shore towns so familiar to me from the songs of my hero Springsteen – Asbury Park, Atlantic City and so on. Cape May was a lovely sea side town and I stayed in a beautiful old tall clapboard house B&B. After a couple of days I took the ferry across Delaware Bay, made my way up through Lewes and found the Ace Hardware Store on the edge of town.

I stood and waited, doubting now the information in the travel guide that had become my bible. However, just a couple of minutes late, suddenly the bus appeared and I was on my way to Washington DC.

The conference was good, I met some fine people from the homeless sector there, and made a bit of a rabble rousing speech as

I tended to do which seemed to ignite a bit. Still flying the flag, as ever. The red flag, that is.

Then I flew off to Chicago and then on down to Memphis, Tennessee.

My Mum and I loved Chuck Berry and 'Memphis, Tennessee' was a favourite so I just had to go. When you add in Elvis, Sun Records and the Blues then it was a must.

I flew into Memphis on a very hot, humid July afternoon. As we drove to the motel, I had booked I asked the taxi driver why there was no-one about on the streets. He was a mixed race, surly dumpy guy with a greasy complexion and a very miserable air about him. "Because it's only tourists stupid enough to come out in this heat," he growled. Fair enough.

The motel was on two floors with an iron staircase linking the two floors at either end of a long open corridor past all the flimsy room doors. It was a typical low rent American road motel.

I went downtown. There was a tense air of imminent violence everywhere. I had not experienced anything like it anywhere (I later would in Johannesburg). Maybe it was just me, feeling alone and nervous. I don't know but I was spooked.

That night in the poky motel room I watched some TV then turned in. I could not sleep. Every now and then there was someone climbing up the iron stairs and walking slowly along the corridor outside. It was nerve-wracking in the humid night waiting to see if the footsteps would halt outside my flimsy door. I hardly slept at all.

Funnily enough next day I discovered it was the armed security guard who would make regular patrols through the night that had been clumping along keeping me nervously awake all night!

I went down to Beale Street and ate in BB Kings Blues Bar – some rather good BBQ ribs, as I recall – but again was too nervy to stay out late and was back in the poky motel before 9pm. The next day was a Sunday and I read in the local paper that Al Green, the soul singer – actually the Reverend Al Green now - was scheduled to be preaching at a church in Memphis. To my eternal regret I chickened out of going.

I decided to rent a car and get out of the city for a bit. I drove over the Mississippi – it was a thrill to see it and I was amazed by how wide it was that far inland – and into Arkansas. I was heading on Highway 40 through Shell Lake towards Little Rock. I decide to take a detour inland and see a bit of the beautiful lush Arkansas countryside. It was lovely, dirt roads, little towns with town squares and fine looking farming land. I stopped at a roadside stall and bought two huge peaches.

As I drove along, I ate the excellent peaches then decided to work my way back towards Memphis. Somewhere near west Memphis two things happened simultaneously. Firstly, the peaches began to have a dramatic effect on my stomach. Secondly, I got caught up in a huge static traffic jam. I was absolutely jammed in and absolutely desperate to go to the toilet. I began looking around frantically – was there somewhere off the road I could dash to with some handy bushes? No, there wasn't and what's more I was jammed into the middle lane and could not move – I could hardly abandon the car there. I even began to search the car for something to empty my stomach into. There was the paper bag the peaches had been in but I didn't think that would hold. I was frantic. There was a plastic shopping bag – could that work? As I searched around, I noticed two young guys in the next car laughing at me – was it that obvious? My stomach boiled and growled. Any moment there would be a dramatic and very unpleasant explosion in my trouser area.

Then suddenly the traffic began to move. There was a slip road. I took it. There was a petrol station. I stopped, flung open the car door and sprinted to the toilet along the side of the building. It was a dirty smelly toilet but I did not care. I sat down, the world fell out of my bottom and I have never, ever felt so relieved.

Somewhat pale and chastened, I made my way back to the Motel and slipped quietly into my room and lay on the bed and slept for six hours straight.

So I did not make the best of Memphis. I loved Graceland and Sun Studios and the Memphis food but there was a lot I did not see and I never got the feel of the place.

Next stop was LA, a city I had been to before and really liked. I picked a car up at LAX and drove south down Highway 5 to San Diego, stopping at Laguna beach and La Jolla along the way. I stayed at a hotel in the Hotel Circle in Mission Bay and found San Diego a lovely city in the sun. There were great beaches, a pleasant downtown, good shops and Mexico just down the road. I went to a homeless people's event – a 'cook out' for ex-Vets in Barboa Park set up just like an army field kitchen and enjoyed that.

After a couple of days, I drove back up to Los Angeles and stayed in one of my favourite hotels in the world – the Angeleno, on the crossroads of Santa Monica and Beverley Hills just on Highway 405 in Sepulveda Canyon. I loved Santa Monica - I knew then I could live there for sure – and along the coast but I also liked Beverley Hills, Brentwood and Hollywood. I certainly did get a feel for LA and have enjoyed every visit there.

Soon I was flying back to New York and a few days with my wife there doing the tourist stuff. It was a great trip, a great experience overall.

If you want a travel adventure – and fancy getting someone else to pay for it. I recommend the Churchill Fellowship to you. In the year I got one, when I went to the Awards ceremony, I read that someone else had travelled the Silk Road as they were into textiles and fashion. Someone else was scuba diving of the Great Barrier Reef.

Thank you, Winston!

For all the bleakness we came across from time to time, we did well with Off the Streets. We learned how to write really good funding bids and brought several millions of funding from funds like the European Social Fund into the sector. We put over 1000 people into jobs in our first three years and many thousands into training schemes. It was good work and an honour to be part of. After a while I felt that Carole and Vince - and our growing team then of around ten people by then – didn't really need me around anymore. I had done what I set out to do, what I was asked to do and got the charity set up and got the partnership working. It was time to move on.

I felt like I had paid a bit of a debt off. I had been very aware of those days as a young kid when me and my family were homeless and I felt my Mum in particular would be pleased I had gone back to try and help.

I started looking round for a new challenge. I applied for one job but didn't get it but the recruitment agency involved – Odgers – seemed to like me. The consultant involved, Frances Bell, a tall elegant smart woman, took me under her wing. Over the forthcoming years Frances would put me into my next three jobs. The pattern was she would take me out to lunch and ask what I wanted to do next. I would have some half-arsed idea. Months later she would call and say "I've got something for you" and that was it. She did very well for me but given what they charged the companies they worked for, I guess I did okay for them too. Nevertheless, Frances was a good friend and guide.

She put me forward for a role as Chief Executive of a children's hospice based in Surrey called CHASE. They were just about to open a state-of-the-art new children's hospice called, coincidentally, 'Christopher's' near Godalming. I got the gig. I wanted to work in an operational charity, not only raising the money as I had at 'Off the Streets' but seeing through the delivery. The Children's Hospice movement was just moving from the phase of initial founder-based charities into a more professionally managed grown up service. People like me at CHASE, my mate Ted Gladdish at Demelza House in Kent and David Strudley at Naomi House and then Acorns, were the new wave of managers, I guess.

For those of you who have not been to a Children's Hospice you might have a dismal image of somewhere children go to die. In one sense of course that is true as the children looked after in such places are all having limited life range. However, they are places of life, places of play and fun, all dedicated to making the most of the often too short time that is left to children and their families and supporting everybody concerned up to and beyond the invariably inevitable death of that child.

My first week at CHASE coincided with the opening of 'Christopher's' so I soon learnt my way round as I was doing guided tours for the public all day every day for that first week. Then we got down to delivering the service we were there for.

We had a great team and a mass of volunteers too. There was such a lot of goodwill around for a children's hospice service. I used to say to our fundraising team – 'if we can't raise money for these dying kids then we should pack up and go home'. A tough message perhaps but it focused the mind.

The first child to die on Christopher's was a lovely lad from Camberley called Matthew Aston. Matthew was watching football on TV one day at home – he and all his family were big Chelsea fans, as it happens – and he said to his Mum, Tina – "there's something wrong with the tele, Mum". But there wasn't. There was something wrong with Matthew. It turned out he had a brain stem tumour. A couple of months later he and his family are with us in Christopher's having been released from the hospital to us because there was nothing else they could do.

I was actually out in London, walking in Covent Garden with a couple of my kids, having a day off when I got a call from work. It was the excellent Director of Care, Bridget Turner.
"We have this family in with their son, Matthew." She explained the situation. Matthew did not have long. All the family were staying with us and our team were supporting them and doing what was needed to make Matthew as comfortable as possible.
"We asked them if there was anything they wanted desperately to do," said Bridget. "You know some people at Chelsea, don't you?"
"Yes," I said warily.
"They want Matthew to meet Gianfranco Zola. He is his hero."
A crazy idea. It was mid-season. How could we possibly do that?
Two days later a very nervous Gianfranco came to visit Matthew. Matthew's room had Chelsea flags and pictures all round. The whole family were there. Matthew was heavily sedated by then but seemed to come round when Gianfranco sat on his bed and held his hand.
"When you get better, you come to training with me," said Gianfranco. He knew Matthew would not get better. Maybe Matthew did too because he was getting tired and it was time for Gianfranco to go but Matthew would not let go of his hand. Everyone was in bits.

Matthew died two days later. Gianfranco was a real gentleman throughout, an absolute star who stayed in touch with the family.

A week or so later I went to Stamford Bridge to watch Chelsea play Norwich. It was a night match. In the closing minutes Gianfranco scored a marvellous goal, backheeling in a Graeme Le Saux corner. As he left the field, he was interviewed by Sky Sports.

"Was that the best goal you have ever scored, Franco?" he was asked, live on TV, in the tunnel as he came off the pitch.

"I don't know, "he said, "but I dedicate it to the memory of Matthew Aston, a boy who just died in Christopher's children's hospice."

Social media went crazy.

My phone went as I left the ground, pushing through the crowds on Fulham Road. It was one of my sons.
"You seen Sky Sports?"
"No, I was at the game, just leaving. What a goal!"
He told me what happened.

We got people donating from all over. Gianfranco put us on the map. Matthew's lovely Mum, Tina, stayed in touch and years later came to work for us at CHASE as a fundraiser and we are still in touch to this day.

I couldn't help in terms of nursing or medical services. I wasn't a play therapist or a family support worker. I couldn't even cook for the families and provide for them in that way when they were staying in the beautiful hospices, or fix the heating system if it went wrong. My way of contributing was to manage the charities as efficiently as I could to make the best of what we had available and, in particular, to help raise money to support these families through their difficult journeys.

I used the public speaking skills I'd learnt in the labour movement and tried to move people to raise money for the children's hospices. In all honestly it was not usually a difficult case to make because every day I was surrounded by stories that would break your heart. I would go around to supporter groups or to business groups or big charity events and sing for my supper in the sense of at some point standing up and trying to paint these pictures and turn emotion into money.

I remember at one cheese and wine event at Godalming, which was very well attended, the woman who was running the event introduced me by saying "and now I want to introduce the only man other than my husband who can make me cry". I walked up to the front of the room just trying to process that a bit and I recall being very aware of a rather stony stare from the husband in question.

There were some wonderful Gala Nights or charity balls. These could be wonderful events from masked balls in the Royal Courts in London to a series of wonderful summer nights at the home of our supporters like Grant Bovey and Anthea Turner, where the road leading through their beautiful country estate to this huge marquee was lit by flaming torches till you met the valet parking outside the magical setting. We made a lot of money at such events.

I can remember Grant saying to me one year that he had the idea of auctioning one thousand pounds in cash. I felt this was a daft idea and told him so but he said "no just trust me, it will work".

The auctioneer on the night was Chris Tarrant and he did very well. A woman bought the thousand pounds in cash for £1250 on her credit card. Chris Tarrant got the woman up on stage and said "I have to ask you, tell me why have you just paid twelve hundred and fifty pounds for a thousand pounds in cash?" The woman just shrugged and said "it saves me going to the cash machine." Hey-ho. It was all about getting the right audience and getting them wanting to impress each other after a few glasses of champagne.

At one such event we were sharing the proceeds with another wonderful charity called Debra. Their patron who was speaking on their behalf that night was Michael Portillo, the former MP. Now I, along with thousands of others, had enjoyed the news at the previous general election when he had lost his seat so you could comfortably say I was not a fan. However, I must say he did very well on that night and from a professional point of view I very much appreciated his speech which painted a wonderful picture of the possibility that they could find a cure to the particular awful skin condition that his charity was concerned with. Basically, Portillo had a message that with one more push the cure for this awful condition could be found. It was a wonderful uplifting and positive message and I had to follow it.

As I made my way to the stage to make my speech, I really did not know how to paint a positive picture for my charity after that and as I walked up it was this very fact that came to my mind and I knew I had to make a virtue of that difficulty. I trusted my instinct from street corner speeches.

"I can't offer you any happy endings", I said. And I had them then in my hand.

I went onto tell some of the stories of the children and families that we worked with and you could have heard a pin drop. I am under no illusion that it was any wonderful oratory from me that worked the magic that night, but rather the power and emotion of the stories of children taken too soon and their families that lived through and beyond that experience that held the crowd that night and on many other nights.

I was proud to work in such an environment. We were able to do things for the families that our colleagues in the NHS could not do. I remember, for example, just before I left the Children's Hospice world to go back full time into football I was at young adults' Hospice we ran near Winchester. We got a call from the local NHS about a young woman aged nineteen who was within the last couple of days of her life. She had a brain tumour and as ever the NHS do not give up until the very end. But they had contacted us and said there was nothing more they could do so we took the young lady and her family in and tried to look after them and help them for the few days that were left.

Close family and friends came to say their goodbyes. However, the family said that there was one visitor in particular that they knew the young lady would most want to see and who hadn't been able to see her in hospital. It was her dog. He was a border collie and her devoted friend.

We said of course we can do that. They bought the dog to the hospice and into the room. The young lady was drifting in and out of consciousness at this stage and surrounded by her family. Her Dad said the dog usually slept on her bed. We said that was fine. The dog got up on the bed and lay down beside his owner. The young lady woke up, saw her dog, reached out and put her hand on the dog's head and smiled, and they lay together.

The young lady died later that night.

The children's hospice world allowed me to get involved in all sorts of events including crazy challenges home and abroad – like trekking up to Everest Base Camp which was really tough, the London Marathon and bizarrely cycling from Saigon in Vietnam up through the Mekong delta to Angkor Wat in Cambodia with my mates Tim Lee and Michael Morgan.

I think of all the challenges Everest Base Camp was the toughest. I had done the London Marathon in the April of 2004, turned fifty in the May and we were set to go to Everest in the October. So, I was pretty fit. I was going to do the Challenge with my great mate, Bill Davis, who was HR Director at CHASE. We flew to Kathmandu, the capital of Nepal and the stopping off place for the Himalayas. It was a long flight and we were tired and we knew we had to fly on up to Lukla, right up in the mountains at the foot of the Khumbu Glacier, the highest glacier, which would lead us to Everest. But we decided we would take this chance to get out and see a bit of Kathmandu.

I am so glad we did. It was really my first sight of an Asian city and I loved it. The colour, the noise, the drama on every street corner with monkeys on the roofs, the occasional working elephant on the street and the traffic, sounds and smells of this exotic city. We found our way to the Ghats or cremation sites on the river and watched the body of a member of the royal family, wrapped in white sheets, being ceremoniously burned.

We wandered through the old hippy streets with the colourful shops leading to Durbar Square. How I would have loved to have been there back in the day. It was fascinating as it was, to be fair with the tourists, the bustle of local life and the old Sadhus, the wandering holy men with their long matted hair and dusty saffron robes, who have renounced their worldly lives and families and lead a life of celibacy, meditation, the search for enlightenment and yoga.

I had my camera out and was taking pictures everywhere I looked. There was one striking sadhu standing majestically in the square, tall and wild eyed. He saw me watching him, I gestured down towards my camera and then at him. He nodded, I approached closer. He reached out towards the camera. I was unsure what to do. This guy was big and wild looking.
I handed him the camera. He looked it over then handed it back.
"Good lenses those Minoltas, aren't they?" he said in faultless English.

The group of about a dozen trekkers gathered together at the airport the next day to fly up to Lukla. Our guide told us we would be flying with a local airline called Yeti Airlines. We walked out onto the tarmac with our bags. The plane was tiny. It took about ten people at a go. We strapped ourselves in and off we went.

Lukla Airport – actually known as Tenzing-Hillary Airport - is one of the most dangerous and extreme in the world. In fact for twenty years, it was rated the most dangerous airport in the world by the History Channel. It is cut into the side of the mountain with a dramatic drop off at the end of the short 527 metre runway up at just under 10,000 feet. As you approach it you seem just to be flying into the side of the mountain and it's only at the last minute that the runway appears, looking like a driveway outside a house rather than a proper airport runway. When you leave you just seen to drop off the side of the mountain.

As soon as we stepped, gratefully, out of the little rickety airplane we noticed it was difficult to breathe. The air was really thin and our breath seemed to catch in our throats and we were always panting. This was only the start. Over the next eight days we had a further 8000 feet to climb up as we progressed along the glacier to Base Camp.

We had a gang of hardy, cheery sherpas to guide us up and the luggage was loaded onto yaks – big hairy lumbering beasts. The sherpas were very impressive – wiry, smiling, fit as fuck. A couple of them would go ahead and set our tents up for us each day. When they learnt one of us had a birthday coming up, one of them ran back to Lukla, got a birthday cake, and ran back to us – all this while we could hardly put one foot in front of another. They had a terrible sense of humour – when they found out we were game for a laugh they were up to all sorts – putting stones in our day packs, hiding boot laces and so on. I must say we gave as good as we got.

We were just about the last trek to go up that year as winter was coming. It was bright and sunny virtually every day giving us incredible clear views but it was seriously cold at nights, getting down to minus 10 and eventually minus twenty at night when we were camping.

The Himalayas were so stunning. Our path along the valley to the glacier going higher and higher took us around the lovely Ama Dhablam mountain – 'the mother's arms' as it had two sort of side wings that looked like open arms. We made it up to Namche Bazaar. The last town n we would go through and the trading hub of the Khumbu region. It was there up at the museum which was in Sir Edmund Hillary's old house looking along the valley that we got our first sight of Mount Everest.

Namche Bazaar was great. A lively little town with tea houses and cafes – it even had an Irish pub, allegedly the highest Irish pub in the world. It had shops selling climbing and trekking gear – invariably knock offs brought over by Chinese traders apparently. I bought a 'North Face' wind jacket here for about a fiver.

Sadly, the knock-off jacket was not the only thing I picked up in Namche Bazaar. I woke up in the night needing to get out the tent urgently – no easy task given the layers and sleeping back and so on – and it was soon apparent something was very wrong with my stomach. We had a Nepalese doctor join the team and he and the Head Sherpa stood over me as I sat on a rock by the tents in the morning, grey faced and wrung out.
"Food poisoning," the Doctor said. He was a nice young lad, we called him "Doctor Diamox' because he was forever doling out the Diamox anti-attitude sickness pills for us. The Doc and the Head Sherpa conferred.
"OK," the Doc said at length, crouching down next to me." You have two choices. We can't get a medivac helicopter up so you either stay here and wait for us to come back down or you come with us."
"I'll keep going," I said, not fancying sitting there on my own for ten days or so.

I had often wondered what I would be like faced with danger of real physical challenge. When it came in the form of food poisoning and days and days of very tough trekking, I felt like I had no choice. I was completely washed out, barely able to eat anything other than plain rice, exhausted. But I just kept going, one foot in front of the other. I noticed the Head Sherpa was never far away, keeping an eye on me. So many times, at first, I was just picking the spot by the side of the track where I would fall when I collapsed – which I expected to do any step - trying to ensure I would not tumble over the edge if I did collapse, but I just kept going. There were no glamorous moments of bravery. I had no choice, keep going or be left behind.

At the end of that first day out from Namche Bazaar we were aiming for Tengboche Buddhist Monastery, an impressive place built in 1916 and destroyed a couple of times by earthquake and fire – but rebuilt each time. I can remember trudging round the corner and there it finally was. I was so pleased to see it. I did collapse then, falling onto a bench outside the monastery. After a bit I recovered enough to go inside to the cool dusty interior with the smell of old incense.

Each day I got a bit stronger, encouraged and supported by Bill and the other trekkers, and the Sherpas too. Up and up we went, above the tree line. We visited the ghostly graveyard with its fluttering prayer flags as we approached Everest – an eerie place.

Then we were clambering cross the glacier – which was a jumble of black ice blocks. Some were the size of cricket balls, some the size of cars, all in a mix. The air was so thin, it was so tough, but the Doc's Diamox got us all up there. Finally, we were there at the head of the glacier, underneath Everest and you could see the pathway over the other side of the glacier up to the higher reaches of Everest. We had reached Base Camp.

This was where the teams going all the way up Everest would gather, particularly in April and May, and prepare for the last climb. I don't know quite what I expected but I did expect a flatter area where you could envisage tents being pitched not this crazy jumble of huge black ice blocks and boulders.

We hugged each other. The Head Sherpa came over and lifted me in a big bear hug.

"You big man," he said in my ear, and I felt honoured.

Going down was much easier and only took about four days. What with the exercise and the food poisoning I had lost a stone and had a dark beard. When we finally came out of arrivals in Heathrow, Keir and Oscar, aged about six and four then, didn't recognise me.

The Everest Base camp trek was a fantastic if gruelling challenge. I could not have picked a better mate to walk beside all the way, and share a tent with in those freezing temperatures and face those challenges with than Bill Davis. He was good humoured, supportive and a joy to be with throughout.

I loved the Himalayas and promised myself one day I would visit them again. I loved Kathmandu too – it's life and colour, sounds and smells. I knew I would go back to Asia again.

The Sherpas were very impressive too. On the last night we all sat round a camp fire at Lukla and they sang their folk songs and entertained us, telling the stories in the songs and the places they referred to. It came time for us to sing something. We just could not think of anything. We sang 'American Pie' the old Don McLean song in the end but it felt so lame after their display of heritage. We all gave them a load of our trekking gear and they seemed to really appreciate that.

I did these challenges to raise money for the children's hospice and to lead by example. We did raise a lot of money. But to be honest, the main reason was to test myself, to travel, to meet physical challenges and to see what I learned about myself.

One evening on the Everest trail the Sherpas had said that the next day we had a choice of two routes for our day's trekking. A shorter quicker route which was a tougher climb or an easier longer route. A group of the younger fitter guys came over to where me, Bill, our mate Bob Watts and a couple of the other 'oldies' sat. The younger athletic guys wanted the shorter harder route and generally the older trekkers wanted the steadier option.

"We've been talking about this, "one of the young guys said. "We all reckon we'll leave it to you, Chris. You decide."
I had recovered from the food poisoning by then so couldn't see why they would ask me. They went back to their tents.
"Why am I deciding?" I asked Bill and Bob.
They both smiled at me.
"Because you are the leader," they said. "Though you don't realise it."

I was honoured and more than a little taken aback.

Some of these events did show my competitive side, though.

From his game you can tell his character, what interests him, what he fixates on and his motivation. I remember reading Malcolm X's fine autobiography and he said there that you can tell if a woman would be good in bed by the way she dances. After a lifetime study I am not sure if I agree with him or not.

But I do think you can tell a lot about people by the way they play whatever games they do play or actually will not play. Funnily enough I do not like to join in with the parlour games when there are family or friends' gatherings. You know that dreaded point when someone says "lets play a game!" and people squeal and clap their hands and say 'Oh yes!'. Whereas inside I am saying, "Fuck, no.."

I have become quite notorious amongst friends for not taking part. I usually say, "no, you all play, I'll watch."

I wonder what this says about me.

There are two reasons I demur from the games. Firstly, I find a lot of them mind-numbingly boring. I can't help that. Some years ago, I resolved I would not do something just because other people wanted me to. It gives me a sense of enormous well-being, as Blur would say.

Secondly though, is a deeper darker reason. I am too competitive. I hate losing. Knowing this and knowing this Mr Jekyll will appear at some stage with a surly snarl, I would rather not engage and thus not embarrass myself or kill the party vibe. Shouting "that's not fucking right!" has, I have found, not usually added to the joie-de-vivre of the evening's social family gathering. It is not good.

Let me give an example. For the last twenty five years or so I have split my working life between spells full time in football and spells working for charities, mostly children's charities. When CEO at CHASE I persuaded a group of family and friends to take part in a 'Dragon Boat Race' as part of `Marlow Regatta one summer. It was a fun, money-raising thing, a lovely family day, nothing serious. Except to me, of course.
I think you needed a team of eight rowers and there were a lot of races. So once I agreed to take part I worked out you really needed a squad of nine so that you could rest one rower per race and pace yourselves through the day. I put a good strong team together. Whilst none of us had ever done a dragon boat race before, we had some fit lads. My three eldest sons, all tall and sporty were in, some good mates and a few 'ringers' who just happened to be top athletes of one sort or another. (In another later dragon boat race, I enlisted a good friend who just happened to be an Olympic medal winning rower. Competitive? Moi?)

Now we had a squad of nine then at Marlow, as I say, for the eight - man races. As it happened, there was another boat racing for the same charity, led by a vicar, funnily enough. Just before the first race the vicar came over to me. Now, please bear in mind, I may be the CEO of this charity, and this was indeed a fun family event, but at that moment, I am in the zone. We have just had a team briefing from the ex-Marine boat specialist who was going to be our cox and he did know what he was doing. I was focusing on what he had said we had to do.

Over comes the vicar.
"I say," he said to me with a cheery smile, "we're a man short on our team and I understand you have one extra. Could we borrow a man?"
"Fuck off," I growled and got into our boat.

Now, I am not proud of this story. I repeat it here somewhat shamefaced. However, I think it paints the picture.

We got to do some glitzy things. Grant and Anthea's summer balls were spectacular. They really worked hard and roped in their friends like Max Clifford – who I have to say was a great supporter of CHASE – and through him Simon Cowell and so on. We auctioned off a flat in Docklands one year and Simon Cowell and his brother were competing against each other in bidding for this apartment and right at the death a property developer there nipped in and got it. £138,000. On a night out.

Uri Geller was there one year and put up some lovely jewellery he had designed for auction. As it happened my best mate Tim Lee bought it. It cost a fortune so I felt I should try and add something. I asked Tim and his lovely wife, Lucy, both dear friends, if they would like to meet Uri. We walked round to the table where he was sitting.
"Uri, this is the couple who bought your jewellery."
He got up and was friendly and enthusiastic.
"Let me introduce you to the person who actually made the piece,' he said and graciously did so as we stood by their table.
"Let me do something else for you," he said, looking round. He grabbed a heavy spoon from a random coffee cup. He held up in

front of us and before our eyes, lightly rubbed the stem and the bloody spoon bent over like it was plasticine. He gave it to Lucy with a laugh.
I don't know how he did it. I'm just telling you what he did.

We had royal visits too. Sophie, then Countess of Wessex, came round for a formal visit. There were a lot of media there. She and I went into the Butterfly Suite – which was the suite of two rooms where the children's bodies lay after they died so family could visit and so on. It was always a moving thing to see and I explained how the rooms were used, how we would decorate the rooms how the families wanted and play whatever music they wanted and so on. I told Sophie how one Mum just wanted to lay here a while with her two year old daughter who had just died.

Sophie had tears in her eyes. She dabbed at her face with a tissue and turned to me as we got ready to go back out to the media.
"Do I look OK?" she asked as she stood in front of me.
"You look fine," I said with a smile.
"Oh," she said.

I got on well with Sophie. She agreed to become our Royal Patron. She invited me for tea at Bagshot Park where she and Edward lived. She would support our events – she came to one of Grant and Anthea's grand events as I recall too. Later I was invited to a reception at Buckingham Palace. She and Edward were working the room and she came over.
"At last," she said quietly, "a face I recognise."

We got some good celebrity support. It was important. It raised our profile, helped us raise more money, helped us therefore improve and sustain our services for these families going through awful times.

I wanted to get in touch with Eric Clapton. I knew he lived nearby and, as it happens, I was a big fan but I just couldn't get to him. I was telling this to one of our many excellent volunteers over a coffee.

"Well, that's easy, "she said, "I've known him for twenty years." It's amazing what connections are there if you ask.

Eric came round for a visit on a Saturday morning with his young wife and two young daughters. We walked round, I told him my stories.

At the end we sat in my office.

"I'll do whatever you want," he said.

I told him I had this idea of putting on an outdoor gig at Losely Park which was nearby and owned by the More-Molyneux family who were key supporters. Christopher's was actually named after their son who had died in a tragic accident while the hospice was being built on land they donated.

"We could do that, if you want" said Eric, "or what might be easier is next May I'm doing a run of dates at the Albert Hall. They are all set up and sold out already. Why don't I give you what I earn from one of those nights?".

Eric struck me as an intelligent, pleasant and caring guy. May all our heroes do so well!

He told me the dates and said to pick one. I picked the 5th of May. My fiftieth birthday. He got us a lot of tickets for the families and staff and so I spent my fiftieth birthday watching one of my favourite artists at my favourite venue. I sat there looking round trying to guess how much Eric would earn from a night's work at the Albert Hall.

Those Albert Hall dates were part of Eric's world tour. We had to wait till the whole tour was done and all the accounting completed. I went to meet Eric's business manager – a really nice guy called Roger who had a solicitor's practice in Dorking. He explained how the Albert Hall was not a big earner as venues go as it had a limited size and there were a lot of 'debentures' or season ticket holders who were not counted in the income. Then you have all the musicians and technicians to pay and so on.

"So," said Roger. " what Eric actually earned from that night is about £32,000., He wants to top that up to £40,000., If he makes out a personal cheque to you, I think you can claim the tax benefit back?"

We could indeed. So, for sitting watching a superb gig on my fiftieth birthday we picked up about £50,000 for the charity. Happy days and well done, Eric!

I had five years at CHASE. It was an honour to work in such a fascinating field and I learned a lot. We raised millions of pounds every year. It was a real community effort.

But the time came when I thought I should move on. The same problems began to come round again so I was ready for a new challenge.

When I was out for one of my lunches with Frances Bell, the recruitment consultant, she had asked me what I wanted to do next, as usual.

"I'd really like to work for an international charity. See a bit of the world. But I've never worked for an international charity before."

"You hadn't worked for a children's hospice and we got you in there."

Fair point. Several weeks later she phoned.

"I've got something for you."

"Right to Play' came out of the Olympic movement and was formerly called 'Olympic Aid'. It was set up and run by the impressive Johann-Olav Koss, the Norwegian speedskater and double Olympic gold medallist. It was based in North America and in fact its heads office was in Toronto. It raised money from the west, basically, and used it to fund programmes in the poorest countries of the world using play and sport to promote health and community development initiatives. However, it was unknown in the UK and my role was to be the first UK National Director and to lead on football issues across the world. Most of the end user countries in Africa and the Middle East and so on were football countries but `RTP' knew little about the sport and had few connections from its North America base. It was my job to try and put us on the football map – and London 2012 was a few years away so we had an eye on that too.

"We need a partnership with a Premier League club," said Johann at one of our first meetings.
"Leave that to me," I said. There was only one club I wanted to partner with.

I had some connections with Chelsea already. The Gianfranco Zola thing had worked very well for the club, too and I had actually helped them out when a player got into some problems and they needed a couple of connections to help on the public relations side.

I reckoned I could get a meeting with Peter Kenyon, the new CEO and Simon Greenburg, the Director of Communications. One shot. I did my homework. They had hundreds of charities contacting them every day, I had to find my angle. I looked at their business plans and they wanted to hit the China and USA. I sat and thought.

I went in and made my pitch.
"We get a lot of contact from charities wanting our support," Peter said.
"Oh, sorry, this isn't a charity pitch," I said. 'This is a marketing pitch. I want to help you deliver your business objectives."

I explained about our new deal with the Chinese government delivering play education packs to thousands of schools in China.
"We can put your logo on every one," I said.
I talked about our USA profile and how we could help them there.

I explained how if they nominated us as their 'international charity partner' they could pick another charity as their UK partner. This would then give them a ready reply to all the thousands of charity requests they got – they could say they worked through their charity partners. I then talked about London 2012 and how we were the only charity allowed to set up in the Olympic village itself.

Right to Play became Chelsea's first International Charity partner, initially for four years but this was later extended to eight years taking us beyond London 2012. When Chelsea won the Champions League in Munich in 2012 beating Bayern Munich on their own manor, there was 'Right To Play' on the back of the Chelsea shirts. It became the biggest partnership between a football club and a charity in the world.

I'll talk later about some of the adventures I had with Chelsea in Africa and the Middle East, like travelling to Ghana with Jose Mourinho and Michael Essien, and how I got to know the people at the Chelsea Academy very well.

But with Right to Play I certainly got my wish to see a bit of the world. I travelled to some of the poorest parts of the poorest countries in the world and met some incredible people.

Now, I am a big fan of travelling, particularly for the young as part of their education in the world. All my older kids have been travelling, indeed my lovely daughter is in Australia as we speak.

However, what was on my mind was the conversation my son Keir and I had about travel insurance as we were driving back from Lancashire one weekend with Oscar, no.5 son, having visited the older boys and families and grandchildren and had a great time. We got to talking about Keir's upcoming trip to Thailand, Vietnam and points east with a couple of mates, Binny and Matt.

"Have you got travel insurance organised?" I asked. Inevitably he had not and almost equally inevitably it was going to be the Dad Bank that sorted it.

The next day, on my way out to work, I said to Keir "I've sorted that travel insurance for you, sent you the policy by email."
"Oh, thanks," he said, "has it got motorcycle cover?"
"What?"
"Well, we're going to be hiring motorbikes when we are travelling. Only up to 125cc."
Now, again, I must say, I like motorbikes, having had a couple myself in younger days but any of you parents will understand this little exchange was somewhat on my mind as I walked through the woods with the dog the next morning.

We want our children to have adventures and learn about life, but we want good insurance cover at the same time. We want them to enjoy the sunshine but remind them not to stare at the sun. We want the thrills of the well-maintained theme park not the back street Saturday night in Bangkok.

It got me thinking about my travels. I didn't get to go far when I was in my early twenties like Keir and the other boys. It was not until I worked for Right to Play in my fifties that I really got to see more of the world than the usual Western Europe destinations. I was fortunate to go to places like Brazil, China, India, Namibia, Zambia and so on. Because I was working for a charity, I got to see the poorest parts of those countries and meet some extraordinary people. When I started that travelling, I said I was going to add a day on every trip and see a bit more of each of the countries.

Great plan, but it didn't happen. It got so I was travelling so much and missing my family I just wanted to get home after the work was done. The one time I did add some days on was one trip to India. It was around my birthday (May 5th, in case you've forgotten) and that also happens to be around the time the Buddha's birthday is celebrated. (Me, Marx and Buddha having the same birthday? Oh, and Michael Palin too. I know, go figure.)

I was going to be in the north east of India and flying though Patna so I worked out I could take a few days and travel the 111 kilometres south and visit Bodh Gaya, the little town where the Buddha found enlightenment. He famously sat under a tree there – the 'Bodhi tree' – and was enlightened. Apparently, a direct descendant of the same tree was there still on the same spot. Seemed like a place to go.

I stayed at a three-star hotel rather modestly called the "Royal Residence Hotel' just outside the little town which was full of Buddhist temples from the many and various Buddhist traditions from around the world. After a rather hairy taxi in one of the famous Ambassador taxis so common in India which seemed to involve driving at breakneck speed on a warm dark night through crowded little towns and villages, accompanied of course by the ever-present shrill car horn tooting, I arrived in Bodh Gaya.

On the way, after about an hour of this noisy travel I asked the taxi driver, a neat dapper tubby little guy:
"Have you ever tried driving without blowing the car horn every thirty seconds? You know, just for a trial, for a change?"
He thought about this as I leaned forward from the back seat, arms on the worn leather of the Ambassador front bench seat. Then he waggled his head and replied:
"No, no, sir, I could not do that," he smiled, "it would be like not being able to speak!"

So, the first morning in Bodh Gaya I stepped out into the sunshine of the hotel drive. There waiting, under a scraggly tree, was an equally scraggly wiry man with a battered, once yellow now mostly rust-coloured bicycle rickshaw. He immediately waved and cycled over, the old bike clanking alarmingly.

'Hello, sir," he said cheerfully, "my name is Lailesh and I am your top personal taxi driver!"
I had no idea where anything was in the town so I put my reservations aside and climbed in.
"I'd like to go to the temple where the Bodhi Tree is," I said.
"Ah yes," said Lailesh," I know that place, but first we go somewhere else."
I was going to suggest this was not the way the customer-taxi driver dynamic usually worked but what the hell, I was in no rush.

And so it started. Lailesh would be waiting for me each morning and take me to all sorts of places. He was great company. We went over one day to the little stream where the Buddha, having tried the ascetic approach eventually collapsed from starving himself and was revived by a local girl who, funnily enough, fed him rice pudding. Or so Lailesh said. There was a little temple on the site but no tourists. It was great, though walking through the field to the stream Lailesh suddenly grabbed my arm and pointed to a small thin little snake sliding away from us.
"Mister Chris! Be careful!"
Now, I hate snakes but this one was very small.
"It doesn't look too dangerous, "I said, as much to myself as Lailesh.
"No," he said, looking round the field at our feet, still holding my arm," it's not. It is baby cobra."
"Oh, OK," I said, also now looking round.
"It is not a problem, "said Lailesh, "but Mama is!"
We hurried on.

One morning Lailesh got the bike going and announced where we were going. I had long given up any semblance of me deciding the itinerary.
"This morning we go see our cow," he announced as he grunted and groaned getting the bike going, the muscles on his stringy thighs beneath his ragged shorts working hard.
"Why do we want to see your cow?"
"No, no, Mister Chris," he laughed," not my cow. OUR cow!"

"Our cow? We don't have a cow?"
"No, not yet but we buy it together. Very good cow. Only twenty five dollars."
"Why would I want to own a cow? I don't even live here."
"No, no, Mister Chris," he explained, "you would own half a cow."
"OK, so we pay half each, I still don't want half a cow."
"Mister Chris!" Lailesh said patiently, as if to a simple child, "You pay all price. I have no money for cow."
"So how come it would be ours then, not mine."
"You buy it, I look after it! You don't live here."
Fair enough, I suppose, but I still was not convinced.

Anyway, we went to see this cow – a very acceptable fine cow, as far as I could tell – and Lailesh enthused about it, pointing out it's many fine features.
"Keep whole family in milk," he said triumphantly.
"Not my bloody family, it won't, not from here," I said in exasperation.

Every day, every half hour or so, Lailesh would mumble something about 'our cow' just to remind me.
"Our cow lives down there," he would say, pointing down a dusty lane. Or, if we saw another cow wandering about he would shake his head and say dismissively:
"Not as good as our cow."

On the last morning, I went out to get into my taxi to go back to Patna. Another Ambassador car, indistinguishable from the one that brought me there, was waiting. There was also another trim, dapper little driver in immaculate white shirt and black trousers – Lailesh's cousin, apparently. Lailesh was there to supervise the departure.
I shook his hand and passed him a tip. He looked at it in his hand, a small fold of notes, his eyes lighting up and his brown creased face illuminated by a wide smile. For once he was speechless.
"Look after our cow," I said, climbing into the taxi.

One of my first visits to Africa was with Greg Rutherford and John Regis to Sierra Leone. I liked Sierra Leone. It was then apparently the second poorest country in the world. (Which was the poorest? No googling. Come on…….Mali. Did you get that? Well done. Next week you can hand the pencils out.). In Freetown the capital there was usually no electricity for most people so at nights shows and stalls were lit with kerosene lamps. It was a poor but spirited place having just come through years and years of wars.

The main airport in Sierra Leone is Lungi airport which was originally an RAF base. The airport is across the river estuary from Freetown and this presented the problem. The quickest way to travel across then was by helicopter. These were Russian built Mi-8 helicopters. OK we said we will go with that.

I found out later these were notorious and in fact they no longer run. Our bags were dumped in the back of this rusty old helicopter. We all sat in bare seats around the edge of the hold with our bags between us. There was an armed guard standing by the door to the pilot's cabin. The pilots were noted for two things – they were Russian and they were usually drunk. When the old helicopter took off everything shook and rattled. By the time we had made it across the estuary I was checking all my fillings were still in place. This was 2004. In 2007 one of these bloody things crashed killing all 22 people on board.

Going inland the people were great and good fun to be with. I was taking a lot of photos with a new Nikon camera I had been given. I took some of some kids playing by a rough football pitch. Later when I looked at the photos on my laptop I notice that the thing they were climbing on and jumping off was an unexploded bomb.

Mines were a terrible issue in Sierra Leone but I later had the chance at the national stadium where I had gone to meet the Minister of Sport and talk football, of watching the Sierra Leone disabled football team train. These guys were all on crutches with a foot or leg missing, blown off by mines. I thought I loved football but these guys put me to shame. They were really keen, really athletic and really good. The Minister of Sport told me how they were reviving football in this football mad country. He later spoke to my worldwide boss, Johan Koss and said they needed a new manager for the national team. Johan said "you can have who you want as long as it's not Chris Robinson." I would have been tempted.

Sierra Leone was an education. Poor people, ravaged and scarred by years of war, putting their lives back together with enthusiasm and spirit.

My work with Right to Play took me to the poorest countries and I usually met the poorest people there. I think the slums in Mumbai were probably the worst I saw. I remember being down by the shanty town in the port area one early morning and saw a stream of people – old men, young children, women – make their way down onto the smelly mud flat where the dock tide had gone out and squatting down to take a crap, leaving a steaming pile in many cases for the tide to hopefully wash away. As the sun rose and the heat grew the stench was unbelievable.

In one of the nearby corrugated iron and mud block shed-like dwellings, crammed in together, a woman explained to me via an interpreter that the illegal electricity they were all hooked up to with a maze of tangle overhead wiring was organised by a local slum lord who charged them exorbitant prices.

In Delhi I was followed by two young men from the station area. My street antenna was working though and I hid behind a pillar and watched them saunter past, searching for me. I slipped away in a different direction.

I know who I am. I've stared at the sun.

Just might get some sunglasses for my boy though, if I can.

I am not a massive Christmas fan, certainly not the religious side, however I have to say I see the 'Christmas Spirit' as a positive warm human reaching out and I like that. I just wish it was more in evidence throughout the year.
Bah, humbug?
Yeah, Ok, just a bit, I suppose.

But I do get Christmas messages from friends old and new and that is one of the positive things about that time of year. I guess it's a positive thing about the much-maligned social media too in that it does give you the opportunity to re-connect or keep in touch with people that our busy lives drive us off from in different directions, like bouncing pinballs.

I think this was probably started with 'Friends Re-united' – remember that? Many thousands of people got onto that site to re-connect with old school friends, and later work colleagues. It got a bad reputation though, in that it took the blame for a lot of affairs starting up as people met their old flames and tried to re-connect with their teenage selves by re-connecting with the people who had been their boyfriends or girlfriends back then. I guess it worked well for some people but for others may be less so. We can't go back in time.

There's a saying that you can't step in the same river twice and of course that rings very true. Everything and everyone has moved on and is different. That actually usually becomes very clear when you meet an old friend and think 'blimey, do I look that old, too?'

For all that, though, we know that some connections do endure. There are people I have met through my life who I have found a real bond with – even if I have only met them quite briefly. I do wonder what it is that makes that connection - what are the elements that forge the almost immediate bond? Why with this person and not that one? It is not necessarily a romantic or sexual attraction at all. In fact, in my experience, it is usually not that because that can feel like something else altogether and takes you in different directions with an altogether different dynamic. It is more an almost mystical, maybe even chemical fusion somewhere in the narrowing space between two people.

I did get some messages from abroad over Christmas and they got me thinking on these lines. I got messages from people who don't even celebrate Christmas as such. Different places, different religions. And yet they still reach out and let you know they are thinking of you because of past connections made.

I got a 'Christmas hug' e-message from Fadi El Yemani, my Palestinian friend living in Beirut. Fadi is Palestine's most famous footballer, retired now from playing but a celebrated coach. Walking around with him in Lebanon was like walking up Newcastle High Street with Alan Shearer (I imagine). Everyone knew 'Captain Fadi'. He was trained as a coach in the Ukraine and his wife is Ukrainian, as I recall. He may be a local superstar but Fadi also happens to be one of the nicest people I have ever met, too.

Back in those days when I worked for Right to Play, my favourite region I got to visit was the Middle East. We had a big programme there. I loved the region and met some incredible people there.

I was at an international Right to Play meeting in Toronto, where the world-wide head office was, and talking to my old mate, Michael Bedford who ran Right to Play USA.
"Who is that?" I asked him, pointing across the crowded room.
"Who?"

"The beautiful young woman with long dark hair who has just walked in", I said.
"Oh yeah, that's Rasha. Rasha Salah, she works in the Middle East office. She's Palestinian. You don't know Rasha? She's great. Come on, I'll introduce you."
And so I met the lovely Rasha Salah, beautiful, long dark hair, slim, very smart, very determined, and we got on well. We connected.

Sometime later I visited Beirut for the first time and was met like a long-lost brother by Fadi, Rasha and Abdul Hafiz who ran the region. Over the next few days I was taken round that beautiful battered city by my Palestinian friends who had grown up there, in exile.
I remember sitting with Rasha down on the beach, near my hotel, where amidst the building rubble someone had made a café. We sat and drank rich Lebanese coffee in beautiful sunshine. It was extraordinary to think we were having such a 'normal occasion' in such a tormented city. Lebanon generally is a beautiful place (where, incidentally, in my rarely humble opinion, you will find the most beautiful women in the world. I have made a close study of this international subject and speak with some authority, albeit with a lot of bias and a considerable amount of ignorance.)

Fadi and Rasha took me into the 'refugee camps'. I expected these to be sort of transit camps – and at one time they may have been - but they have been there for so long they are now almost regular neighbourhoods, with apartment buildings, concrete, electric wires running loosely along, dust and small dusky shops. We were going to see a friend of theirs who was a film maker. A young man appeared out of a derelict looking building opposite us, wearing an adidas t-shirt and jeans, casually carrying a skeleton machine gun. I looked at Rasha.
"Don't worry, "she said, taking my arm," they are just letting you know they've seen you. You are fine with us."

I went to Rasha's stylish apartment for a lovely meal, I met her parents who lived nearby and were very involved in Palestinian politics, and met her two fine teenage children from her marriage (she was now divorced). Rasha had been educated in France at University and spoke French of course, and faultless English. However, hearing her speak Arabic was a thing of beauty. She had an almost husky voice and as we sat opposite each other at her dining room table and she tried to teach me a few words of Arabic I was mesmerized. I found it hard to focus on the language and get beyond the sound of her speaking it.

Through the Chelsea partnership, we took a group of coaches and young players to Jordan. We visited the Dead Sea which was extraordinary. We all swam in the salty, oily water and the feeling of being held up was strange, almost like being weightless. Rasha walked into the sea wearing a bikini and stopped all conversations. It was a bit of a 'Dr No' moment (for the James Bond fans out there) except as I recall Ursula Andress walked out of the sea. Rasha walked in. We sat next to each other in the shallows.
"The minerals and oils in the water are very good for your skin," she said, with a smile, running the water over herself.
"Evidently," I said, and she laughed at me.

We all visited a Greek amphitheatre above Amman. We walked around the old site, in the sunshine, high above the white walled city buildings. I said to Rasha how much I liked the city, how fine it was.
"Oh, Chris, you should see Damascus," she said, "it is even better, a beautiful city."
I wonder if it is now.

We talked about growing up a Palestinian in another country, as a refugee, less than half welcome, a perpetual visitor.
"It is like having a mother who does not want to know you," she said.

We were walking in Beirut with another friend and he enthusiastically greeted a young woman walking the other way and introduced us.
"She is from the same village as me," he beamed.
Later, talking to Rasha I realised he meant the village in Palestine where their families were from. A village they had never seen. But it was still 'their' village.

The life experience of Rasha and Fadi and their families is so different to mine. Different continents, different religions, very different lives as refugees living in what has often been a war zone, exiled from their homeland which they all yearn for, faced with injustice and discrimination every day. Yet, they send me a Christmas message of love and friendship. When my son Danny died eight years ago they were in contact straight away.
"We can't come to see you," they said, "you know the limitations, but you must come to us. We need to hug you."

We found we could sit together and talk about our families and our lives and loves and connect as people back then and have continued to do so over the intervening years.

This is the connection, where we as individual dots find a line is now joining us to another dot. On the blank canvass of our lives, we are no longer a solitary dot. It is a wonderful thing and I have been privileged to make many connections with many dots over the years and I value each one more and more as I get older. It is maybe in these connected dots that we find true wealth and achievement. Once connected I don't think you ever are alone again.

When it came to say goodbye to all the people in the Right to Play Middle East office in Beirut, they all of course made a big fuss and said some lovely words. It was to be my last visit there but we didn't know that then. I went round each of them in turn, talking about them and what I had learnt from them and how much I

would miss them. I had some words for every single person, except one. When I was finished there was a clamour:
"What about Rasha? You've forgotten Rasha!"
I looked at her, and she frowned sadly at me.
"No, "I said, "I haven't. It's just I can't say goodbye to Rasha."

I don't think I ever have.

As part of my seeking football connections, I managed to get a meeting with Sepp Blatter then President of FIFA in Zurich. Our Swiss National Director knew him and made the connection. FIFA HQ is an impressive set up above the city. Sepp Blatter's office was also impressive. There were subtly lit cabinets with various trophies and signed memorabilia around.

I had done a deal with adidas that they were going to produce a version of their current ball but with the RTP logo on it. There had just been a World Cup final where Italy had beaten France.

Mr Blatter got up from his desk and took an adidas ball out of the cabinet and handed it to me.

"Like this, the World Cup ball?" he asked.
"Yes," I said "like these."
"No," he said, "this is THE actual World Cup ball, the one used in the final."

The meeting continued but I have to say I was in fan heaven and totally distracted by holding the ball used in the recent World Cup final in my lap. I realised later it was probably a ploy he used quite often to put football fans like me off their stride. Anyway, we reached an agreement so it was not too painful.

I met a load of top athletes who were keen to help. I went with Greg Rutherford – a handy footballer himself even if a Villa fan – and John Regis to Sierra Leone, for example.

As London 2012 came closer there was a plan to develop an international legacy programme in advance of the Games. Five agencies were asked by UK Sport to nominate one expert each to be part of a team to assess various proposals from the selected countries where the international programme was going to happen. The five agencies were the Youth Sport Trust, the British Council, Unicef, UK Sport and RTP. I was the nomination from RTP so we all travelled round to Brazil, India, Azerbaijan and Zambia assessing projects. It was a great experience but given I was also travelling for RYTP to China, Ghana, the USA and Canada, it was exhausting.

The nominee from Unicef was Beth Nicholls and we became good friends. She knew RTP and knew Johan, the founder, well. Beth was a fan of the TV series '24' and I was working my way through 'The Sopranos' so on all the flights and in all the hotels we were both watching our laptops.

Brazil was fascinating. We went to Rio. A local guy told me "here we have heaven and we have hell." The London 2012 contingent were staying in a hotel on Copacabana Beach so I got to see some of the heaven but every morning when I went for a run along the beach – I was training for the Edinburgh Marathon then. The beach was lovely, with beach volleyball and football goals set up and glorious looking people all around. The mix of races and types in Brazil was wonderful.

But we saw hell too. I guy I knew from London had set up a Boxing project ion one of the favelas – the ghettos run by the drug cartels. This project – 'Fighting for Peace' – was good. Boys and girls could train there if they also signed up for some IT training upstairs from the gym. I arranged for us to visit. We were in a small minibus. We stopped where a big, tarnished chrome bumper off a big truck lay across the entrance to a street. My mate Luke had arranged for a local guy to meet us there and bring us through the favella.

The guy got on board sitting next to the driver. He put the interior light on – "so they can see it is me" – he said. The old bumper was dragged aside and we drove in. W drive down a very normal looking street with lights on in the bars and shops. It was a Saturday, early evening. The guy was telling us about the favela and the cartel. He spoke good English.
"They don't like the kids to go outside the favela. They like to control, see? So, there were two kids, about nine and eleven, kept slipping out to go swim the reservoir over the hill" – he waved a hand off into the soft inky evening.
"The gang did not like that, no," he went on. "they had warned the kids before. So this one time last week they caught the boys coming back from the reservoir. They could not argue they had not been. Their hair was still wet. They shot them and hung their arms and legs up there along the wires." He pointed above us to the electric wires running from post to post along the street, festooned with some dark shapes. I looked away. I can remember thinking that my Keir and Oscar were just about the same ages as those poor kids.
Hell indeed.

The travelling got too much in the end. I turned down the chance to visit Beijing for the 2008 Olympics because I had been to China twice that year already and I was just tired. Travelling for a charity invariably meant traveling Economy and ten to twelve hour flights overnight were no fun. I was perpetually tired and aching.

The only time I ever travelled First Class was when a TV company was paying for me to visit Kenya for a promotion of a new football channel where we in RTP were to be the charity partners. I travelled Virgin First Class from Heathrow. It was only when someone asked me about the drive in to Heathrow that I found out that a limousine service from home to Heathrow was included! I'd travelled on the bus!

In Nairobi, I was with my mate, the sports presenter Matt Lorenzo who was introducing the launch event at a night club and the great

Marcel Desailly, French World Cup winner, Milan and Chelsea legend. Matt was a very funny guy, a good presenter – when he was introducing us to the night club, live on TV, he said 'and now, two of the greatest footballers of our generation – Marcel Desailly and…Chris Robinson!"

Marcel and I fell onto the stage laughing. I think it was the only time I had ever featured in the same sentence as the great Marcel Desailly.

My sons needed me more at home. I wanted to watch them play football, go with them to watch Chelsea, see my friends, go home.

I phoned Frances.

She called back a bit later.
"OK," she said, "you'll love this. They are starting a new charity called 'The Mayor's Fund for London'. It's Boris's idea. They need a CEO. Fancy it?"

"Me – working for Boris? Are you sure?"

Frances laughed, "It's not quite like that. Let's meet for lunch and I'll explain."

The next adventure was waiting.

Meanwhile, over the years, there was another current flowing in and out of my life. I had first become interested in Buddhism reading Kerouac as a student. I had wanted to try Transcendental Meditation back in Sheffield but couldn't afford the joining fee. As an avid reader I began to read more and more about Buddhism. I first attended a meditation course in 1986 in Oswaldtwistle in East Lancashire with a group called Friends of the Western Buddhist Order - the "FWBO' - and enjoyed it. I have been meditating on and off ever since.

Wherever I lived I would try and find a local Buddhist group or centre and also of course still be reading whatever I could. When I lived near Bicester, working for 'Off the Streets' I started attended a Tibetan Buddhist Group called the New Kadampa Tradition in Reading. I used to ride down there on my Kawasaki motorbike. In typical Tibetan style they had a very structured formalised learning programme. Although this did not always sit well with me it certainly helped me learn the basics.

I liked the honesty of Buddhism. "If this doesn't work for you then don't do it," the Buddha had said. What other religions were saying that? It's basic message of suffering and it's causes and personal responsibility explained a lot about life to me.

After a couple of years studying, the people running the Reading NKT Centre asked if I would like to teach meditation because they wanted to open a centre in Woking. I was living in Surrey and working at CHASE by now. I studied and became a teacher of meditation, teaching one night a week at a community centre near Woking station. I went up to the Lakes to get teaching straight from the leader of the NKT, the Tibetan lama, Geshe Kelsang Gyatso. All great experiences in this crazy life.

I enjoyed it and learnt from it. The ritual and cosmology of Tibetan Buddhism didn't really work with me though. Later I lived near a more traditional Theravada Buddhist Centre at Chithurst which was – and is still – a beautiful place. I stayed there on retreats where you lived the same traditional pattern of life as the monks and nuns– getting up at six o'clock for the first meditation of the day and not eating after twelve midday. After a couple of days staying there the Abbot invited me to tea with him.
He was a really kind, humorous English guy about my age, tall and thin, wearing the long ochre robe of an ordained monk in this Thai-based order.
"How are you finding it?" he asked then before I could answer he said with a grin:

"No, let me guess. You didn't think you'd be able to do the early mornings or the not eating after midday – but in fact you've found it far easier than you expected!"
He was right. You soon adjusted to the gentle rhythm and expectations of the monastic life.

When later living in Rogate, just a couple of miles from Chithurst, I would go to the Sunday evening pujas or services regularly. I loved the meditation hall and its quiet and peace and the sound of the chanting monks and nuns. It was a real joy.

I don't think I would be suited to the monastic life but I have learned a lot along the way.

I think most people who know me would mention how laid back I am, how calm (unless watching Chelsea!). if that is so then I do think a lot of that comes from the years of studying Buddhism, of meditating and of listening to the Dharma teachings from all sorts of traditions and teachers.

I learned more stories, of course. Buddhism is full of stories and many of them illuminated a path forward for me.

For example, I often have thought of the pace of modern life and our jumbled minds and never finding time to do one thing properly. I look back on my life and wonder if I should have focused more on one thing than try so much – yet it has brought me so much variety in experience. But closer in, in my mind, every day, I have tried to focus and it's here, close at hand, every day, that it makes a difference.

I read that there was this young Buddhist monk and he was determined to find the teacher who could give him the answers to all the big questions in life. He walked many, many miles and sought out a guru he had heard tell of who could explain the Buddha's teachings on the meaning of life better than anyone. He found the guru but after some years began to think that this was only part of the answer. The teachings were great and it was good to hear them all explained but…

He went off and eventually found his way to yet another teacher who was a master of meditation. This must be the way, he thought, this guy meditates for eight hours a day, this is impressive, this is the answer, I want to learn these techniques. After a few years he again began to feel he was missing something still so he set off again.

He came upon an old monk gathering wood.
"Hi," he said, "I am looking for a teacher. What is your teacher like?"
"Oh, he is wonderful," the old wood gathering monk said.
"Really?" our guy said, getting interested. "What does he do? Does he teach you about the Buddha's sutras? What meditation techniques does he use? What does he do?"
"Well," the old wood gatherer stood up and scratched his head, "he chops wood."
"What? What's so good about that?"
"When he chops wood, he just chops wood."
The monk sat down, stunned.
"That's the teacher I need," he said.

8. It's Hard To Be A Saint In The City

Boris Johnson had been elected Mayor of London in May 2008. One of his first actions was to announce he would be setting up a 'Mayor's Fund for London'. Other cities – New York, Melbourne – had similar things. The idea was that successive Mayors would be the Patron.
It was a non-political project, with whoever was the Mayor at the time as the Patron. However, there was a lot of suspicion around. Political opponents saw this as a possible cunning play to side step local authority systems and fund Boris' pet projects.

Boris made one smart move right at the start. He asked Sir Trevor Chinn to be the Chairman of the Fund. Trevor was a well-known Labour supporter so it established this non-political stance. Trevor had taken on and expanded his father's motor business then moved into the private equity world, working for the American company CVC. He was put in as Chairman of companies they bought – like the RAC and Kwikfit – and led them forward. He also had a great track record of philanthropy, having chaired the 'Wishing Well' appeal for Great Ormond Street Hospital – for which he got his knighthood. He was a multi-millionaire, in his mid-seventies, full of energy and drive.

I went through the hoops of the recruitment process then finally it came down to a 1:1 meeting between me and Trevor at his office at Marble Arch. I knew that it would be the relationship between Trevor as Chairman and the CEO that would be the key. We got on well.

I got the gig.

Sir Trevor Chinn turned out to be one of the most impressive and influential people I have ever met and certainly the best Chairman I ever worked for. He was very smart with great instincts about people, and very kind. He had a wealth of sayings – 'Trevorisms' I called them – that stay with me yet. For example he would always start meetings on time even if everyone wasn't there yet.

"Never disadvantage those who are on time for the sake of those that are not," he would say.

We came obsessed with evidence and data.

"An opinion-based conversation is more enjoyable but an evidence-based one is more productive," was another Trevorism which I took to heart.

When Boris first approached Trevor he said he wanted the Fund to focus on gangs and knife crime.

"Boris," said Trevor, "if you want me to do it then it must focus on the causes not the effects." Trevor was adamant the Fund should focus on child poverty in London and Boris was persuaded.

Trevor got other high profile Jewish business people on board as Trustees – Sir Stanley Fink, later Lord Fink, and Michael Sherwood of Goldman Sachs, for example. The idea was to get money from the city then spend it on child poverty projects.

Straight away there were huge challenges.

Firstly, I started work in October 2008. The month before had been the virtual collapse of the financial system with major players like Lehman Brothers going under. The city was in turmoil and the 'credit crunch' was at its height. Not surprisingly, many people in the city had other priorities other than some new Fund after their money.

Secondly, unlike other major funders – like the Lottery or the City Parochial Trust – we had no income stream. We had to raise the money before we could spend it. It was very difficult to get people committed without having a specific project in mind but difficult to get a project going if you had no funding. Particularly if it was something new and different.

Here Trevor and I made it difficult for ourselves. We became convinced too many existing funders were not basing decisions on evidence and as a consequence far too much money was being gambled on projects where there was no evidence they actually worked but just looked good. We saw this everywhere.

We were both hugely influenced by the work of Dr Michael Little and Dr Louise Morpeth of the Social Research Unit at Dartington and the whole 'evidence-based' prevention approach that was picking up speed around the world. We asked them to help. They said they would, for free – if I would join their Board. Trevor agreed and I became a Trustee (and later Chairman) of the Social Research Unit board.

Trevor and I agreed we would give ourselves the first six months to get some funding behind us and establish exactly what we wanted to do. We did not want to be just another fund. We want to do it differently based on evidence.

It would have been so much easier just to pick a few projects here and there around London and got them some funding. This is what Boris' team and most of our Trustees wanted us to do. However, Trevor and I were convinced that would be almost a waste. We wanted to change the way funding worked and make a lasting impact.

This again caused us some problems because some of the existing funders felt we were criticising them (we were) and so were not going to come in and play ball.

However, largely due to Trevor's indefatigable spirit and contacts we raised several million on the first six months. Rather than supporting a project here and another there across London we decided to take a starting pint as a 'square mile' around Shoreditch and try and link new evidence-based poverty prevention project together there. This was again based on the idea that the issues were all joined up in families but the funding to help was not – a lesson learned from my 'Off the Streets' days. We decided on the area around Shoreditch because it took in parts of different boroughs, had a lot of deprivation and was on the doorstep of the city.

It also happened to be where I grew up. I spent a lot of that first six months literally walking the streets in that area around Old Street, into Hackney, around to Clerkenwell, the white working-class estates off Central Street where I was from, through Whitechapel and so on. I got to know projects, people, places. I studied maps, evidence, data, school reports.

Also, we had to get the Fund launched and I had to put the start of a team together.

In my first week it was arranged that Trevor and I would have lunch with Boris – this would be the first time I had met him. He hadn't been involved in the recruitment process. The idea was we would brief him for the launch event to be held at the old Shoreditch Town Hall the next day. Boris' office had asked for some notes for the speech he was going to make at the launch.
"Why don't you write the whole speech?" suggested Trevor. I did so and we sent that to Boris and the next day we met for lunch at the 'Pont de la Tour' restaurant just under Tower Bridge, a short walk from City Hall, and apparently a favourite of Boris'.

He came bowling in, a little late, in that now very familiar way – blonde hair all over the pace, jacket slightly askew, tie a bit mangled. In all the meetings and discussions I had with Boris over the next four years – and we would do a lot of events together – that first impression remained. He was just as he appears on TV. He was blustery, personally charming, funny, very clever and all over the place. But at that stage of the first meeting, I was still learning all this. Putting our political differences aside I was trying to keep an open mind. I had discussed that with Trevor.

"I believe Boris is a decent man, with a good heart," Trevor had said, "the people around him…" he shrugged.

At that lunch table Boris waved some papers.
"This speech," he said, "who wrote it?"
"I did," I said.
"It's..it's excellent, " he enthused, "a wonderful speech! Marvellous! If ever you need a job – "
Yes, that would work, I thought and looked at Trevor who grinned back.

The next day we had the launch. It all went according to plan. There were a lot of people there and a lot of interest.

Boris made his speech. It was a great speech, very funny and very smart.

Not one word of it was what I had written.

I had to get a team together. I think I have been good at building teams. At 'Off the Streets' I had Carole Coulon and Vince Murphy and then we built from there. At 'Right to Play' I had Mike Emery, a bright young man and good footballer as my Deputy Director and the ex-Rugby player Ben Pegna looking after out Athlete Ambassadors and we had had the lively, smart Jen Barratt but she'd been poached away to run the England footballers in-house charity. When we established Right to Play in Soho – in free offices provided by a marketing company – I had recruited a very smart young woman called Emma O'Meally as my PA/Office manager. Emma became invaluable. She was always one step ahead of me and would say 'you've been asked to do this event but I've turned it down because you won't want to do that." She had worked in Sierra Leone as an administrator in the International Court hearings. We became close friends.

I always said when I was a football manager "once you're one of my players, you're always one of my players." That's probably why I am still in touch with so many of my ex-players. It's like an extended family. It was the same with these teams in the charity world. These people I have mentioned are all friends now, still keeping in touch.

I must say though that Emma was special. When Trevor said, even before I had actually started the Mayor's Fund job, "you'll need a PA." there was no second thought in my mind. I needed Emma on board.

Emma joined and we started the Fund up together. She was more than a PA, she got the background research together and helped develop the ideas and approach. She was my confidante and my friend.

Two years in she came to me one day and said she was going to leave. She had been offered a job in Barcelona. She had been learning Spanish for a while. I realised this was something she had thought about a lot. A new start in a new city, a new country, a new adventure. She was single with no ties. I could see the sense of it for sure.

I still missed her though.

Meanwhile I was slogging away at the impossible challenges of the Mayor's Fund as Trevor and I saw it. We were living in Haslemere then so I was up early on weekdays, usually catching the seven o'clock train into waterloo and I was not home much before nine or even later if there was an event. At least I was mostly free at weekends so I was getting to see the boys play football, do a bit of coaching and going up to our beloved Stamford Bridge with them. But those week days were long. Suited and booted in my dark Boss suits and overcoat it was a real slog and the political setting made it all very stressful.

As part of my walking research, I went back and visited my old primary school – Moreland Street school in Finsbury off City Road. The old Victorian era school had been knocked down not long after I left in the mid-sixties and they had even knocked down the one they had built then! The new building was smart but felt soul less. There was a temporary head, they had difficulty recruiting teachers. I sat and spoke with the temporary head – an earnest but tired young fella. I told him I was there from 1958 to 1965. It appeared I may have been one of the first kids from that school to go to university.

"It's no more on the radar of these kids here now that it was in your time," said the Head Teacher and I found that really depressing.

As I went around the area listening and learning I was struck by the isolation of the inner-city kids. I met some teenagers at Kings Cross who had never seen the River Thames – just a couple of miles down the road. At another primary school they told me how they asked kids to bring in a book for international book day. One kid brought in the Argos catalogue because it was the only book in the home. At a training project they told me about a teenage they got onto a building site apprenticeship but he had given it up because his family got fed up with him getting up early to go to work and waking them up – as none of them worked.

I sat talking to a group of teenagers at a project just off Aldgate in the shadows of the City's gleaming towers. They were talking about how much people working in the City earned compared to people they knew.

"How much do you think they earn then – these people working in the banks and that?" I asked.

They all shrugged. Then one skinny black girl spoke up.

"About, like, thirty grand a year," she said.

A young guy opposite, was dismissive.

"Nah! Way more than that. I reckon the big earners are on, like, sixty grand."

Just before the crash, million-pound bonuses were not that unusual, just down the road we were on. They had no idea. These were separate worlds.

Boris and I did events and meetings together. He would often travel on the tube or on his bike. We were doing an event at the Dorchester together, a black tie event. I was waiting for him at the entrance talking to the hotel manager. Up bowls Boris on his bike, gets off, takes his bicycle clips off and hands his bike and clips to the doorman.
"Hello!" he brays, "here we are!"

Once I went to see him because he had made some claim about a project that was not right.
"Look," I said, "I'm just telling you this so you don't end up with egg on your face."
"Chris," he said, "my face is a veritable omelette."

He was a good speaker, I'll give him that. I had studied the craft and had shared platforms with some really good speakers over the years – Tony Benn, Denis Skinner back in my political days, and Denis Healey was a good pro too. But Boris was funny and clever and people loved him. When we did a charity ball or dinner together, I would usually do the charity message stuff first then he would get up and entertain. It made me raise my game, my old competitive spirit coming out though I knew he was the one they had come to hear. Once at a black-tie event at the Inns of Court, I hit good form on the literacy and numeracy theme, telling my stories then introduced Boris. As I stepped down and he was coming up the stairs to the stage he paused and grabbed my arm and leaned in.
"Damn good speech, Chris," he said, and I appreciated it.

His office was always on pins as to what he might say because he invariably went off message with some clever quip or joke and it used to give them palpitations. Initially they asked me for briefing notes for each speech but after that launch speech experience I ignored their requests. Before one event with London Citizens they were particularly nervous. Now London Citizens was a project I really had time for. They got people together in neighbourhoods, got them talking together, set up local open forums and helped the community campaign on whatever was important to them. They did great work on the London Living Wage and I loved attending their lively open meetings when I could and had great respect for Neil Jameson, the Director and community organisers like Dan Firth.

However, open agenda community forums made politicians nervous and whilst all the established politicians would court London Citizens and their hustings became a key part of the Mayor election process, they still were very wary. It shows what open democracy can do to politicians who have grown up with the stately Oxford Union debate as their comfort zone. For an old Shop Steward and rabble rouser like me it was happy days. However, before Boris was due to speak at one of their meetings his office phoned me.
"You've got to watch what he says today," pleaded the assistant, "keep him out of trouble,"
"Do me a favour," I said, "you can't control him and it's your job to look after him not mine."

Travelling with Boris on the tube was illuminating. People believed him to be approachable and would just come up and have a chat. He was approachable and just as he seemed on TV so he was appealing and popular to many.

One thing I could not – and do not – understand was his appeal to women. Many times, at events, when the speeches were over there would of course be a line of people waiting to speak to him. I noticed though that there were always a high proportion of women of a certain age and style – often posh, late thirties or forties, stylish, a but tipsy shall we say. This mystified me a bit. I just could not envisage Boris's sex appeal – but my wife assures me it is there even yet!

Working for the Mayor's Fund was tough. We had built in challenges, as I have explained, and we were operating in a very political stressful rarified atmosphere.

But there were some good times too. My favourite restaurant was Roast, upstairs at Borough Market just a short walk from City Hall. The food was always excellent. It was owned by Iqbal Wahaab, who became one of our Trustees. One day Iqbal said to me:
"When you want to impress a possible donor, where do you take them to lunch?"
"Well, to be honest," I said, "as a charity, that's not something we can do really."
"OK," he said, "I'll tell you what. Anytime you want to take someone for breakfast or lunch then just ring me and bring them here on the house."
So that's what I did. If I was taking someone to lunch – and Roast was always busy – the waiter would usually appear at some stage with two glasses of champagne.
"Mr Wahaab's compliments," he would murmur. I would look round the restaurant and somewhere Iqbal was sat in the busy throng, giving me a little wave.
At the end of the meal the maitre d' would come over.
"That's fine, Mr Robinson, it's all taken care of."
I realised early on that as I didn't pay I wasn't leaving a tip so got into the habit of leaving a fiver under my plate. The staff soon cottoned on to this and I would get the very best table and the best service and was always greeted with big smiles and their best attention.

At one of the business breakfasts we ran at Roast with Boris speaking I met Kiaran McDonald then the General Manager of the Savoy. We got to know each other and I found him a really good guy. One time I was sat having a coffee with him and he asked what events we had coming up. I mentioned that I was due to speak at a big charity ball at the Inns of Court. "That's right opposite us," Kiaran said. 'where do you stay when you do these events?"

"Well, if it's a late night do like that my office usually book me in the Premier Inn over the river."

"You must stay with us!' he said but then someone came up to us and the moment passed and that was that. I was walking back to City Hall feeling I had missed out on something. However, by the time I had got back Kiaran had emailed me and said I was booked in at the Savoy for that night of the Ball.

On that day I was working up in London so my wife brought my dinner suit and so on with her when she came up that evening. It was all a bit of a rush. As we entered into the Savoy a young manager came up and said:

"Ah, Mr Robinson. Compliments of Mr McDonald, welcome to the Savoy. Please come this way."

There was no registration or anything, this charming chatty American young man took us up a couple of floors and showed us into a luxurious suite of rooms overlooking the river. The Hotel had just been extensively renovated – as featured on a 'fly on the wall' TV documentary series, and was immaculate. There was champagne and chocolates on the heavy sideboard.

We were in a rush though so had little time check out the luxury. It transpired my wife had forgotten my cuff links. It was about six o'clock in the evening. I dashed out onto the Strand but couldn't find anywhere one that sold cufflinks. I made my way back. As I entered the Savoy I came across Kiran.

"Is everything Ok with the room?" he asked.

"Yes, it's fantastic, really appreciate it. Bit of a rush now though."
I must have looked a bit hassled.

"Is there a problem, Chris?"
I explained about the cufflinks.

"Here, "he said, pulling back his jacket sleeve, unfixing his cuff. "Take mine". He handed me his solid silver cuff links.

"I can't take these off you!" I protested

'It's no problem, I've got others in the flat upstairs. Go on."

I took the cuff links. We finished getting ready and hot-footed it over to the Inns of Court which had been done up spectacularly for the Ball. It was a successful night.

When we got back to the suite late that night, we polished off the champagne and chocolates and, in the morning, – on Kieran's recommendation – had a superb breakfast brought into the suite and served on the table by the window overlooking the Thames.

When it came time to check out, I had a flash of working-class panic – what if the champagne and the chocolates and all that had not been complimentary? What if I had misunderstood? As we came down to the big reception lounge the same smart American was there and hovered over.

"Was everything ok, Mr Robinson? Mr McDonald sends his apologies as he as a meeting this morning and can't be here to see you himself – and of course everything is taken care of. Thanks so much for staying with us."

I remembered to give him Kiaran's cufflinks at least.

It was such a kind thing for Kiaran to do. I really appreciated it.

Working for charities has meant I have seen the best of people on many occasions in many difficult situations.

And got to stay free at the Savoy.

I was up in Dundee visiting a childcare programme there getting some information first hand on what worked when I got a phone call. The Evening Standard wanted to do an interview with me. The message was they had been told about my past including the bankruptcy. They were going to run a story.

I was very shaken. Although the bankruptcy was not my fault in that it was as a result of someone else's criminal act, and once that was established, I got an automatic discharge, nevertheless it was not something I was proud of and had not made public at all. I realised the story could be twisted to get at Boris as anything approaching scandal was fodder for his many enemies. In fact, I later learned that it was someone associated with the Labour Group on the City Council that had known me back in the day and was trying to cause mischief.

I got straight on the phone to Trevor and told him the whole story. He was, as ever, terrific.

"I don't give a shit about your past, "he said, "you're doing a damn good job now. That's what matters."

When I was back in London, we had taken soundings from our Trustees. The consensus was I should do the interview straightforwardly and paint the picture to the journalist - who happened to be a young woman.

"Charm her," said one Trustee. "You can do that."

I met up with the journalist and told her my story. She asked a lot of questions but seemed friendly and positive. Having said that I was very wary. I knew it was a story that could be spun a number of different ways.

The story came out as a two-page spread in the Evening Standard. It was very balanced and very positive. The reaction was terrific. The Trustees were delighted and felt it was very good for the Fund. Trevor was happy.

I was relieved.

A couple of days later I joined a crowded lift in City Hall. Boris and his Director of Comms, Guto Harri, were in the back of the lift. As we went up, I heard that familiar voice:

"Great story in the Standard, Chris, well done."

It's a funny thing. Someone seeking to do me harm spread a story to the media. It ended up very positively for me and in fact, once the whole picture was out in the public domain it was a relief all round. Again, I was learning to take life's ups and downs, it's congratulations and brickbats with a calm mind where I could.

In the summer of 2011 when I was in fact off on leave following my son Danny's death, the Board decided to get rid of Trevor. His three-year term as Chairman was up but he had said he was ready to do another three. One or two of the Trustees were plotting against him and once Trevor got wind of that he was not going to stay, in typical principled fashion. I said to him I wanted to resign if he was not going to be Chairman and I felt the Board had not treated him well. He would hear none of it.

"No," he said, firmly, "you have a family. You can't just walk away. Take your time. Pick your moment."

And that is what I did. I resolved that summer that I would go when the time was right and I had something else to go to. That November my mate Ted Gladdish died and I resolved I would change my life. I wanted to stop commuting and go back to football.

Stalin said "you decide what you want to do. The rest is organisation."

Fair enough, Joe. I started organising. I joined Chelsea part time in May 2012 and started as CEO of Naomi House Children's Hospice in nearby Winchester soon after.

Being the first CEO of the Mayor's Fund for London and setting it up with Sir Trevor Chinn was a great experience. Trevor has been a major influence on my life with his example of a brave and principled persona. Working with Boris Johnson at close hand when he was Patron of the Fund and me CEO was very enjoyable overall. However, the stresses and strains built into the structure of the Fund, it's timing just after the financial crash and the political environment all made it very difficult. When you add to that the commuting and pressure and the personal tragedy and other stresses near to home that I had to bear then it was definitely time for some changes.

I can do changes. I have had to.

We all have to.

It is one of the immutable laws of being.

Everything changes. All the time.

Chris Robinson – Over, Under or Through

9. Living Proof

I have tried in my way to be free.

I have tried to love my children well and be the best father I could be for them.

I have tried to teach my children well.

Back when I was managing Cheltenham Town, having just had the lovely time with Carole Coombes, I met a young woman on a players' night out in Birmingham at the end of pre-season training. We got together, got married – my third wife – and were together twenty three years. We had Keir and Oscar, my two youngest boys, and mostly lived in Haslemere in Surrey. Eventually our relationship broke up because of some issues on her part though it was all quite amicable.

I remember years ago, when Keir and Oscar, were about nine or ten, we lived in Camelsdale near Haslemere. We used Camelsdale recreation ground – the 'rec' - a lot. It was not big. There was a playing field and then a grass bank leading up to the playground and over to the side the paths through to the ponds. We played football there, me and the boys. And cricket. And just about anything else. Keir learned to ride his bike there, freewheeling at first down the grassy bank. Oscar did too. The boys would walk through the park or right by it every day on their way to Camelsdale School, their excellent primary school.

One spring when we had a lot of snow we were out there with our friends, and their kids, sledging down the now snow-covered grass bank. It was that lovely luxury of a 'snow day' when those of us who commuted up to London had a sudden day off because the trains were not running, or we couldn't get out cars out of the side roads.

The playing field was just about big enough for a full-sized pitch and both boys played there and I think at least one of them later refereed there. One year when Keir was about seven, he said he wanted a football party for his birthday so I set up a little training session for him and about ten of his mates and we did that at the rec and then we had a picnic there. It was what he wanted.

So, 'the rec' meant a lot to us.

One day I said to the boys, who then were about nine or ten, "OK, come on. We have a challenge to do." I gathered some plastic shopping bags and they dutifully followed me along to the rec. When I had been running through there that morning, I had noticed there was a lot of rubbish and litter around the bench at the top of the grass bank looking down over the playing field. So when we got to the rec I explained our job was to put the litter into the bags, which I duly handed out, and then into the big rubbish bin by the entrance.
They looked puzzled.
"But we didn't put the litter there?" said Keir.
"No, I know," I said.
"And it's not, like, our garden or anything, is it? It's just the rec," said Oscar.
"No, also true. Look, do we use this rec? We play football here and cricket and you used to go on the swings and that."
They nodded.
"So, we get use out of it. Who does it belong to?"
They shrugged.
"It's sort of run by the local council, "I said, 'but really that means it belongs to all of us, the community So it's up to all of us to keep it clean."
"But it's not our fault there's all this crap here!" said Keir.
"No, I know," I said, "I'm not saying it is. But it's our park, in a way. It doesn't matter who did it, really. That is down to them. We can't control what other people do. We can just control how we react to it. This is not about them, it's about us".

I don't know if they got my point but we tidied up and then, yes, ice creams from 'Cee-Gees' the corner shop were involved.

Sometime later when they were with me in London, when they were teenagers, I gave some money to a rough sleeper in a concrete space under a flyover stairs by Waterloo, as we walked along.
"What will he do with that money?" asked Keir.
"That's up to him," I said.
'Wouldn't it be better to give him food?"
"Well, no-one tells me how to spend my money, do they? So I can't really tell him what to do. Besides I didn't do it for him."
"What?" Oscar looked genuinely puzzled.
"No."
"Who did you do it for then?" asked Oscar.
"For me."

That had them quiet for a while. I must ask them if they ever worked that one out.

Conversation. Listening. Waiting. Considering. Thinking.
The dying arts.

Pat, Nye and Micky – 'The Boys' – my three wonderful sons from my first marriage. On the too rare occasions we do all get together I look round the table at these three, now grown men of course, with their own lovely families, and am so proud. They are good people to be with – kind, smart, loving and all three very good fathers themselves. A week or so after my recent wedding my mate Richard Shadforth said to me how he was so impressed by the boys at the wedding, how good they were to be with, how welcoming and friendly they were to everyone, such good company. It was good to hear though I of course already knew it.

I am sure my first wife deserves a lot of credit too for how they have turned out.

My first child was born when I was twenty-seven years old. Patrick Blair Robinson was named after Patrick Pearse of the Easter Rising in Ireland and Blair Peach the teacher I knew who died after being hit on the head by the police in the anti-racism demonstration in in 1979 in Southall that I was on too.

When Pat was about two years old, and we were living still in Bacup, Lancashire, one winter night he had a real bad throaty cough. It got so bad we called the Doctor out. A young locum called Dr Williams came out. Pat was in a bad way by now. The Doctor seemed nervous, a bit shaken by how bad Pat's breathing was.
" I think it might be croup," said the Doctor. "I'm..I'm going to give him an injection and call the ambulance."
The ambulance came and I went with Pat in it to Burnley General Hospital. I held him in arms, he was struggling to breathe, a terrible strangled hoarse noise in his throat. We got to the Hospital and they soon had him sorted, the injection that young Dr Williams gave him apparently saved his life. He came round quick and was soon sat up in bed, much the same as ever. Two things struck me.
Firstly, well done Dr Williams for your knowledge, you're training and your nerve.
Secondly, as I recalled how I felt holding my son in my arms, in the back of that ambulance, going to the hospital, feeling sure he was going to die, I knew I would never ever forget that. I haven't. I have seen at too close hand how awful it can be for a parent to lose a child. Maybe the writing was on the wall back on that wintery night in east Lancashire as the ambulance rattled us over the hill to Burnley.

I remember when we knew our second child was on the way. I sat on the floor of Pat's little bedroom in the house on the hill in Bacup up at the top of Bankside Lane. I was worried. I just could not understand how when this other little baby arrived, I would have any room to love him as I loved Pat with all my heart. I am sure countless parents have wondered the same thing, had the same worry. Of course, as it turns out each baby arrives with their own supply of love.

Every child is a blessing.

Aneurin James Robinson followed in November 1982, named after Nye Bevan and James Connolly – two of my heroes. (You can do the Googling now for those – you'll have to do some of the work!).

Nye had a big disadvantage growing up (apart from his name, I hear some of you say, you philistines!) - that was as a child he looked very much like me. I remember going to pick him up from football training when he was about twelve. The coach was an old mate of mine, Jimmy Clarke, that I used to play with and as Nye came over to us, Jimmy said:
"Bloody hell, don't you look like your Dad!"
We laughed at that and as we got into the car Nye said:
"Every day someone says that to me."
"What?"
"That I look like you."
"Oh..sorry."
"No," said Nye, smiling, "I don't mind."

Michael Anthony Robinson (Davitt and Benn) came in September 1984 when as it turned out my first marriage was on its last legs and falling away.

Micky was a sturdy child but has grown into the tallest and slimmest of my tall, slim handsome sons. He was excellent at Maths all through school, blitzed through his 'A' levels and went to Leeds University to study Maths. Within a few weeks though he was telling me he was not enjoying it. It was a different subject at university. He switched courses to 'Media Studies' and really enjoyed that. He saw a problem, sorted it and fixed it. Impressive.

All three boys grew up loving sport, football in particular. They all played to a good standard – Pat and Nye at Burnley, Nye played for Lancashire too and Micky played for the District team. They loved their cricket too – Nye played Lancashire League cricket for Bacup at sixteen.

Sport – and football in particular – was our 'lingua franca', our common experience, our training language. We always had something to talk about and it was the same later on with my two youngest boys, Keir and Oscar. Football became our memories, our shared experienced, our connecting point.

There are very few people that I will actually choose to watch a live game sat next to, particularly a Chelsea game. Mostly I am so engaged in the game I would rather be on my own. However, all five of my sons are in my exclusive little club – I know, it's probably another sad reflection on me, but it also says something about them and me.

I have had to work hard at keeping a relationship going with the three older boys and I have made some mistakes as usual, along the way. But I kept at it and get the reward every time I see them and spend time with them.

But it was tough. To explain I would need to go back.

It was my fault my first marriage collapsed. Firstly, in retrospect, I married the wrong person! However, seriously, I was at fault so let me take the responsibility.

It was not surprising therefore that my first wife was very bitter. I tried to say that I had left her and not the boys – that much was true of course, but maybe not helpful for me to say it. I desperately wanted joint custody at least but back in those days it was very difficult to get that.

It also must be said that denying me time with the boys was just about the only weapon that could be used against me.

It was very difficult to sort any arrangements out. I would turn up at an agreed time and no-one would be there. It happened so often. Then there would be long periods when I was refused any access at all. It was, of course, torture for me – as it was intended to be, I guess.

My solicitor was a football mate of mine – Mark Gosnell – now a judge, funnily enough. Mark guided me through the court system though made it clear that it was very difficult to get access orders enforced. There were endless orders, some adhered to and some not. Christmas and holidays were particularly difficult. Anyway, I kept at it, kept going. My ex-wife's solicitor stopped representing her. I kept going.

Eventually one Christmas, as I've mentioned before, when I had been denied access again, I got an unexpected phone call from my ex-wife. "You might as well come and pick them up, "she said. "They are refusing to do anything till they see you."

I was there. I knew I had won through. This is what I had been working for over the years. The boys had voted with their feet.

We settled into me having them two out of three weekends and in holiday times. But along the way I had made a mistake which I see clearly now as I look back.

I had needed to earn a living. When my work moved from being Manchester and then Rossendale based to being Preston and then the Lakes as I moved into financial consultancy, I felt I had to follow the work, had to earn. Then I was ill and back in Lancashire but with no job or money so again followed the work down to the Midlands. All through I fought for and then kept the contact going until it got regularised.

Years later I was talking to Nye about those times. We had some good memories. He asked why I had moved away, and I explained about the work and trying to earn a living and so on which he understood. He said though that particularly when he was about fourteen, he would have wished I was closer.
"I would have loved to be able to call in on my way back from school or something," he said.
I thought a lot about this and realised I had done wrong.

I don't honestly regret my first marriage breaking up other than for how it affected the boys. I do regret not staying closer to them in terms of location. I should have stayed where they could walk to me when they needed to.

I will always regret that.

One day when Pat was about six or seven, I got the local paper, and his photo was in it. He had won some art contest at school – which was great, the paper had his name as Patrick Brennan, not Robinson. I was dumbstruck. Brennan was not even my ex-wife's maiden name but her mother's maiden name. It all seemed weird.

So, the game started again. The divorce papers clearly said the boys' name could not be changed without my permission. Mark got on the case but there was no solicitor at the other end making sense of the situation. It dragged on. Eventually after various court orders and solicitor's letters and so on it went to court – but it took ages to get to that.

I had a barrister presenting for me in court. There was no legal defence really at all. Finally, the judge said he had decided to leave the Boys name as Brennan as so much time had passed. I was mortified.

"So, if I rob a bank and keep the money for eighteen months it's all OK?" I said.

But that was it. It was a crazy situation. On the steps of the court house I said to the Barrister

"I feel like I've lost the boys all over again."

The boys were too young to understand what was going on, but I promised them that when they each got to eighteen if they wanted to change their name back to their real name, I would pay for it and organise it.

When they did get to eighteen years old, I took each of them out to lunch and we went over the story. In each case they said that so much time had own passed they were used to being called this other name. I think they also knew I was easy going and we communicated so well that they could talk it over reasonably with me whereas that might not be the case with their mother. I have paid a price for being so easy-going on more than one occasion!

I must say it still really hurts when I see them called the made-up name not their real one - and of course my grandchildren are called that too. It bites me every time it comes up or I address an envelope or whatever. But I guess that was the point of it. My ex-wife can call herself what she likes, of course, but it was simply morally wrong to change the names of the boys at an age when they could not decide for themselves. It was legally wrong too so the judge's decision was mystifying to say the least, but I could not afford to appeal.

I still have their original birth certificates with their real names.

However, overall, I have a great relationship with the boys and their lovely families. Better than I really could have reasonably hoped for, I guess. Some years ago, when I was working for the Trade Union, I knew a guy who had been married before, marriage split up and he had effectively lost contact with his children from that marriage. I can remember pontificating with the certainty of naive youth along the lines of:

"I can't understand how any father can lose contact with his children. It just would never happen to me."

It didn't happen to me, but I came to understand the pain and emotional cost of battling for access. It is awful. I will never criticise anyone who struggles with it all.

I had two children from my second marriage – Danny born in 1986 and then Rachel – finally a daughter - two years later. Danny always struggled with ill health. He would keep getting recurring chest infections and it was a mystery as to what was causing it and we went back and forth to doctors and hospitals right from the start.

We weren't planning a second child and my first reaction was a pause of exasperation – but then I was caught up in the joy. Every child, as I say, is a blessing. However, my second wife seemed to think I didn't want another child and even though that was not the case she got it into her head.

For whatever reasons, a few years down the line, I found myself with my second marriage collapsing and here I was battling for access again.

About two years ago, during lockdown I walked along the lane in Rogate where I was living. I was often out walking in those times, ranging through the lovely surrounding woods. But this particular walk was just a brief stroll to the old rather battered looking little red post box up the lane, just before one of the paths into the woods.

This letter was to my daughter, Rachel, who is in Australia. I guessed it would take weeks to get to her but that does not really matter. I actually photographed it and emailed it to her that way so she could read it straight away, but I feel the original is something she might want to keep so I sent it off into the world. I hope so, anyway.

Rachel is my only daughter, as I have said, a child of my second marriage. She and my son, Danny, were brought up in Salford and she went to university there, too. When their mother and I broke up it was very bitter and difficult all round. I don't want to re-hash the sad story. It's water under the bridge and, besides, still painful. Generally, in my life, I take responsibility for each and every one of the mistakes I have made – and, unfortunately, there have been quite a few! I take responsibility for every one of the tears whether I have shed them or caused them. I find that is easier overall. I don't have room in my life for recriminations, in any direction.

It was a difficult time back then. I had to go through the courts access route to see my children at all which I would not wish on anyone. I remember one time having to go through what was then termed 'supervised access' which meant a social worker sat in the same room at a scruffy family centre in Bolton while I played with Danny and Rachel. I cannot describe to you what that was like. I said to the social worker while we were waiting for the kids to arrive:
"Have you any idea how this makes me feel?"
But I did it. I jumped through the hoops.
Ah, it was a long time ago, another life and time. Does it matter now?

Yes, in some ways it does because it was part of the background to why Rachel and I did not get so much time together as I would have wished for, as she grew up. We stayed in touch of course. I would send the birthday presents and cards and the Christmas presents, and I would get to see her and Danny occasionally. We had a long-distance relationship, I suppose, even before she went to Australia. I will talk more about Danny in the next chapter.

Over the years Rachel and I have kept in touch and met up occasionally before she went to Australia – far too occasionally – and I have watched her from afar grow up to become a beautiful young woman, now in her early thirties. She went out to Australia a few years ago – her mother is Australian so Rachel has dual nationality, as I recall, which must make the immigration thing easier.

One of the benefits of the much-maligned social media is that it helps us keep in touch with family members and friends who are far away. I am sure we have all felt the benefit of that in this lockdown limbo, too, by the way, in particular. I know I have. I have had great contact with old football friends, in particular, and that has been so heart-warming, reviving so many memories of us all, in many cases years ago when we were young and strong and in our prime.

Recently Rachel and I have been messaging a bit more, and Rachel said she had been thinking about family quite a bit. Then Julie sat me down and gave me a talking to, metaphorically. I had been saying I had not seen as much of Rachel as I would like, and I really regretted that.
"Have you told Rachel you love her?" Julie asked in her usual direct perceptive way.
"No, I guess not." I finally said, head down.
"About time you did then?"

So, I did. I wrote Rachel that letter that I mentioned. I won't go through exactly what I said in it here because it is between me and Rachel. But I can say, encouraged by Julie, I referred back to what had happened, but just briefly, and mainly said how much I missed her and that I loved her.

I said that I hoped it was not too late to be the father for her that I wanted to be.

Maybe it's never too late to love. Although sometimes it can be. Life happens. The moment passes. The wheel turns. Someone walks away. The page turns. You move house. You move countries. Maybe sometimes someone dies. You get older and there are other things in front of you to do. The sun goes down and when it comes up it is another day.

Perhaps there is someone out there who you need to tell that you love them? I don't know but you will. Maybe there is someone there you think knows that but maybe you have not told them enough. Again, you will know. Maybe it's hard to pick up the phone. I don't know. Maybe it's time to get some paper and a pen and write your letter. I did and I'm glad I did.

I have a daughter I love. I have told her that.

And, you know what? It turns out she loves me, too.

When it came time in my third marriage (are you keeping up here?) I was ready for children – I do love kids – but I was determined that whatever happened I was going to be there for them as dad all the way through, at least until they were through University age. Keir was born in Hereford in January 1998 and Oscar in Harrow in London in 1999.

I got to do all the first steps and first words, the first days at school the parents evening and everything all the way through as I promised myself I would. The boys had little choice but to love sport of course. I coached each of them in their local teams for a couple of seasons each and that was great (though I am not temperamentally suited to kids' local football – I am once more far too competitive!).

And we had Chelsea. It was when we were living in the little village of Middleton Stoney, near Bicester and I was working at 'Off the Streets' that I decided I should try and get a season ticket at the Bridge. My then wife agreed but on one condition:
"That's OK," she said, "But you'll have to take the boys with you."

Keir was about two and Oscar literally a babe in arms! However, it turned out all was possible at Chelsea. They had a free creche under the East Stand at Stamford Bridge. You could only book a week ahead so you had to be off the mark sharpish each week, but it was great. I started taking them up, installing them in the creche and then going round to my seat and then picking them up. So, they literally grew up at the Bridge and got used to the crowds and the noise.

The creche was great. They even had a Xmas party for the kids. It was not much publicised, and I think Chelsea were one of very few big clubs to provide the service but it was vital for us.

When Keir got to four years old he was avidly following games on TV, so I tried him out at a couple of local games and then got him a season ticket and we switched to the Family Stand. When Oscar got to four and also followed games on TV well enough, I got him a ticket too. So, for many years the three of us would go to every Chelsea home game in our season ticket. We had our rituals as most fans do – parking in the same place, going to the McDonalds in North End Road before the game and so on. I think Oscar's first game was Jose Mourinho's first game (Eidur Gudjohnsen scored, I think, for us to beat Manchester united 1-0) so we enjoyed some great seasons together.

This crucial common connection of shared experience in going to Chelsea together for about fifteen years has been really important for me, Keir and Oscar. It has created shared memories that we will never forget.

I have thought over the years how lucky Keir and Oscar have been to go to see their team so many times. There are many thousands of kids around whose parents just could not afford to do that. It has been a real privilege.

As a kid myself I would go with my dad virtually every Saturday to one game or another – Arsenal, Chelsea, West Ham – all the London clubs. But that was a different time when admission prices were geared for working class families and you could just rock up to any game and get in on the day – although given we were always in the standing areas on the vast terraces you might not as a small child always see so much of the game. I have no illusion that the seating and better views and better amenities are obviously so much better these days but it's for a different audience now. Keir and Oscar were just fortunate they could be part of that new audience.

As for a slice of a whole generation of working-class kids who went on to go to university and got better paid jobs than their parents and experienced a bit of what we now call 'social mobility' of some of the sixties and seventies, I have been able to give my children many more material things than my parents could give me. Because I have earned so much more in relative terms than my parents, the boys have experienced us owning our houses, very nice houses of late, having many holidays abroad, nice cars, new football boots, and on and on – including season tickets at Chelsea for Keir and Oscar. Many of us parents who have been through that have questioned whether this has always been to the advantage of our children.

Of course, it has overall – again harking back to the old Max Miller line "whether you're rich or you're poor, it's nice to have money" – and having been really poor at least twice in my lifetime, I know which I prefer. But I think of my children and at times do think that Keir and Oscar, in particular, have that sort of sense of security knowing the Bank of Dad will bail them out if it really comes to it. Is that a bad thing? I am not sure it leads to growing up and taking responsibility quite as well as it should.

This is something Julie and I talk about a lot, and we do with our friends too who are in similar positions. It is a bit of a conundrum – again it's a first world problem, I do understand that, and one born of having good choices about resources, but it is something to consider.

I do believe it is important for children to grow up knowing the value if things, not just their price. By that I mean they need to understand what most people have to do to earn the money to buy those things, what it costs in human effort and sweat.

Over the years, from necessity I also got a lot of experience of long-distance parenting – and more recently, grandparenting.

As I write this, I have five lovely grandchildren, three boys and two girls, all up in Lancashire.

 Keir and Oscar are relatively local, being about forty minutes from where Julie and I live, just outside Worthing. Julie has two daughters who live in Worthing, with two grandchildren now and Freddie, her son who is severely autistic and lives with us. So, we have a lot of family connections down here in the South here too, and a lot of friends. And, of course, my work is still down here – that old issue – and still very demanding.

So, however you look at it, given this spread-out extended family, wherever we live there will be some distance involved somewhere. Like many people in the lockdown, I thought a lot about priorities and how much I wanted to see more of my family.

The practicality is difficult. The Lancashire lot are a five-hour drive away. We are busy, they are busy, all getting on with our lives.

This is not an unusual problem these days. My mate Derek Mead who sits next to me in my season ticket at Chelsea has a five-year-old grandson up in Scotland – also autistic, funnily enough – and at a recent game we talked about the difficulties of being a Grandad at such a distance. We agreed you have to adjust the way you think about them and accept – as hard as it is – that the relationship with your children and grandchildren at a distance is not the same as it would be if they lived five miles away. You have to adjust, and you have to make the best of it you can – and both ends of the relationship have to work at it.

I once heard Malcolm Muggeridge say on TV that there was no such thing as progress. For every step we took forward on one sphere we took one back in another. You invent safer cheaper more reliable cars but add to your traffic problems and have to carve up more lovely countryside for bigger and bigger roads.

However, this always felt a bit of a negative, depressing view and I don't absolutely agree. I do know the issues and problems, along with the opportunities and advantages, of my life are very different to those of my parents'. Not necessarily bigger nor necessarily smaller but certainly different. I think, looking back, my parents did really well meeting their challenges.

I can only hope I do as well facing mine.

10. One Minute You're There…..

I take our lovely chocolate Labrador pup, Dixie, out for a walk two or three times a day, mostly around here in the South Downs. There is one walk I like to do in the early mornings up behind us long a narrow sandy path through some trees up to where there are fields of horses and some stables, high up on the chalky hill. This morning as we trudged along, Dixie suddenly went off into one of her lunges to the woods on my left. I was ready for her, though, and held fast and managed to stay upright. She was staring into the woods. I stood and looked too. Often at such times I will see a bobbing disappearing white tail of a deer, or the slinky scuttle away of a cat, or maybe a fox turning curiously to look back as he made his way over the hill in the woods. But there was nothing that I could see.

"You're chasing after ghosts, Dix," I said as I pulled her away and we resumed the steady trudge up the path.

It got me thinking about what she could see. There was probably an animal I missed as often her fine senses will pick up something that I cannot see or hear or smell. But maybe she sees other things, other remnants of lives lived or gone, maybe she can see ghosts or images, who can tell?

Now I don't really believe in ghosts. Having seen that spark of life leave a body and leave a pile of inanimate bones and flesh only, I have a feel for the magical mysterious essence we all enjoy. So maybe that incredible spark lives on in some way. But why are ghosts that people say they have seen always clothed? I mean, just maybe that human spirit can live on in some ineffable way but their clothes? I would be happier with naked ghosts, not of course in a pervy way, I hasten to say, at least I don't think it is, but in a more appealing logic sort of way.

My Mum died twenty-nine years ago. Sometime before she died we were talking about whether there might be life after death. We were both sceptical but open-minded.

"I tell you what," she said," if it is possible to come back after death then I will come back to you."
"Right," I said, "it's a deal" and we both laughed. I did think about this for a few years after she died but there was no sign, so I put it away in my file of 'conversations with Mum' and was okay with the realisation that I was none the wiser.

It can be so hard to separate out the remembered past from the actual now. I've read of how those collective family memories and myths that we all have can be as real to us in memory as if they all really happened, and some of them may not have really happened at all. But they become real to us by repetition.

The key people in our lives are often so vivid we know what they would say in almost any situation and can almost hear their voice, even after they have died, and that is normal and fine.
When Mum died I was talking to my son, Nye, who then about eleven I guess, and we were talking about how in some ways those you love are always with you.
"Yes," he said," When I go out and it's a cold morning I bet I can hear Nan telling me to put a vest on!"
And, of course, in that way he was right. They live on with us in what they have given us and taught us and how it effects our lives going forward.

I don't believe in heaven or hell. I think I have seen a little of each here on earth in life.
They call the blues, which I love, the 'devil's music'. Well, if in the event that I die (very likely) and I do find there is a heaven (very unlikely) and realise I have actually made a terrible mistake (extremely unlikely) and I do get to the pearly gates (almost

inconceivable), and they are playing hymns and not a bit of Muddy Waters or BB King then I think I'll head for the other place.

I have sat in the dark hours, looking out onto a summer night in the moonlight, thinking of my child who had died the day before. I have been homeless, I have been suddenly unemployed with a family to feed, I have travelled in an ambulance with one of my children in my arms and really not thought he would make it to the hospital, I have read lies about myself and my personal life in national papers. And you tell me there is a hell somewhere else?

What would heaven be? Every working day I get to go to the training ground of the club I have supported, and lived for, for over sixty years. The security guys wave me in and know my name. I have seen my seven children born and held them in that sudden wonder and joy. I have seen most of them grow up. I have loved and been loved. I have experienced that look in that someone's eyes when you catch them looking at you and they smile and hope to again. What could heaven show me?

My Mum had barely ever been ill as far as I can recall. At sixty she looked fifty. She was careful what she ate, never smoked in her life and was not a big drinker. She watched her weight too and was in good shape.
Mum and Dad had sold their council flat in Barking ("I know you don't agree with it, but we need to do it,": she'd said. I told her I was fine with it; it was their decision and they'd be daft not to. It was the overall policy I was not a fan of.) With what they got for that they could buy a lovely little terraced house in Worsthorne, an attractive village up near Burnley, close to the Boys, her beloved grandchildren.
One day she asked me to come over to see her. I did, of course, and dad let me in when I knocked. Mum was sat in the armchair, pale and stricken. I leant over and gave her a kiss and a hug and sat on

the edge of the sofa opposite. Something was up. Mum took a gulping breath.

"I've got cancer," she said.

"What?"

"Cancer. Lung cancer."

She told me the story. She had been troubled with some back pain, high in her back. Her GP referred her to the hospital, there were tests and so on, all leading to this.

I struggled to take it in.

"What happens then?" I said" What treatment?"

"Well, first thing is I've got to go in to hospital. They are going to remove a lung."

Her eyes filled.

"I'm scared," she said in a little voice. I sat on the arm of the chair as she cried, and I hugged her.

I told her about Malcolm Allison, one of my football coach heroes. "He had a lung removed," I said, "and he's fine."

After the operation I visited her in Burnley General Hospital, the hospital where Pat, Nye and Micky had been born. The hospital where I had gone in that ambulance with Pat years before.

She had just come round. I sat on the edge of the bed and held her hand.

"How did it go?" I asked brightly.

"They couldn't do it" she said.

"Why not?"

"There was too much...it's right through..nothing they can do now."

So, she had had the trauma of being opened up for the operation then they had seen what was there and closed her up again. This was July 1992.

On 23rd February 1993 I was on a train travelling from the Midlands where I was living on my way up via Manchester to Burnley. My Mum was dying in hospital.

I thought over the last seven months since Mum's diagnosis. She had battled on, mostly in hospital, sometimes better, sometimes worse. There was no treatment they could give her really. All they could do was try and make her comfortable. She began to decline.

When Christmas was coming she announced she was coming home for Christmas. We were all amazed, if doubtful. She wanted Christmas with her children and grandchildren, she said. She was fed up with hospital.

I can remember standing by the doorway into my lounge down in Evesham on Christmas Day., Mum was dressed and smiling, looking a bit frail and thin but her eyes were bright and alive as she watched the noisy boys and their Christmas presents in front of her. It was the usual raucous lively scrum of family life. She looked up and our eyes locked. She nodded at me slightly and smiled and I smiled back and winked. Then I turned away into the kitchen, my eyes full of tears. I knew what was going on.

She was determined to have a last Christmas with her kids. Typical of my Mum, it was a matter of character and a determined will against cancer. No contest, then. Not for a while anyway.

Straight after Christmas she was back in hospital, worse than ever. My sister, Pauline and I took it in turns to go up and visit Mum and Dad. Pauline travelled up and down to Burnley from Somerset and me from Evesham in Worcestershire.

In February I had sat by Mum's hospital bed. She was asleep, heavily sedated against the pain by then. She came round a bit and looked over at me and gave a tight little smile as I kissed her. I sat on the side of the bed. She looked up at me.
"You know," she said, "I could just turn my face to this wall and die."
"I know," I said.

Then Dad had phoned me. I had just returned from Burnley, and I knew Pauline was going up the next day.
"You'd better come back," said Dad. "Not long now."

I'd gone back to the station and got that train north. I just knew that Mum would have died by the time I got there. I thought of the last seven months of illness and struggle. I thought of Christmas and of course thought of growing up and all the love from Mum over the years. By the time I got to Burnley I had made my peace with the memories and was as ready as I'd ever be to face this.

I got a taxi to the hospital. Dad was in the foyer. I don't know how long he'd been waiting there.
"She's gone," he said. He told me she's been asleep and then woke up. She just said to him.
"Tell the kids."
He knew what she meant so he'd phoned me and Pauline. Mum had died shortly after.

Dad and I went upstairs to the ward. There were two nurses attending to her. I stood in the doorway.
"Do you want to have a while with her?" one nurse kindly asked.
"No, "I said, "I've said my goodbyes."
And I had. On that train journey up, I knew I would be too late, and I had said my goodbyes amidst reliving all those memories on the way.

The family gathered for the funeral. The night before we were all gathered at the little house in Worsthorne feeling miserable. After a while someone spoke up:
"This is not right. Nan would not have wanted this. Let's all go out and do something."
They were right. We went out ten pin bowling as a family. Mum would have loved it.

The morning of the funeral was OK. I was doing all right getting ready. We knew a lot of people would be coming. However, when the flowers started arriving I fell apart. The messages were so lovely. As we knew Mum had touched a lot of people's lives with her good heart and this showed. My sister was really struggling at that point too.
I went out through the village for a walk on my own.
I had tears in my eyes. I spoke out loud:
"Mum, I need your help. I've got to hold it together for the kids."
I took a big breath and straightened my back, put my shoulders back and looked the world in the eye, just like she taught me. I walked back. I got through it.

I have heard other people say that it is only when one of your parents die that you come face to face with your own mortality. I knew then what they meant.

One of the things that really struck me over the next few weeks was that every time in my life when something happened to me, be it good or bad, my first thought would inevitably be – "what will Mum say about this?" She had been that sounding board for all my life's events. I have missed that.

We arranged for Dad to sell the Worsthorne house and buy a little house in Shepton Beauchamp the village in Somerset where my sister lives. It seemed to everyone the right thing to do.

Dad was lost without Mum. She had organised him and every aspect of their lives. She had particularly organised their money. Selling the Barking flat and buying the little terraced house in Worsthorne had been a shrewd move meaning they had no mortgage and a good chunk of money in the bank. One day my sister was round at my dad's now down in Somerset and she found a bank statement. Dad had been going through money like the proverbial hot knife through butter.

Basically, the nest egg was gone and some more besides. Pauline called me, I went down, and we both sat down with Dad and sorted his finances out. We bailed him out of debt between us and my sister took over his finances. It had been his money so he could do what he wanted with it, but he had gone beyond that and got into debt. Mum would have been mortified. He was a silly old sod. Fortunately, my sister and my niece, Clare, were on hand to keep an eye on him now and, although always so bereft without Mum, he had a good life in the village from then on.

Dad's death remains a bit of a mystery. Just getting towards Christmas in 2000 my brother-in-law Dave called me. We were living in Middleton Stoney then, near Bicester.
"I don't know how to tell you this, Chris, but I have some awful news. It's your Dad. He was involved in a car accident and I'm afraid he's dead."

On Friday nights Dad would drive his old Rover over to the next village, a few miles away, and have two pints playing snooker with some old mates in the Legion there. He had done that as normal on this particular Friday night and parked his car a street or so away from the club. Maybe the car park was full. His old cronies said he was the same as normal. Couple of pints and a few games of snooker.

He was killed walking on the A303 a few miles away late that night. As far as the police could make out for some reason he had left his car and started walking the three or four miles back to his village. This was very strange because we couldn't imagine Dad choosing to walk anywhere with his car at hand, especially on a cold winter's night. Dad walked on onto the A303 – which is virtually like a motorway at that point – and was walking along that towards the junction for his village when a car came from the London direction behind him, and Dad was somehow in the middle of the inside lane. There are no street lights there on that section of the A303. Dad was hit by the car and died soon after.

Why had Dad left his car? When the police recovered it, they said it did not have much petrol in it but probably enough to get him home. His old mates said he had not had any more to drink than usual – not that that would have stopped him driving in all probability. Maybe he forgot where his car was? Who knows?

I drove down to Somerset on my motorbike. I met the police liaison officer with my sister, and he was very helpful. He took us to where Dad had died. I went and spoke to Dad's old mates. However, like the police officer said, we probably would never know exactly what happened.

We had the funeral. I told my stories about Dad.

A few days later I had another death to deal with.

Way back when I lived up in the Lakes I got a dog – a yellow Labrador puppy. I had always wanted a dog but living in a flat as we mostly did there was no chance growing up. So, one day I drove to a house in Carlisle and there picked out the biggest of the litter as he seemed interested in me and brought Charley home.

He was with me for about twelve years, going with me from new start to new start. He was my best friend and my dearest companion. He was a big daft typical Lab – loving, loyal and food mad. He was great with the kids – they used to crawl all over him, pulling his whiskers and poking fingers in his eyes. He just rolled with it, maybe giving them another lick. He was very adept at nicking the odd biscuit off them though.

At one stage, while living near Evesham I thought I really should try and get him some training. As it happened, I had seen a notice for dog training to be held in the village hall just down the road. I went along and signed Charley and me up.

There were a lot of dogs and owners there, so it was bedlam at times with dogs kicking off and yapping. At one point the trainer – a middle aged woman – took Charley down one end of the hall and got me to stand at the other.

"Now," she said, straining to keep hold of big old Charley. "If I let Charley go and you call him, will he come to you?'

"If you let Charley go, he will come and take me through this wall behind me whether I call him or not."

She clearly doubted me. She released the straining Charley. I muttered 'here, Charley' but I knew it was unnecessary. Charley hurtled down the hall, brushing aside several other dogs who wandered out in the process, scattering them like nine pins. He launched himself at me from about ten feet away. As I lay on my back against the hall wall, with Charley over me, enthusiastically licking my face, I heard the trainer say:

"Ah yes...right. OK...now let's try with Toodles shall we?" She went off to the next dog and owner and I presumed she had given us up as a lost cause.

At the end of the class, she called over:

"Ah, Mr Robinson! I wonder if we might have a word after class?"

Now Charley had by then had a bit of a run-in with a yappy King Charles Spaniel which did not go well.

"Bloody hell," I thought, "we are getting expelled after the first night!"

So, me and Charley waited. She eventually finished up and came over.

"Mr Robinson – what I wanted to say was have you ever thought of training Charley for Obedience Competition? I have never seen a dog so attentive of its owner in thirty years. You could be at Crufts in a couple of years!"

"Crufts? I'll be happy if I can get him to walk alongside me."

We never went back.

As is sadly too common with labs, gradually Charley's hips and back began to cause him trouble and then got worse and worse. I took him regularly to the vets and he was on expensive tablets but the dose had to be regularly increased as time went by. However, they did help him enjoy some more years in the family, at the centre of things, being fussed and fed by everyone, which is what Charley loved. If I was to leave the room, even just to go to the toilet, Charley would immediately jump up and follow. He was totally dedicated to me.

Just after my dad had died, Charley was taking a turn for the worse. It was a day or so after Christmas. Charley could barely get upstairs, and I was frightened he would fall down them and really hurt himself. I knew what I had to do.

The vet was sympathetic.

"I am really glad you've brought him in," he said." It is time."

He gave Charley an injection. Charley lay down across my lap as I held him on the floor of the surgery. The vet left us alone.

As I write this, I have tears rolling down my cheeks. God knows what I was like then as I held and kissed my dear old friend who was dying in my arms.

The young vet came back in to check Charley.

I was in bits.

"He was my best friend," I sobbed. "And my dad died last week, too!"

The poor vet! I had not actually cried when my dad died nor at the funeral. But I did for Charley. Maybe it was all joined up.

When I got home, funnily enough, my sister was there. She had driven over from Somerset just on spec to see me. As I got out of the car, without Charley, she knew what had gone down. She came out to meet me, holding out her arms. I collapsed sobbing into them.

I swore I would never get another dog. I had had my dog. He was so lovely; how could I ever get another?

I stuck with that for twenty years and then this year Julie persuaded me – not only that we should have a dog but that it should be a Labrador. Now as I sit here, I can hear, snoring somewhat less then gently behind me as I write in my study, Dixie our chocolate lab puppy. I can't help but think though that Charley would approve of her.

Later there was an Inquest for my Dad. The driver of the car – a middle aged lorry driver actually, who had been driving from London to see his girlfriend, told his side of the story. Dad appeared out of nowhere, right in the middle of the lane in front of him. No, he said, he wasn't speeding.

The coroner was kind and helpful but there was not much to say. As the Inquest finished I said to the police officer I wanted to speak to the car driver. The police officer looked at me carefully.
"OK," he said after a pause. He walked me and my sister over to where the car driver was with his girlfriend. The police officer stood almost between us.
"Look, "I said to the car driver, a burly balding ordinary looking guy, "I just wanted to say on behalf of my family that….this must have been an awful experience for you. Obviously you are not to blame in any way."
The guy slumped like all the air had been sucked from him and burst into tears. I shook his hand.
"My Dad used to be a lorry driver, "I said, "you'd have liked him."

I did have one close call myself with mortality. We were on holiday in Fuerteventura one Easter. Keir and Oscar were about seven and six years old. My son Nye was with us – he was in his early twenties maybe.

It was Easter, the weather in Fuerteventura was good but it was not busy at all. Me and Nye were playing football with Keir and Oscar on a beach. My wife was sunbathing further up the beach.

For some reasons the island did attract a lot of German tourists and the beaches on the east side of the island did have a few areas where some of these tourists went naked. Not always an edifying sight. I had vaguely noticed an elderly couple walking further down on the beach nearer the water's edge and the guy - a pudgy, sturdy grey haired fella maybe in his early seventies – looked like he was one of the nudist wanderers.

Anyway, we got on with our football then I noticed the old woman waving frantically and shouting at us, but she was too far away for me to hear anything. The old guy had gone swimming, and he was thrashing about in the water about thirty meters from the shoreline.

"Nye, come on, that fellas in trouble!" I told the boys to go back to their M<um and Nye and I ran down to the woman on the water's edge. She gestured towards her husband frantically.

"He is drowning! He can't get back!" she said in heavily accented English.

We just ran into the water. We are both decent enough swimmers, but this bay had a fierce rip tide which we knew nothing about. We got out to the guy easily enough. He was puffing and struggling. He could not swim back against the rip tide, and he was losing strength. As I got to him he reached out desperately for me, clinging to me.

I wrestled with him, trying to turn him so I could hold his head on my shoulder and swim backwards.

"Stop fucking struggling!" I shouted at him. A bit irrational perhaps but there you go. I eventually got him turned round though he was still heavy to move around in the swirling surging water. I later learned of course that you need to go sideways against a rip tide, but I did not know that and we struggled. Nye and I were trying to get back to shallower water dragging along this dead weight of a German who had more or less passed out by then. It was such hard going, we were making no headway. After a bit Nye gasped:

"I've got to go in," he was just so tired, and I knew what he meant. I can remember so clearly thinking 'that's good, Nye will be safe.'
I held the German with his back to me, head on my shoulder, me trying to keep us both afloat as Nye managed to get back to shallow water.
I was losing strength; my legs and arms were so heavy. I looked back at the shore, and I could see Keir and Oscar standing with my wife and there were two local garbage collectors in their orange uniforms waving at us as they stood with the German woman. I realised later they were trying to tell us to go sideways but I was past understanding now.
I can remember thinking "Well, OK, I'm going to die, going to drown here. It's not so bad, just a shame the boys will have to see it."
I was not afraid. Just tired.
Then suddenly my weary leg strokes and the twisting current must have moved me a bit sideways because suddenly I felt a rock under my left foot. I stood on it, it took my weight and relief flooded through me. I held on to the German and then Nye was back. Together we managed to get him in to the shallows. There was a small crowd there by then and others came into the shallows and took hold of the German guy and dragged him on to the sand. There was an ambulance and people milling round. I saw the German guy had regained consciousness. Nye and I sat in the shallows exhausted.
"Come on, "I said, struggling up, "let's go."
We slipped away.

It was a strange experience altogether. Those morning sin Fuerteventura Nye and I would go for a run along the sea shore together each morning. The next morning we met up as usual and started jogging along. The sky was already blue and the sun getting warm.
"You sleep OK?" I asked.
"No," he said, "couldn't settle at all."
"Nor me, "I said. "How you feeling?"
'Shit," he said.

"Me, too."
As we ran along we talked about how strange it was when we felt we should have been in a great mood, having saved someone's life the afternoon before, when in fact we both felt quiet depressed.
Some weeks after we were back I told the story to a psychiatrist I knew, and she said it was not unusual or surprising at all that we felt down. She explained it was probably the after effects of the massive adrenalin surges through our bodies during the rescue.

I have out it down as one of life's experiences and just noted it and not tried to explain it any further. However, those moments when I had my own death in front of me remain very clear. I was weary but not at all frightened. There was just a feeling of peace. It was OK. I don't know if I can draw any conclusions from it for me, you or anyone else. I am just telling you what happened.

My son, Danny, had health problems all through is life. This was essentially from a blood disorder that effected his immune system and made it virtually impossible for him to fight off specific chest and lung infections. At first in his childhood it was not even easily detected or identified but as medical research advanced they could be more specific.

By the time of his late teens and early twenties he managed to get through University doing film studies – he loved his movies - and had in many respects had what we would call a normal life. He was a happy lad with a lot of friends and other than being an avid Manchester United fan, he was a good lad. He was however having to have these regular sorts of major transfusions which virtually changed his blood over. These were intrusive and exhausting and every couple of weeks.

Early on we were told he would probably grow out of his condition. However, that was probably before it was really understood. As he got older it was getting more damaging to his system.

Now this has to be set in the context of me not seeing that much of Danny and Rachel, as I have said. I sent the birthday and Christmas cards and presents and phoned and tried to get to Manchester to see them when I could, and we would meet for lunch. Sometime Danny would come to those lunches, sometimes it was just Rachel.

Danny and Rachel came to visit in Middleton Stoney, and they did when we lived in Haslemere. I have a photo of all the kids except Pat – who was working by then – at Legoland. Oscar looks about three years old then. I can remember Danny and me going to an England game at Old Trafford – I seem to recall Paul Scholes getting sent off.

So, we did meet up and I did stay in touch, but it was not ideal. Then Danny told me that he had been told by the consultants that if he had a bone marrow transplant and it worked he could be home free – an end to the transfusions, a 'normal' life. However, as his immune system would be reduced to zero after the transplant it would be dangerous. There was risk. However, if he didn't have the operation he would probably not live much past thirty. At this time Danny was twenty-four years old. He had decided to take the risk and have the operation if it could be done. I understand both his Mother and I agreed with this though it was very much his decision. He was now waiting on the bone marrow match.

On the 2nd of June 2011 I had been down with the family on the beach at West Wittering. We were living in Haslemere. That was a difficult time for me in my then relationship but that's another story.

Back at home in Haslemere the phone went, and it was Nye. I took the call on my mobile in the conservatory.
"Dad, we've been trying to get hold of you!"
"Oh hi – we've been down at the beach. No reception probably."
"It's Danny," Nye said. "I've terrible news. He's died."

I reeled back, holding the top of the armchair in the conservatory to keep from falling.
"Oh, Nye," I said, "how awful for you to have to tell me."

Nye told me what little he knew of the events. It turned out that Danny had had the bone marrow operation, but he caught an infection – 'PCJ' as it is now termed, I believe – and died. It was not until many years later, just recently in fact, that I learned via Rachel that Danny had actually died the day before on the first of June. How and why it took so long to contact me, I have no idea. We had only been down to the beach that day, the second of June. Nye got a phone call from a family friend, and he had got straight in touch with me.

I had not known Danny was actually having the transplant. I had not known he was in hospital at all. I was told at least twenty-four hours after he died.

Danny was twenty-four years old. I had a fierce mix of feelings – grief, guilt, anger, sadness. I was very concerned for Rachel as I knew how close they were.

I walked round to my mate, Tim's. As soon as he saw me he said:
"What's happened?"
I told him.
"Fuck," he said.
Indeed.

The days past in a blur. I was working at the Mayor's Fund then. Trevor was great and very supportive. I got a lovely hand written note from Boris, which I still have. When I did go back into work a few days later Carole just got up and walked over and hugged me. I got messages from all over the football world as the word went out.

The funeral was arranged in Eccles near Salford, quite near the hospital where Danny had died and where he had lived. It was arranged I would go up and stay with Pat who was living at Edenfield then and me and the Boys would go to the funeral together. It was felt that Keir and Oscar were a bit young for the funeral. There was to be some sort of wake at a working men's club nearby after.

"Listen,' I told the Boys. " We'll go to the funeral, then call in at the wake and see Rachel is OK then we will bugger off and do our own thing."

They agreed.

We arrived where the funeral cars were leaving from. It was rainy miserable day in Salford. As we got out of the car I walked along with Nye.

"I am not looking forward to this," I said grimly. I was so angry and hurt but was determined not to make any scene. I was sure I would not be welcome at the event by Danny's Mum.

Nye took hold of my arm.

"We are here with you," he said. "Remember, 'Over, Under or Through."

We went to the little chapel in the crematorium. It was packed with loads of young people in particular, overflowing outside. It felt heart-warming to know Danny had so many friends. I hugged Rachel briefly then we were inside. I sat next to Micky in the back row. I was stone faced and set. It was a good service overall. I was barely mentioned but I did not blame the humanist celebrant for that, he was only going off how he was briefed.

We endured. Then we were back out in the rain and drive to the working men's club. In there Rachel, who was lovely, introduced us to some of Danny's friends and they were real nice and welcoming. Rachel sat with is a good while. The Boys' Mum was there but the Boys stayed with me. A team.

Rachel then got up to present a film she had made with some help from some of Danny's friends of lots of old family video and so on. There was Danny as a toddler walking across the floor of the kitchen at the house in the Lakes. There he was playing on the stairs. I wondered why I was not in any of the old films then realised it had been me holding the camera. I had taken the film. I could not be edited out of his life altogether.

Rachel did brilliantly putting it together and presenting it and I told her so.

We chatted a while with Rachel and Danny's friends. I looked round at the Boys.
"Come on, "I said, "time for us to bugger off."
We said our goodbyes to Rachel then slipped away.

We went back to a pub in Edenfield near Pat's. We sat down, the three Boys and me and had a few pints and something to eat. We went through memories of Danny. I told stories of living in Bacup, and we all laughed. We had a great afternoon. Micky's lovely partner, Chloe joined us later. It was a warm, soulful close family gathering and I loved it. It was just what was needed after the stress of the funeral and all that had happened.

Danny's death was a stunning event in my life. It was a major turning point in some ways as we will see. It raised so many different emotions it was impossible to process them then. There was a lot going on. I was right in the heart of the stress of the Mayor's Fund whose Trustees were conspiring right then to get Trevor out. Although I did not know it there was also a lot going on around my marriage that I was unaware of – again right at that time as I grieved for my son.

On top of that was that mix of emotions Danny's death had immediately provoked. I don't think I dealt with them then. I am not sure I ever have.

I came to think that maybe you can never 'come to terms' with a child's death. How can it be dealt with? What would that mean?

I recalled my time in the children's hospices. One time I came in early one morning and there sat all on her own at the breakfast table was the mother of a young baby who I knew had died overnight. She said hello. I said I was getting a coffee; did she want one?
She said:
'No but come and sit here."

I got my coffee and sat at the table. I said nothing. After a while she looked up with red rimmed but now dry eyes. It had been a long night for her.
"He died," she said simply.
'I know," I said gently.
We then sat in companionable silence.

I had learned at the children's hospice that there are no magic words, nothing right or wrong to say in the face of such grief. You just have to be there for people as they struggle through. Sometimes all you can do is stand there and maybe hold their hand.

When my own son died I learned these lessons all over again at first hand. It does not really matter what people say. It's just important that somehow they express their support, that they are there. You can't put what has happened right. You can only be there.

Later that year, in November 2011, I heard that a mate of mine, Ted Gladdish had died. Ted was about my age, maybe a year or two younger. He had been made CEO of Demelza House Children's Hospice in Kent at the same time as I took over as CEO of CHASE. We became good friends, and we stayed in touch. We had even met recently to talk about going into business together.

Ted was a fit guy. He exercised – in fact he was playing golf abroad when he died from a heart attack. He was not overweight. He had had no warning signs or other trouble.

When I stood at his funeral on another cold wet day in Kent, seeing the grief of his lovely family, his children and grandchildren and his friends, it all really hit home to me. The lessons from Danny's death and now Ted's and the stress and strains of my life all were suddenly very stark.

Life is short. You don't know what is around the next corner. You need to enjoy it while you can.

I was still in the stress of the Mayor's Fund, commuting up to London every day, working very long hours and not enjoying it at all by that stage with Trevor gone. I resolved to make some changes then in my life. It was, as I say, November 2011.

In the summer of 2012 I started as CEO of Naomi House Children's Hospice just outside Winchester – an easy, lovely forty-minute drive from where I lived in Haslemere through the Hampshire countryside. I knew there was a very experienced and capable management team there and I knew the charity was in very good financial shape. I knew the change, particularly when you took the end of the commuting into account, would slash down my working hours and my stress levels. It was time to enjoy working life a bit.

However, perhaps more significant was that in May 2012 I had started a new, initially part-time, job just as I started my notice period for the Mayor's Fund.

I was going to work for Chelsea FC.

Some years before, when Keir – who is in his twenties now– was about four years old, and Oscar, my youngest, about two, we went to Fuerteventura for a holiday – not the time we had the lifesaving incident with the German but a couple of years before that. After a long tiring exhausting stressful journey – parents who have been crazy enough to take their toddler kids on longish haul flights will know what I mean – we arrived at the hotel. The guy from the hotel was showing us round to our rooms. It was sunny, the swimming pools were busy and looked very inviting and blue, there were happy family sounds and splashes and the poolside noise and music. My wife was ahead with Oscar in her arms, next to the hotel guy. I was next trudging along with the big, wheeled cases and Keir was just behind me and we walked round the edge of the largest pool, following the hotel guy.

In the midst of the noisy poolside of the big hotel complex, I heard a very familiar, instantly recognisable voice call my name.
"Chris!"
I turned, and Keir wasn't there. I looked instantly at the pool and will never forget seeing his little face, deep under the water where he had jumped in. He couldn't swim. Time stood still. I cast aside the cases and jumped straight in, clothes and all, I pulled him up and out of the water. He gasped and choked and then was breathing fine, crying from shock and surprise, but okay. I held him tight. Such a close call. Such a brush with understandable, unbearable tragedy. A four-year-old child sees a pool on a hot day and just follows his instinct. In the crowded noisy hotel surrounds he drifts unnoticed to the bottom of the pool. But he was fine. We all lived to tell the tale.

Sometimes in life something happens, and you cannot make sense of it. All you can do is shrug your shoulders and walk on.

The voice that called me and got me to turn round was as easily recognisable as my own. I have never been in any doubt who it was. How could I not recognise that voice?

It was my Mum.

11. Chasing Wild Horses

My Chelsea adventures began a couple of years before I started to work for them. I got to know the Academy in particular when I was working for Right To Play and we had the partnership with Chelsea. Part of the deal was we would take Chelsea players and staff out to see our projects – though I knew in practice the timing of this would be a problem given the full-on nature of current players' lives and schedules. Football is a full-on line of work for all the jobs involved and I knew finding extra time would be tricky.

We launched the partnership at the House of Commons in 2006. Jose Mourinho was then the manager, and he brought all the first team squad to the launch. I had the feeling this was going to work well.
I thanked Jose for making the time and bringing the whole squad to the launch event. He shrugged.
"I'm happy to help. This is more important than football."

We had a big programme in Ghana, and I had been out there and knew it was well organised and well run. I hatched a plan with Simon Greenberg, the Chelsea Director of Communications, to see if we could get Michael Essien, Chelsea's Ghanaian star to visit the projects. He said he would.

The Academy then said they would put together a group of young players, probably youth team players and staff, and they would come too. It would be a good education for them, they said. I happily agreed – Chelsea were paying for everything anyway!

Then Simon told me that Jose Mourinho had said he would come too. He would give up a week of his short summer holiday to come to Ghana with Essien and us. This was huge. Jose was news wherever he went. This was an incredible coup for us.

Firstly, we had to have a 'recce' visit. Darren Grace, Head of Local Recruitment at the Academy, who had been the Project Manager on the 'Soccer Idol' TV series Chelsea had been involved with, would come out and have a look at the hotels and projects with me. The Right To Play (Ghana) manager was a smart local woman called Rose. I had met her before and knew she would have things well organised.

We went out there and all the visits went well. The best hotel, the Golden Tulip, was near the airport and fine for what we had in mind as base. One evening after we had been out to projects Rose said she would take Darren and I for a local delicacy. We drove to a bit of waste ground on the edge of Accra. It was dark now – the way it can suddenly be dark in Africa – and the waste ground was murky with the occasional glare of a vehicle's headlights or the blaze of a brazier fire. There were a lot of people there and they seemed to be milling around. We got out of the car and followed Rose in. There was smell of BBQ and smoke.

The local delicacy turned out to be barbecued guinea fowl – like a small chicken. It was grilled and then put into one of the ubiquitous small black rubbish bags that were everywhere in Ghana and West Africa. It was then battered with something like a rolling pin and then you ate the grilled meat (and bone and skin) from the bag. All this we had to take on good faith from what Rose said as it was pitch black everywhere and we could not see a thing. We sat down on a couple of turned over ten-gallon barrels and ate blind. Whatever it was, it tasted good.

The next day we drove past the BBQ waste ground in day light. The field next to it seemed to be full of black flowers. As we drove by closer I realised the black flowers were actually hundreds and hundreds of the discarded little black plastic bags. It was depressing.

When it came to the actual visit we had Jose Mourinho, Michael Essien, about eight Chelsea academy players and about six staff plus a TV crew from Chelsea TV. Ben Pegna and I were there from Right To Play UK, and we had the help of our local Right To Play staff too. We arrived at Accra airport at around midnight. An airport official came to me as we got off the plane.

"There are too many people in the airport. We can't even physically open the terminal doors to get you to your bus. You will have to wait a while and we will try and find another was round."

It was not so surprising as Michael Essien was like a god in Ghana and Jose Mourinho was a world-wide celebrity by then. We waited in a little room just inside the terminal building. Jose was not blessed with a lot of patience. He came over:

"What are we waiting for?" he asked.

"There are too many people, "I explained, "they can't even open the doors."

"I will find a way out," he said, "see you at the Hotel." He strode off followed by his faithful sidekick, Silvinho Louro. After about ten minutes he came back.

"There are too many people, "he said, "they can't even open the doors."

The trip was a huge success. Jose and Michael were great, the projects were impressive, and we were greeted everywhere we went. At that time Jose and I had similar haircuts and the Chelsea TV crew kept going on about how much alike we looked. One day when I was getting on the bus after Michael Essien they took a photo and put it on the club website saying, 'Jose Mourinho and Michael Essien getting on a bus to visit projects in Ghana' and nobody noticed. Little things…

We went on a short flight up to Makeni in the north of Ghana. Jose decided to sit the day out by the hotel pool. He was not a bad judge as it turned out. The football pitch up at Makeni was just a slightly flattened piece of spare dirt ground on the edge of the town. At first there were hardly any crowd watching but I noticed that it grew steadily. I spoke to our security guy, David about it. He was ex-Military Police from my mate Bob Taylor's Fusion security company. "Yeah, I know," he said. "Seems it's been broadcast on local radio that Michael is here, and people are walking in from the surrounding villages from miles away." By the time we were getting near the end of the sessions there were several thousand people around the edge of the makeshift playing area, singing and chanting.

David came over to me and Ben Pegna.

"Walk Michael over nearer the bus," he said, "just as it you are showing him something. Then we will make a break for it. This could get difficult."

We did as he suggested. The Chelsea academy guys were edging near the bus too. The crowd sensed what is going on and surged. We ran for the bus and somehow got away without leaving anyone behind.

The Ghana trip was a real success for Right To Play and Chelsea. The positive PR stories were terrific, and we got a great improvement in brand recognition. Our people out in the field also told us they found it a great boost as it put them and their projects on the map.

Michael Essien and Jose Mourinho out themselves out for us, taking precious holiday time to come out on the visit and they were both good to work with and very helpful.

There was going to be a tournament to formally open the Cobham Training ground and Chelsea asked if I wanted to bring in a team to represent Right To Play. This was a great opportunity but a tough ask as there were teams like River Plate from Argentina, Dinamo Moscow and Bayer Leverkusen taking part. It was at an u16 age.

I had the idea of putting together a team of Palestinian refugees from Lebanon to represent Right To Play. I spoke to my dear friend Fadi El Yemeni, and he said it could be done. Chelsea were not so sure. They were ok with the idea in principle but did not want a refugee team to come over and get completely hammered by some of the best young teams in the world. It was arranged that I would take Darren Grace and a top very experienced Chelsea Academy coach – Frank O'Brien – over to Beirut so they could check out the standard of the refugee squad that Fadi had put together.

Off to Beirut we went. In a scruffy little well-worn football ground in the backstreets of Beirut Frank out the refugee squad through their paces. As the session finished, Darren and I asked Frank what he thought.
"They'll do," he said, and it was game on.

That evening – a Saturday evening - near midnight Darren, Frank, Fadi and I sat having a coffee outside a cafe in the main square in Beirut. There were a lot of young people about, out meeting up with friends and milling round. As there was basically no alcohol on sale, everyone was drinking coffees and mint teas and so on. It was a lovely soft balmy summer evening, and the atmosphere was very relaxed. After all the media images of Beirut this was an eye opener for Darren and Frank.
"You know,' Frank said shrewdly, "you couldn't sit outside a café in Guildford this time on a Saturday night and it be so relaxed!"
It just went to show what the absence of alcohol and a drinking culture could do.

Having said that, we had no illusions about the real violence and trauma that the streets of Beirut had seen. When we had got to the little ground for the training session we noticed one outside wall was partly fallen down on one side of the ground.
"Ah yes," said Fadi, "There was a car bomb there last week."

The refugees squad came over with Fadi and did very well and had an amazing time. They didn't win any of their tournament, but they were competitive, only losing narrowly. It was an incredible experience for them. River Plate u16s beat Chelsea u16s in the final. I spoke to the Argentinian coach afterwards and congratulated him on his top-level team.

"Your club must be very proud of them," I said.
"I don't know,' he shrugged. "We do produce players for them, but we have no equipment, no resource – they give us nothing. In fact, could we take a bag of balls back with us because we are so short?"
It again made me realise how fortunate we were in this country on all sorts of different levels.

A year or so later we took a Chelsea academy group over to Jordan and that was a good experience too. We visited the Dead Sea which I talk about elsewhere. The Chelsea group were then flying on to Tel Aviv, but I did not want to visit Israel so made my excuses and returned to see my Palestinian friends in Beirut.

The next adventure took me back to LA. Jose liked LA as a pre-season training base and so the first team squad were heading out there and would play games up at Stanford and also against LA Galaxy and their recent signing David Beckham in LA. The plan was we at Right To Play would do all sorts of promotional activity around the first team – like getting them to carry out our iconic red balls (now made by adidas, then Chelsea's kit sponsor) and kick them into the crowd.

There's a story about the red ball which was Right To Play's symbol and logo. When we were first discussing the deal with Chelsea Simon Greenberg and Peter Kenyon asked if there was any chance we could turn our red ball into a blue one. This would have been very difficult for us.
"There's no need," I said," the red ball is part of Chelsea history too. It's even on the club badge."

Peter and Simon were doubtful about that, but we searched around for a picture of the badge and I showed them the two red balls that are actually featured on the Chelsea badge. I pointed out how there were actually two red roses and two red balls on the badge recently revived from the 1950s original. This seemed to do the trick and the issue of the red ball was not raised again.

So we had things to do in California and off I flew, booking once more into the Angeleno. The players were all booked into the Beverley Hills Hotel and training at the UCLA campus nearby, so it went well. I flew up with the first team to the game at Stanford in a private jet borrowed from the LA Lakers. It was a bit surreal sitting there watching Arjen Robben, Frank Lampard, John Terry and so on playing cards and hearing Petr Cech behind me talking French to Michael Essien. I was very much a fan edging onto the fringes of my heroes' lives.

All the promotions went well. Once more I enjoyed being in LA. On the last night we were all told to report to an address on Hollywood Boulevard at 7.00pm. I went along with my friends Gary and Carine Ireland who had bene helping with all the Right To Play promotional stuff. The address was a multi storey car park. This seemed strange. As we drove in we could then see there was a line of valet parkers and waiting minibuses. Our minibus whisked us up into the Hollywood Hills overlooking LA.

There was a party house up there which had been hired for the evening. It was a dazzling white multi-level house set on the side of the hill with a sparkling blue pool behind looking out over LA. It was spectacular.

The party seemed full of beautiful young women with very short dresses and very long legs. I later learned a local models agency had only been too happy to get their girls to come to the party to meet the Chelsea players. The Chelsea Academy boys – all aged about seventeen or so – seemed particularly happy though the free bar might have had something to do with that. The party crowd was sprinkled with celebrities too.

One of my Right To Play team was out in India and was having some problems so I had to take a call from her. I went back outside to escape the throbbing music around the pool and actually went back onto the red carpet. As I emerged all the photographers lifted their cameras but when they saw it was only me, no-one famous, they all let out a collective sigh of disappointment. Very grounding, I thought.

As I made my way back round the side of the party house my mind was still full of the issues out in India, and I was very distracted. When I recoined Gary and Carine by the pool they were talking to some other people.
'Ah Chris," said Gary as I approached them, "have you met Paris Hilton?' he was introducing me to the striking blonde on his left. I however was still distracted.
"No, "I said, "but I've seen the video" and looked up into her blue eyes. Whoops! I don't know why I said that – I hadn't actually seen the infamous video which had been doing the rounds – but to be fair she took it well and was gracious.

A while later I can remember standing by the pool talking to Frank Lampard about the charity and what we were doing. He was serious and clearly intelligent and good to talk to as well.

The leggy models were very popular and seemed to be enjoying themselves.
"So, "said one of them, yet another very slim, very leggy girl." What do you think of California Girls?"
"Well, "I replied, looking up at her," you're all very…tall"

It was a great evening. I was drinking diet cokes – I am not much of a drinker – but clearly some of the younger players hit the free bar very hard and one or two had to be helped or even poured back onto the minibuses at the end of the night.

A party house up in the Hollywood Hills overlooking LA? It was a long way from the terraces of Stamford Bridge. It was even further from the tarmac cage by the King Square flats off Central Street back in Islington or the cinder pitches of Coram's Fields where I played my first competitive game.

But it showed just how far football can take you.

Then I lft Right To Play and was working for the Mayor's Fund and into all that political stress. By the time I got to November 2011 and Ted Gladdish's funeral I was ready to change my life. Getting back into serious football was definitely a part of that.

The Academy guys at Chelsea that I had got to know had always said I should go and work for them, so I got back in touch with Darren Grace early in 2012 when I knew I was leaving the Mayor's fund and going to Naomi House Children's Hospice and this ending my commuting and cutting my working hours back. Darren and the guys knew my football pedigree and we had worked together well through the Chelsea – Right To Play partnership.

I started as a part time scout for the Chelsea Academy in May 2012. Initially I was covering grassroots football in the area around Haslemere where we were living. I was off every weekend to local games in places like Liphook, Petersfield, Beacon Hill, Farnham, Aldershot and Guildford, proudly wearing my Chelsea tracksuit as we were asked to do, flying the flag, looking for talent aged from six to eighteen years old.

I had done some scouting for Portsmouth by then and of course back in my non-league days as a manager I had done a lot of my won scouting. However Chelsea had their own way of doing things and the scouting scene was changing and developing. I was keen and I worked hard. I also listened and learned from experienced top scouts like Ray Rembridge, Noel Connery, Fiona Armfield and Alf Blandford. I met people like Adam Brown, Fred Ham and Nick Brown who would become long term friends. I immersed myself in the Chelsea Academy world.

Now the Chelsea Academy is rightly recognised as one of the top academies in the UK and arguably across the world. The ownership changes of 2003 when Roman Abramovich took over changed the whole set up the club as a whole and the Academy in particular. When I was working with the Academy from a Right To Play angle in 2006-8 it was just getting going, finding its feet, establishing and developing their Cobham Training ground, for example. By the time I actually joined the staff in 2012 it was in to its stride.

First team managers would come and go but the Chelsea Academy leadership featuring Neil Bath, Jim Fraser, Darren Grace and Hayley Prior was consistent – and consistently good. Neil Bath, the Head of Youth Development, is one of the most impressive managers and leaders I have come across in any industry. Always looking to improve, striving for excellence in every facet of the work but treating people like human individuals throughout, Neil is a remarkable innovative and effective leader.

Right from when I started we had talked about me eventually going full time and gradually we walked down that path. They asked me to increase my hours, then I was co-ordinating a scouting team and then cutting back my hours with Naomi House so I could do more. I moved more into academy scouting – that is scouting other academies looking for young players from 9 to 19 we can sign from other clubs, as opposed to grassroots scouting. I began to get involved in training scouts and did some work internationally, travelling to France, Belgium, Holland and Portugal to watch and report on players.

In 2015 Darren asked me to meet up with him, Neil and Jim for a meal at a restaurant in Epsom one evening and they asked me to go full-time. The role would continue to be about finding talent and I would continue to coordinate a team of academy scouts but now I would add in the Integration work – connecting up different parts of the club, in particular the Chelsea Foundation and the Academy. I knew the Foundation well. It was the community and corporate responsibility arm of the club, and it was huge, working with over a million children worldwide on social courses, in schools and various projects. 750,000 of those kids were in the UK so we reckoned there must be some talent in there too. The idea was I would set up links and pathways for this talent to be identified and recruited. This would mean setting up tournaments bringing the best of the Foundation players together across the ages so we could identify the very best and training over 250 Foundation coaches in what we were looking for – effectively giving them our scout training.

We agreed we would aim at me starting on 1st July 2015 in this new full-time role. The Academy could not pay me the salary I was on now as a CEO of a major charity, but they made a good offer. In order to be able to take it I needed us to downsize our house – which we planned to do anyway as Keir and Oscar got nearer to University age – reduce the mortgage even further by taking a chunk of pension money and reorganising. It meant overall a big pay cut – the second time I had taken a pay cut to go full-time in football because I did when I became manager at Cheltenham Town back in 1996.

It was the right thing to do and after some stressful times selling and buying houses we got there.

Cobham was very much my base now and I was working from there most days. It is a fantastic training ground with the equivalent of 32 full sized pitches in over 125 acres, featuring a £5m indoor arena - and we even have our own lake! It is always being improved. The whole set up including the excellent healthy food was first class and it very much quickly felt like home. I loved going in to the training ground. Every time I pulled on the Chelsea kit or drove into that drive with the sign at the end saying 'Chelsea FC – Training Ground' I felt a surge of pride. Yes, every time I drove in and that is still the case. It takes me back to the times as a kid on the terraces of Stamford Bridge watching my heroes from afar – sometimes very much afar given the old ground! Now I felt like I was on the inside and part of it. Much more so that even I did when I was travelling with Chelsea as part of Right To Play. I felt now like I really was part of the club – and that still moves me.

We roared through success after success in those years, winning six FA Youth Cups in eight seasons, for example. For many of those I went to every round home and away and we all loved the staff coach trips to the away games (when we won!) and we also won 2 UEFA Youth League cups in Nyon in Switzerland, and they were great trips and events too. We had the best people and we all worked very hard.

The culture is very strong at Chelsea and at the Academy in particular and Neil Bath has made that a real priority.

I still had my own season ticket through all this time – although these days I hardly get to use it because I am always working. This seems a bitter irony to me – I rarely get to watch the first team of the club I love despite having my own season ticket – because I am usually off working for that very same club!

I have been asked many times what I think is the secret to the success of the Chelsea Academy. Neil Bath always talks about the three elements – recruitment, coaching and opportunity. You need to get the very best players you can. Brian Clough used to say it starts and ends with good players. For an academy if you can sign them at u9 – ie eight years old when you can first actually formally sign players – then you can work with them over the years, and they grow up with you. If you can get the very best then – and that means the right structure bringing them in at six and seven years old – then the theory is you only have to add one or two as they go through the years.

The best of our players now – Mason Mount, Reece James, Trevoh Chalobah, Ruben Loftus-Cheek, Connor Gallagher – have all been with us since seven or eight years of age.

Then you have to develop those players and that means the best of coaching and preparation. I still watch with awe some of the training sessions young coaches like Tom Bird, and George Cole (both products of the Integration project incidentally although both played previously for the academy) put on, week in and week out. The intensity and the quality are superb. There is a lot of support needed other than coaching – education (we have our own very successful school at Cobham), player care, physical conditioning, nutrition and medical support. You need the behind-the-scenes excellence in catering, operations, admin, safeguarding, performance analysis and security and care of the facilities too. It is a big team effort to develop players right. Teams within teams.

Then the players need opportunity. Back a few years ago we had great players coming through the system – Lewis Baker, Nathaniel Chalobah, Ruben again, Charly Musonda – but arguably they were not given their chances at the right time. This was making recruitment difficult, incidentally, at that time because parents could see none of our kids were breaking through.

However, the recent years of the transfer sanctions and the big breaks under Frank Lampard plus the support of Thomas Tuchel since and the emergence of this current crop of top players, has changed that. But you need the right opportunity at the right time for the right player.

I agree with Neil about these elements. I think overall though, you need the right people working in the right culture.

We have that.

The fortunes of the first team and the ups and downs of the various managers do have an effect on us over the road in the Academy. When Jose returned for his second spell I found myself being allocated a seat in the 'Technical Area' just behind the dugout. This was a great experience because although you could not always see well – Jose kept jumping up and I didn't have the nerve to tell him to sit down – you felt you were right in the heart of it all and I loved being surrounded by the players. In one game against Liverpool when Klopp had become their manager it all kicked off with one of Jose's assistants getting involved with Klopp. Keir and Oscar were up in the East Stand behind me, way above. I got a text from Keir "tell me that's not your fault!". For once I was not involved.

It was fascinating watching Jose at close quarters. He was different than he was in his first spell with us. By the second time around he seemed quite bitter, quite negative. His wife and two teenage kids would often be in the seats just behind me, and he would turn to them and throw his arms out as if to say, 'you see, the worlds against me.'

It's a shame how it ended really. I thought back to the first time he was there and his success in bringing us Chelsea fans our first top title for fifty years. When he was sacked that time, I was due to appear on Chelsea TV in my Right to Play role, with Bobby Tambling, as it happens, the day or so after he was sacked. I was not a happy bunny.

Simon Greenberg, the Chelsea Director of Communications, phoned me and complained that I looked miserable and responded badly to the sacking of Mourinho and the appointment of Avram Grant.
"You looked like a member of your family had died," he said.
"That's what if felt like!" I explained.

By the time he left the second time around I think most Chelsea fans were sad about the whole thing but realised a change was needed.

When we had reached the Champions League Cup Final in Moscow against Manchester United in 2008 I was still at Right To Play.

However, Simon Greenberg told me they had put aside two tickets including flights and so on for me.

So, my good mate Richard Shadforth and I flew out the day before the final with the special corporate guests and the wives and girlfriends of the Chelsea players. We were staying in the Kempinski Hotel just across the Moskva River from St Basil's Cathedral and the Kremlin. There was a reception the bight before the game and celebrities like James Nesbitt, the actor (a United fan) and Eddie Jordan, the Formula 1 guy, were around. On the day of the final Richard and I walked over the river to see the eights. There was a British TV crew there and we recognised Fiona Phillips and we realised this was the crew filming live for GMTV back home. Richard phoned home and his daughter was watching it live so Richard got into the act. Fiona was great, really friendly, and told us she was rooting for Chelsea – I recall she said her son was a fan.

That night we had tickets for the after party with the players. The official guests were bussed out to the Luzhniki Stadium built in 1954, which had seen a horrific disaster in 1982 when 66 people died in a fan stampede. By 2008 the stadium was definitely past it's sell by date. It was a huge, cavernous ugly concrete shell. There were hardly any facilities for fans – I can remember having to walk for ages to find a toilet. It was in fact knocked down in 2013 and rebuilt.

It rained and rained. We had really good seats, but the weather was just awful. The game eventually went to penalties, and we lost and it was devastating. Everyone was totally deflated – and soaking wet. The players after party was cancelled and we trooped back to the hotel. We flew home the next day on the plane with the players and their families and it was a very quiet flight.

When I was at Cobham most days we would see something of the managers from time to time (I don't think I ever saw Maurizio Sarri though.) When Antonio Conte was appointed he would come over and was very pleasant to everyone he met. I was sat watching an u18 in-house game one day when he came and sat in the row in front of me. He said hello. We were the only two people in the stand.

Now I love Italy. I always have. I love the style, the country, the people, the Italian way of life. I had in fact been learning Italian then for about two years – partly paid for by the club – and was I thought reasonably fluent.
I plucked up courage to try out my Italian on Signor Conte. I leant forward:
"Mister," I said – the Italians have adopted the word 'Mister' as we would use the term 'Gaffer' in English football, and it dates back to the original English coaches that went over to Italy. However, I digress..
"Mister, the number nineteen for the blue team is on trial with us." I had rehearsed the lines in my head. He turned and looked blankly at me.
"How old is he?" he eventually asked….in English.
This went on a little while, me speaking Italian – or what I thought was Italian – and him speaking English. Then I gave up and sat back and watched the game in silence, feeling foolish.
The next day I had my weekly Italian lesson with my lovely tutor, Agnese. Agnese was from near Todi, one of my favourite towns. She was an excellent teacher, really smart and I really enjoyed learning from her for two years. OK, yes, I admit, it helped that she was very attractive – and made excellent coffee. Anyway, I told her what had happened. She frowned and asked me to say to her what I had said to Antonio Conte.
"That's fine," she said, "nothing wrong with that. I don't know why he didn't reply in Italian."
I was told later in fact that he had promised himself he would only speak English when at work. I don't know if it was true - but it made me feel better when I heard that!

I think scouting is the last part of football to be really professionalised. It is only in the last couple of years that the FA have updated and modernised the scouting qualifications on offer.

A few years ago I went to a Brighton u23 evening game being held at Crawley Town's ground. There must have been a dozen or more scouts there, all sitting together and gossiping. I saw only one of them – other than me – making notes. Now maybe their memories are better than mine – I don't know. Another thing – they were all, like me, white middle-aged men other than the one other scout making notes and he was a bit younger but still white and male.

The field is changing with the arrival of a generation of sport science educated 'Football Manager' game playing, keen, smart young scouts and analysts. Back when I finished managing and knew I really wanted to get into scouting properly I took a course via the League Managers Association in 'Using Performance Data in Football'. I knew I had the football experience, but I was determined not to get left behind by the new graduate class who were very comfortable with all manner of data.

It is changing but there is still too much of the 'back of a fag packet' reporting and too much of a prevalence of the old boy's club.

You do get badly treated at many UK academies. The Premier League's 2011 'Elite Player Performance Plan' revolutionised the academy system in England and set the structure for the much-improved international performance that has followed. Part of it was accepting that scouts were entitled to watch games and set out a process of doing that. However, many academies make it clear they don't really want you there.

Some insist you wait outside the gates until ten minutes before the kick off – no visit to the tea bar (if there is one) or toilet for you! Some mark out a section, usually by the corner flag, where you scouts, the unclean, have to stand. There will often be a security person near you at all times. Not all clubs are as bad as this, it must be said.

Brentford were the worst when they had an academy. They made no bones about it that they did not welcome scouts. They would keep you waiting at the gate then walk you all the way right round the outside perimeter of the playing ground to the pitch your game was on – usually by the longest possible route. They would place you away from the pitch too. It was ridiculous.

So there is a lot of unprofessional treatment of scouts. When I have scouted in the Netherlands or Belgium you get team sheets at all ages. Its only at u18 and u23 you get that in the UK and then not at every game. You can spend half the game trying to work out who is playing and trying to catch a name or two being called out by the coaches or parents. As I constantly remind security people and scouts from the most inhospitable clubs, they don't get treated like that at Cobham. I am delighted to say that once you show the email permission you can go where you like. You can get a cup of tea or a burger. If a scout misbehaves – and the Premier League have a clear Code of Conduct for scouts which includes not approaching parents of other clubs' players then they are dealt with, but the starting position is to treat people as professionals and grown-ups. Sadly we are one of the exceptions not the rule.

Beyond all that, as a scout you are out in all weathers. Recently my mate Dave Allan who works for Manchester United and I were at an u18 game at Portsmouth down on the outside 4G at Portsmouth University. It rained all through the game and I mean really rained. We were like drowned rats at the end, and it was cold too. Dave and I looked at each other and with rain cascading off his face he said to me in his Glasgow burr:
"Hey, big man, what the fuck are we doing?"

Now, when people say that it must be a great job getting paid to watch football I always agree but point out we are not doing it from our armchairs at home or even, moist of the time, from a seat in a stand. As academy scouts we are out pitch side, come what may.

For all that, watching games is the best part of the job. I am quite happy standing there on my own, focused entirely on the game in front of me. Having said that I have had some really good times sitting up in the stand somewhere like Worthing watching their under 18s with my mates Adam Brown, now scouting for Coventry City and Dave Allan, of Manchester United in a midweek floodlit game with half a dozen people in the crowd. We have known each other a long time, respect each other's views on football and the banter is great.

The game is changing and one way it is changing is the increase in video scouting. The cost and time efficiency are obvious and more and more academies are filing more and more games for analysis. The whole process has been accelerated by lockdown although now without a lot of stress where I was concerned.

As I have written earlier Julie and I met just before lockdown started and managed to get through the initial stages of that weird time well enough, seeing each other when we could. Then in November 2020 the family home where I had been staying with the boys after my previous marriage broke up, finally sold after months and months of delay. Keir and Oscar were ready to go independent – in fact Oscar was still at University in Southampton. So I moved into a holiday cottage near West Chiltington for three months. This would just keep me going while Julie and I decided what we wanted to do and when.

However, it was a long dark cold and wet winter. I could not see Julie as often as we would like, at times. The little cottage on a farm was probably fine in summer but dark and small and poky in winter with restricted TV channels and only intermittent internet even. The isolation and the darkness began to get on top of me.

Now Chelsea had been great right from the off of the lockdown. When other clubs were putting staff on furlough, the owner had made it clear that all Chelsea staff would be on 100% salary for the duration. This was great but our management understandably wanted to make sure we were all doing whatever we could to keep gainfully occupied. For the coaches this meant a mass of work filing remote sessions and on-line calls and meetings with kids and parents.

For us in recruitment it meant video scouting. I had a team to manage, and I was under huge relentless pressure to get enough videos to keep them occupied. It was very difficult trying to ring contacts and persuade them to share video. Some did and some didn't. Some just didn't have any staff in work to do anything. It was very stressful, and I really began to struggle.

Julie got me through it, helping me organise my time better and keeping my spirits up. I did get an approach from another Premier League club via an agent during that time asking me to head their recruitment in the south and to be honest I was so stressed I did consider it. However, when it actually came to it I could not leave Chelsea. It was nice to be asked, of course.

In February 2012 I moved to a lovely light airy apartment just outside Arundel, one of my favourite places. The lockdowns began to ease. Julie and I were planning to get married. Everything lifted as spring came and we were out of the tunnel and into the sunlight again.

I had never really had any bout of depression before (or since) so this was a new and scary experience for me. I think there were very particular and unusual circumstances and I know a lot of other people struggled at times during the lockdowns too.

But one legacy has been the increase of video scouting and it is here to stay. Many of the relationships eventually forged in lockdown have continued and many clubs are much more ready to share match videos. Video scouting does not suit everyone. It is OK if you have a specific player to focus on and know who it is. However the filming quality varies hugely – it's not Sky Sports standard at all! Usually there is no sound either. But when it works it can be very useful and has allowed us to get a variety of opinions on a target player much more quickly, for example.

I am sure someone will set up a platform of academy video exchange before too long and we will see more and more grassroots teams foiling games as the technology is so much cheaper and more available.

It will not replace live scouting. There is a lot you can pick up live – off camera as it were – that you don't usually get on a video. You can see much more of the pattern of the game, see more of the target player's interactions off the ball and maybe hear what the coach is telling him. But video coaching is another tool we will increasingly use, and it will get better and more versatile.

I am often asked what it is we look for in a player. There are basic criteria like skill and technique, speed and movement, game intelligence, physicality, character and desire and so on. But really it depends on who you are scouting for. When I was scouting for Portsmouth's Centre of Excellence, as it was then, I was looking for a different type of player than I might now for Chelsea's academy. The key is knowing what you have got and what you want. That may sound obvious, but I mean so many scouts who do not know their own teams well enough.

Many years ago, I visited Nigeria. I wanted to get one of those carved wooden elephants you see everywhere in Africa being sold on street corners. A local guy I knew said he would take me to where they actually make the best ones, and I could buy direct from there. So, he took me into the dusty hot backstreets of Lagos, an area called Mushin as I recall, where the people are mostly Yoruba.

We came to an open workshop which was basically just a tarpaulin shading some crude work benches and he took me to one of the craftsmen – a wiry guy with long fingers and greying hair. I watched him work a while then said to this guy:

"It's amazing, you take a block of wood and create an elephant from it." I was in awe of his craftmanship.

"It's easy," shrugged the guy, "you just knock off the bits that don't look like an elephant."

We laughed. I bought the elephant (I still have it forty plus years later). It was a good line and I have thought about it a lot over the years.

I realised the thing is he was of course right but to do that you really had to know what an elephant looked like. I mean, really know. Then it was easy.

I always say I can tell you the best and worst player in any football game within five minutes. I think any experienced scout can. It's all the buggers in-between that are the challenge. It's also an issue to try and guess what the player in front of you would be like with better players around him and better coaching and conditioning, let alone guessing what shape and size and mentality they will have in five years' time.

I always laugh when I read someone say 'Oh, yes, I saw him play at seven and knew he would play for England." Well, I always think, you need to come and do my job because I cannot tell that far ahead. If they are ten years old I think it is a reasonable question to ask me will they be in our top five if they came into our group now? Would they start if we were playing Manchester City next week in a Premier League tournament final? Will they be in our starting eleven at under 12? I think these are reasonable questions. But don't ask me if he will play for Chelsea when he is twenty. My answer would be I have no idea.

But in scouting, as in life generally, I have definitely found it helps if you know what your elephant looks like.

So, think about it, what does your elephant look like?

11. Long Walk Home

We live a lot of our lives in places that do not exist. In our heads we are often living in the past or the future. The past has happened and has gone so it is not here now. It no longer exists. As for the future, it has not happened. It is not here. It is not yet real.
So as we walk along and mull over what happened, what we should have done, what that person meant when they said that...well, it is lost and gone. And if we are thinking of what we might do when we get home, or that dinner tomorrow night or what we are doing this weekend, then that too is just our mind concocting something we think of as our reality, but it is not actually real.

All that really exists is 'now'. This fleeting moment and the next and the next...just 'now'. A succession of moments that actually are a seamless open space.

What happens when we live more in the now?
What happens if when we are chopping wood, or washing dishes or walking the dog if we just rest our minds on the moment, on what we are actually doing now?
We lose our fears, our anxieties, our panics and our worries.

We rest in the peace that is now.

Now of course there is nothing wrong at all in learning from the past or from re-considering it. After all, that is what I am doing in this book. But when we have done that, we can put it away by focusing on now.

It makes sense to plan, to think what we want to do and how we are going to do it - of course it does. But again, when we have had our planning session, we put it away and come back to the now.

We can develop our capacity to live in the now. We can learn the techniques and build our mental strength and ability by practice.

Practising mindfulness and through meditation. Our minds are so often like our Dixie was when she was a puppy – jumping about all over the place, her mind suddenly attracted by that smell, then this sound or that floating leaf. Now, Dixie is lying at my feet, at rest, at peace, content and relaxed. How did that happen? She has been trained. Well, almost. Like my mind, Dixie will revert to puppy mode at odd times! But she's getting there. I like to think I am too.

So I do try and focus more on the now and be mindful. I fail and try again. That is the nature of life. Failing is not a sin. To stop trying is the sin.

But just occasionally I get a sense of the infinite space and peace there is in now.

I have come to this then. This now, this life. I am at home with myself.

It's been a long walk home.

I first visited Arundel when I was at primary school. At Moreland Street we the two oldest years used to get a week away once a year. We went to this place in Seaford in Sussex. Yes, Sussex again pops up. I can't remember much about the place, but it was run by two elderly sisters and I can remember them giving me extra servings of rice pudding – still my favourite dessert. I don't know why. Maybe they thought I needed feeding up. Or maybe I asked for seconds.

We would have day visits from there. I can remember visiting the caves at Hastings that the smugglers used to use. One other day trip was Arundel Castle.

Arundel Castle is impressive to this day, perched above the lovely town as the Downs unfold. The Castle originates from the 11th century but has been restored and remodelled over the years. It's

£25 to get in the castle now. That seems a lot to me. I am sure it was nothing like as expensive back when I was visiting from Moreland Street because if it had been we would not have been visiting!

When we lived in Haslemere I would occasionally visit the town. It had always impressed me, and I liked the bookshops and antiques and interesting cafes and pubs with the River Arun sweeping by at the foot of the town. I can remember going to the town when Pat, Nye and Micky were down with their families one weekend visiting us.
I was approached by a young clean-cut guy wearing a big purple rosette and carrying a clip board as we threaded our way up the busy High Street on a sunny Saturday afternoon.
"Hello, I'm from UKIP," he said cheerily.
"Fuck Off!" I said.
I heard a laugh from behind me as the young guy blanched white.
"Good to see you've not mellowed, Dad," said Pat.

As much as I have calmed over the years I still cannot abide racism or injustice.

When I was trying to get out of the dark gloomy holiday cottage at West Chiltington and find somewhere for six or seven months while Julie and I sorted out where we would live, I saw an apartment just outside Arundel advertised. This was a chance to have some time in the town I very much liked.

The apartment was bright and airy with wooden floors and part of the impressive development of Torrington Manor on Ford Road a mile south of Arundel. It was just what I was looking for. After the dismal cottage where I had suffered the winter darkness of the deepest lockdown and depression and pressure, this really was springtime. I moved in February 2021. Julie would come over to stay on Wednesday and Saturday nights and occasionally longer – all depending on the care arrangements for her autistic son,

Freddie. She would often call over for lunch or a walk during the day as she was only fifteen minutes away. We both loved the apartment and Arundel from the off. It was a really happy time though I missed Julie when she was not there. I would ring her last thing every night, and she would get me to tell her a story to send her to sleep. I would ramble on about some place I'd been or some adventure or someone I once met, and they must have been really boring stories because I would soon hear her breathing deepen over the phone as she would drift off.

We would walk into Arundel down the back lane, through the fields and down into the town. We would mooch about, have a coffee or lunch and wander back, maybe along the river. Or we would walk over Ford Road and across the field to where the River Arun flowed from the town towards the sea at Littlehampton. Once when we were walking with Julie's grandson Harry there we saw a harbour seal who followed us along the river for a while. The path beside the river was up on a bank like a levee and it gave a lovely view of the town with the Castle and the Cathedral a mile or so away.

In Arundel we would visit cafes like Mott and Bailey's where we would have a great breakfast, or enjoy lunch or dinner at our favourite restaurant, Butler's, in Tarrant Street. We got great Chinese and Indian takeaways from the town and there was a great chippy by the Co-op towards the bridge on the river. We bought a lovely winter scene print from one of the art shops there – the owner turned out to be a Chelsea fan of similar vintage - and it hangs in our hall now as I write this. We would take Harry for a walk along the lane beneath the Castle to Swanbourne Lake where we would get ice creams.

We planned to get married in summer of 2021. I had proposed back in Bramble Cottage in Rogate where I sang Julie a song with my guitar before producing the ring. The song was 'Can't Help Falling In Love'. You old softie, Robbo!

Our dear friends Tim and Lucy have a lovely house in the south of France, just outside the town of Villeneuve-sur-Lot. It is a big old house with a lot of gardens, a swimming pool and the river at the bottom of the garden. Julie and I had the idea it might be a lovely place to get married. We raised the idea with Tim and Lucy, and they were all over it. We all switched into planning mode, and we soon had a plan. We planned the wedding for 29th July 2021, and everything was set.

However, as 2021 progressed we were all back and forwards in lockdowns and there were still serious travel restrictions. Because we would have a lot of people travelling out there, we decided that we would have a decision deadline of the end February. When we got there the travel situation was not good, so we reluctantly cancelled the wedding. As it turned out it was a sensible decision because the restrictions were still largely in place in July.

Julie and I had to come up with a Plan B. The next best option was clear to us – Arundel. We went to see the lovely old Town Hall and gradually all our plans fell into place. Julie planned every detail - the decoration of the Town Hall, the lighting, the music, the food and the entertainment. It would be on 29th December 2021, between Christmas and New Year – a winter wedding.

As the time approached our major concern once again was Covid. Boris had relaxed restrictions for Christmas, but it was widely forecast that he would impose restrictions again on 26th December. We watched the news every day, following the speculation and the alarming increase of Omicron driven infection rates. However, no more restrictions came on – thank you Boris!

The night before the wedding as friends and family gathered Julie and I went to Arundel and met my sister, Pauline and her husband Dave for a meal then we went into the town and called in on friends who were eating at the excellent Thai Time restaurant. We were all set. A few people – about ten in total – had to drop out because of positive Covid tests but other than that, it was pretty much as planned. My son Micky and lovely partner Chloe could not be there because Chloe was very pregnant then and had been advised – again because of Covid – not to travel, which was disappointing but the right cautionary advice. However, they joined us via Zoom in the lovely old Town Hall for the ceremony along with grandson Etienne. Rachel, my daughter, could not travel from Australia as they still had serious travel restrictions there, which was another great shame.

Julie had selected the song she would walk down the aisle to, escorted by our dear mate Richard Shadforth, the Master of Ceremonies, but I did not know which song it was. I had not seen the dress she had selected either so when I stood at the top of the aisle with my best man, Tim Lee, I was not only surprisingly nervous but also intrigued to see the dress and hear which song it was.

The Town Hall looked beautiful with the candle lights all the way up the old stone stairs and the flowers and decoration. Julie has such good taste!

We had about fifty people there – family, friends including a lot of people from Chelsea of course. Everything was just as planned, it was perfect – by some margin the best of my weddings! And finally, to the right woman!

I turned as the music started. It was 'Can't Help Falling in Love' – the beautiful gentle acoustic version by Kina Grannis. It was of course, a perfect choice.

As to the dress, well, what can I say? Again, as expected, Julie looked sensational. As I do remind her from time to time, she is a very good-looking woman.

The whole event went just as planned. Julie and I left just before midnight to go to the Bailiffscourt Hotel at Climping for the night.

According to the videos we saw later the party was still in great flow after that point and we missed a great raucous version of 'Sweet Caroline' too. It was great to see my sons there, my grandchildren, my close friends, my Chelsea family and Julie's family and friends too all together and enjoying themselves.

So, here I am. Married again. In love with the love of my life. Still working for my club. Planning more travels and adventures. Oh yes, there's also this lovely chocolate Labrador pup, Dixie, stealing our hearts and taking me for a lot of healthy walks in the surrounding South Downs.

As I type this the house is a building site. We had originally thought that we would take the equity I had, and that Julie would sell her house and we would buy a house together. But the more we thought about the more it made sense to invest my money into Julie's lovely old house at Findon, just outside Worthing and make that even better. Right now, in the summer of 2022 we are at that point in the building project when it seems it will never be finished, and we just cannot imagine the house being clean and finished or the outside areas smart and attractive instead of looking like a junk yard. However, ever onwards.

But I am taking this moment, this summer, to look back and hence finally getting this book together and reflecting on this crazy life. There are many times when I realise now, I made the wrong decisions, but I made some good ones too. I don't beat myself up about my mistakes to be honest. I have some regrets, which I have shared in this book, but I know I took the decisions at the time based on the cards I thought I could see in front of me. What is done is done.

In fact, I do more regret the things I did not do. I think this is basically true for many people at this stage of their lives. You mostly regret the things you didn't do. If you did something and it did not turn out right then OK, fair enough. But to think of what might have been fascinating.

A dozen lives. Yes, I could have lived a dozen lives. That sounds about right. As I have said I nearly joined the Royal Navy twice – once in the Royal Marines and then in the Fleet Air Arm. Who knows if either of those lives would have worked out or where they would have taken me?
When I left university I was looking around for options. I got offered a job as an Inspector in the Hong Kong police! That would have been an adventure, but my first wife was not keen to go there for two years so I turned it down.
Whilst I was doing the boring management training course working for the transport company I applied for a job in television. Granada TV in Manchester were advertising for a Production Assistant – a nine-month starter gig. This really was the way in to Television – you went and worked hard and made an impression in those nine months and see what happened.

I got an interview. I was about twenty-two, I guess. I was sat with this middle-aged guy, and he was asking what I would like to do in TV. I said I wanted to make programmes that showed young people the consequences of what they do. I jumped up and switched the light on – "that's a political decision." I said, 'because if you take that energy, you are supporting where it comes from and how it is sold.' I waffled on. The guy seemed to like it though.
"Hang on a minute," he said. He made a phone call:
"Richard, can you come in here a minute. Got a candidate here `I want you to meet."
After a minute or two another middle-aged white guy came in.
"Tell him what you just told me," Said the first one. I did my light switch trick again. They seemed enthused and we had a good conversation.
"Have you ever thought of being the other side of the camera? As a presenter?" asked the second guy.
"Well," I shrugged with a smile, "I'm open to anything."

They wrote and offered me the job.

I turned it down.

Looking back, I must have been mad. It was a fantastic opportunity to get into TV and that would have been an adventure for sure. I turned it down because it was only a nine-month contract on very little money and I was married and wanted something more secure. Or so I thought. I ended up leaving the management training course anyway and going back to being a student to do my master's at the LSE whilst working at the Docks with my old man! I had no-one around who could advise me on these career choices really. I was in unchartered waters as far as my family were concerned. But I do think now it was an amazingly stupid decision to turn that chance down.

Over the years in football, I have done a few things on TV. Just a few years ago I was asked to do an advert for Autotrader as they wanted to feature a football scout as someone searching for something. I did it, got well paid – it took me and Keir and Oscar off to Milan for a weekend to watch a game at the San Siro – and really enjoyed it. At one point the Director said to me "that was great, you really are a natural for TV." That made me smile and certainly made me think back to that morning at Granada TV all those years before. Is that what the two TV execs thought back then? Who knows?

Clearly though, when you look at the various working lives I have had, I cannot complain. I have lived a lot of lives from transport to trade union to financial services to leading roles in a variety of charities and with football interlaced into all that along the way as coach, manager and scout culminating in these last eleven years at Chelsea. When my eldest son Pat phoned me to tell me he was starting training to be a firefighter after years working in television on programmes like Emmerdale and Coronation Street as an Art Director he said:

"I'm taking a leaf out of your book, Dad, and changing career direction."

Yet for me, from my perspective there seemed to be a connecting thread each time, although it may seem hard to discern that now from the outside at a distance of many years. I think I was actually trading on my competencies – communication both in person and written, organising, team building, leading, thinking.

I have tried to live my life right, applying the lessons I have learned along the way. Buddhism spoke to me in common sense terms and over the years I have taken a lot from it to help me find my way forward in life. For example, in Buddhism there are five guidelines to living a good life called the five 'precepts'. They are:
1. Refrain from taking life – don't kill anything.
2. Refrain from taking what is not given – don't steal.
3. Refrain from the misuse of the senses - don't act just on sensual pleasure without thinking of consequences and commitments.
4. Refrain from wrong speech – tell the truth.
5. Refrain from intoxicants that cloud the mind – the idea is to see life clearer, don't blur your vision with too much alcohol or drugs, or even things like lust or power or envy.

Overall, I have to say I have found it is a decent code to try and live by. I am not preaching it to you or anybody else – we all have to find our own way and live by our own values. I am just saying these five guides have come to serve me well.

Yesterday afternoon I walked out with Dixie through the village to the village green, a lovely sweep of grass stretching up towards the racehorse gallops on the South Downs. I let her off the lead and we played a while, and her recall was quite good – until another dog walker appeared with a small black dog and Dixie just had to go and say hello! However, I soon retrieved her and had a laugh with the other dog walker as we compared notes on our dogs and their foibles.

Dixie and I walked up to the top of the green and sat on a bench there, looking back down across the Green to the village beyond. Dixie sat and looked at me with her big brown eyes as if butter would not melt then settled down at my feet.

I had left the builders battering away as I escaped with Dixie for some peace. Julie is over at her daughter's house helping paint the nursery for the new granddaughter due in just a few weeks now. Another chapter.

I heard today from my mate Tim who is working out in Singapore at the moment. Julie and I are going out to Tim and Lucy's house in the south of France in August and I'm looking forward to catching up with my mate around the pool. Julie and I are also going to Italy – Sorrento in fact – in a few weeks so we were talking this morning about the issues at airports which are a bit worrying right now.

Next week is my oldest son, Pat's birthday. He's forty-one. I have sent him a new book on cycling – "God is Dead' by Andy McGrath about the rise and fall of Frank Vandenbroucke, 'cycling's great wasted talent.'. My daughter Rachel also has a birthday soon. She is thirty-four and still out in Australia. I can't see her coming back now. We are talking about when we can see her. She is however due back for a visit this summer. I have arranged for some flowers to be delivered on her birthday.

June is a bit of a down time for my work at Chelsea and I have some time off - a chance to take a breather and recharge. However next week I will be back to work and there is talk of a new role and a new challenge and I am looking forward to getting back into it all with my Blues.

It's a sunny day with a cool breeze. I get back up to continue our walk. My knees ache and my back is a bit stiff. I walk about four miles a day with Dixie, and it helps me stay reasonably fit and to deal with the ever-advancing years.

I hold this letter in my hand. This story. I have tried to tell you my truth. I am old. I am in love. I have a lovely family. I have good friends who I would walk through fire for and who would do the same for me. I am busy. I work for the football club I have supported all my life. I miss my Mum every day. I live well.

This is Now.